# Taxation and Development

edited by
# N. T. Wang

Published by Praeger
Publishers, Inc. with
the cooperation of
the United Nations

The Praeger Special Studies program—
utilizing the most modern and efficient book
production techniques and a selective
worldwide distribution network—makes
available to the academic, government, and
business communities significant, timely
research in U.S. and international economic, social, and political development.

# Taxation and Development

PRAEGER SPECIAL STUDIES IN INTERNATIONAL ECONOMICS AND DEVELOPMENT

**Praeger Publishers**  New York  Washington  London

Library of Congress Cataloging in Publication Data
Main entry under title:

Taxation and development.

   (Praeger special studies in international economics and
development)
   Includes bibliographical references and index.
   1.  Underdeveloped areas—Taxation—Addresses, essays,
lectures.  I. Wang, Nian-Tzu, 1917-
HJ2351.T39          336.2'009172'4        75-27023
ISBN 0-275-56010-4

PRAEGER PUBLISHERS
111 Fourth Avenue, New York, N.Y. 10003, U.S.A.

Published in the United States of America in 1976
by Praeger Publishers, Inc.

The Department of Economic and Social Affairs of the
United Nations has from time to time engaged outside consultants
in their individual capacity to assist it in its studies of
fiscal matters.  Some of these consultants have served purely
as advisers, and their experience, insight, and expertise have
contributed to the quality of staff studies.  Others have
prepared specific drafts that have been incorporated to a
greater or lesser extent into studies put out by the staff.
Still others have prepared self-contained studies with the
understanding that they may be issued under the responsibility
of the author in order to encourage the expression of views
that might not be shared by the United Nations.  At the same
time, since these studies are published in cooperation with
the United Nations, a degree of editorial control is exercised,
with particular emphasis on presentation.

The present volume is a collection of such fiscal studies.
The studies included have been selected from a number of
projects undertaken by the Department as part of the effort to
assist governments in tax reform planning and the mobilization
of financial resources.  The chief purpose is to draw attention
to the most important considerations that a government might
take into account in seeking to improve or introduce a
particular tax.  In this connection the experiences of other
countries, especially developing countries, are instructive.
The approach is thus both theoretical and empirical, although
the presentation is not burdened with technical and factual
details so that the study may be accessible to a wide audience
including government officials, students, and the intelligent
general public interested in the subject.  In selecting the
studies, consideration has been given to the unity of the
volume as a whole.  The four authors, who are all from the
United States, are renowned for their academic achievements as
well as their practical experience in advising governments.
The introduction to the volume singles out the main themes of
the papers and offers some comments on the subject matter in
order to stimulate discussion.  It is hoped that a future
volume will explore other important topics and draw upon
authors from other continents or backgrounds.

While many people have contributed to this common endeavor, the following should receive particular credit: Carl S. Shoup, former United Nations Interregional Adviser on Tax Reform Planning and McVicker Professor Emeritus of Political Economy, Columbia University, first called my attention to the publishable nature of these studies and made a number of valuable comments. William Vickrey, who succeeded Professor Shoup as United Nations Interregional Adviser and in the Chair at Columbia, went over all the studies and made detailed suggestions for improvements and alternative formulations. Carmen de la Roche, former Economic Affairs Officer at the United Nations and professor at Universidad del Zulia, Venezuela, and Byron Tarr, former Deputy Minister of Finance, Liberia and currently a colleague at the United Nations, prepared the index. Marianna Oliver turned many passages into more readable form, in addition to eliminating errors and clarifying ideas.

# CONTENTS

LIST OF TABLES AND FIGURES

Despite the importance of taxes in the development process, few developing countries have engaged as systematically in tax planning as in development planning. Development plans tend to concentrate almost exclusively on expenditures. Often, the financing of expenditures is expressed merely as a global statement, and external financing receives more attention than internal, especially when the plan document serves largely as an instrument for applying for external aid.

The unsatisfactory nature of this state of affairs has been emphasized by recent developments. First, with the changing climate for external aid and the growing realization of many developing countries that such aid can at best be of marginal significance in the total development process, more emphasis has been placed on self-reliance in the mobilization of resources. Moreover, with the accumulation of experience in inflationary conditions and the sharpening of reactions and defense mechanisms against inflation among various social groups, the cost of mobilizing resources through inflationary-- and ostensibly effortless--means has increased. As a result, the traditional ways of mobilizing resources by taxation, which are admittedly both difficult and unpopular, have regained

---

In response to a request for possible contributions to this volume, Carl S. Shoup produced a short paper entitled "Some Observations on Developing-Country Taxation" presented at a conference at Northern Illinois University. The paper contains much insight and penetrating analysis bearing on a number of topics covered by this volume. Various ways were explored of making use of the paper for this volume, including publication of the paper in its entirety and joint authorship of the introduction. After some experimentation, it was found that for the present purpose the most expeditious course was to incorporate some of the points of the paper in the introduction, so that duplication would be avoided and extended exchange of drafts by mail to achieve consensus and harmonize the style of presentation would not be necessary. Professor Shoup's contribution to the introduction, in addition to his valuable help to the entire volume, is gratefully acknowledged.

their pivotal role. Indeed, with the exception of such countries as the oil-exporting nations, the capacity to finance has become the chief limiting factor in development expenditures.

The longer that tax planning has been neglected, the more pressing the need to overhaul the tax system. It is true that, despite innumerable obstacles to progress, aggregate growth in developing countries has been in the neighborhood of 6 percent a year in the 1960s and 1970s. Nevertheless, the growth of tax revenues, in real terms, has been more than aggregate growth. In a majority of developing countries, tax revenues have accounted for more than one-tenth of gross national product (GNP). This expansion of revenues has generally been accomplished in an ad hoc manner. Both old and new taxes may be ill adapted to new economic structures and requirements, and their appropriateness is increasingly questioned.

Apart from the question of whether the existing taxes are sufficiently productive from the point of view of revenue, both in terms of total receipts and in terms of built-in income elasticity, serious doubts have been raised from the standpoint of consonance with the basic objectives of development. While the encouragement of savings and investment may be an essential element in speeding the pace of development, the degree to which the tax system actually promotes this objective is frequently uncertain. The promotion of employment is another commonly stated objective, yet many fiscal systems tend to have the opposite effect, through overt and covert discrimination against labor in favor of capital, including very generous tax incentives and holidays for investment by transnational corporations and veiled subsidies to capital-using technology. More equitable distribution of income and wealth is yet another oft-stated goal, but the incidence of taxes is hardly examined, even in the shape of a first approximation of who pays what, and how much of it directly.

The tax-system cannot, of course, be expected to be the main instrument for achieving all the objectives of development. Attempts to exercise influence on too many laudable objectives may in fact so complicate the system as to render it confused and unmanageable. When the objectives are themselves complex, measures designed to achieve one may be at the expense of another. Sophisticated provisions, modeled after practices in developed countries, may be incapable of implementation and enforcement in a less developed setting. The various ad hoc measures and their impacts may not only fail to tackle the fundamental problems but also inhibit meaningful reforms intended to make the system less unwieldy.

Moreover, the precise effect of taxes cannot be analyzed in isolation from the general economic and social framework.

Certainly, taxes have to be examined together with expenditures. For instance, even if taxes are progressive, the incidence of benefits from expenditures, such as urban facilities, or educational and health services, may be concentrated in high-income groups. More broadly, taxes are virtually indistinguishable from other financial arrangements, such as interest rate subsidies and exchange manipulations. Finally, the ultimate effect of taxes must necessarily work through the entire socioeconomic fabric. In a society that is already egalitarian, the progressive tax may lose much of its meaning. Similarly, where resource mobilization is brought about by the direct organization of, and contribution to, productive forces--as in the case of the socialized sector, national service, or voluntary contribution to community projects--the tax instrument assumes a shape different from the traditional one.

A serious effort at reexamination of the tax system must therefore be conducted within the framework of the entire socioeconomic system. It will have to be largely on a country-by-country basis, since conditions in each country are different. This is the general approach of the United Nations in assisting countries in their tax reform efforts. In the case of overall planning, teams of experts composed of various disciplines are available. In practice, however, the participation of tax experts in comprehensive planning missions has been relatively minor, reflecting the separation of planning work from fiscal work in most developing countries. Nor have there been many comprehensive tax missions. Most assistance to individual countries has so far been limited to advice by individual experts on specific topics. The prime objective of most tax officials in seeking external assistance is generally modest. It is frankly reformist, in the sense that marginal improvements are sought within the existing institutions. Even here, however, the solutions offered may have far-reaching implications. For instance, the consolidation of numerous excise, sales, and commodity taxes may very well point to the introduction of value-added taxes, which may be totally new and have a different impact on the structure of the economy, including the overhaul of the entire information system.

In a number of developing countries, the finance ministries are already endowed with trained tax economists well-versed in tax policy issues and, in even more countries, with trained tax lawyers and administrators. Yet, despite the impressive caliber of their intellect, training, and energy, their effectiveness may be limited. Their advice frequently goes unheeded, as political considerations outweigh technical ones. Even if their advice is accepted by the higher echelons, it is often not implemented because of a lack of well-trained and incorruptible lower-rank staff. This situation is aggravated by the low pay in government

service and the drain of qualified personnel into the more
lucrative private sector.  Moreover, tax evasion may be so
widespread that severe punishment of those who happen to be
caught appears patently unfair.  In such cases, even where
external assistance is on a specific topic and with modest
objectives, the advice may touch on sensitive domestic issues
of political significance.  As a result, most of the reports
and studies submitted are for the exclusive use of the
governments concerned and not issued to the general public.

The experience gained in some countries, though not always
relevant in its entirety, is, nevertheless, frequently useful
to other countries.  This is especially the case, for example,
with technical issues concerning a particular form of tax, such
as property tax or value-added tax, perhaps less so with
functional issues, such as tax policy for promoting employment
or the better distribution of income, which are generally more
dependent on local conditions.

It is in this context that a number of tax studies have
been commissioned that draw upon accumulated experience and
existing knowledge in order to provide a general background
for tax officials, facilitate the work of tax advisers, and
stimulate general discussion.  At the same time, new ideas
are also explored, apart from the natural tendency of authors
to advance fresh interpretations of established facts and
theories.

Four studies have been selected for inclusion within the
present volume.  The common theme of all is the tax-planning
problem as it is emerging in the developing countries, whether
it is due mainly to comparative neglect, as in the case of
property tax; to the need for broadening and restructuring the
existing tax base, as in the case of value-added tax; or to
new opportunities and concerns, as in the case of export tax
and pollution tax.  Chapters 1 and 2 are fairly comprehensive
regarding  the issues involved in the property tax and value-
added tax, although they do not pretend to be definitive
manuals or handbooks.  The last two are relatively new
proposals on the export tax and pollution tax, the implications
of which have not been fully developed, either in theory or in
field applications but which are intended to stimulate thought
and provoke in-depth consideration.

Chapter 1, prepared by C. Lowell Harriss, deals with
property taxes, which affect both urban and rural development.
The room for improvement in this area is great, as these taxes
are rarely well administered even in the developed countries.
In most developing countries, basic information on the nature
and value of land and buildings is often defective.  Although
a comprehensive examination of the issues relating to various

types of property taxation is given, the chapter does not endorse a particular model for all countries. It does argue strongly for heavier taxes on land--both urban and rural--than any now in existence. It favors capital value as the tax base, and, where annual rental value is the basis, potential rather than actual income is preferred.

Although the chapter considers questionable the taxing of capital goods, other than land, in addition to taxing the income derived from capital, such a tax at a rate much lower than that for land is regarded as justifiable in comparison with other revenue sources. For the same reason, priority attention should be given to better administration of land taxes.

It should be emphasized that the problem of administration is closely related to the ownership pattern in many developing countries. Any attempt at greater reliance on property taxes is faced with difficulties* arising out of the great concentration of property ownership in the hands of a few politically influential families, and the dispersion of some urban and considerable rural land among medium-sized and small owners or occupants whose titles and boundaries are often unclear. Moreover, communally held lands, as in tribal areas, pose further problems for the application of the usual methods. For practical purposes, it may be prudent to assume that revenue yield from property taxes will continue to be far below the potential. In many cases, the question arises as to whether land reform might not be a prerequisite to tax reform in this respect.

Chapter 2, prepared by John F. Due, concerns value-added taxation, which is a form of sales tax. The organizational structure of the chapter resembles that of Chapter 1 in its comprehensiveness. The chapter should therefore be an aid to anyone interested in various aspects of the value-added tax (VAT), whether with respect to its pros and cons as compared with other taxes, or to methods of administration and enforcement.

The chapter argues that the case for indirect consumption-related taxes in a developing country is relatively strong because they are easier to operate than other taxes and tend to restrain consumption. The sales tax offers a broader base than customs duties, especially as a country moves toward a higher level of development. As between different forms of

---

*This point is emphasized by Shoup.

sales taxes, the value-added tax avoids the evils of the cascade tax, which gravitates toward one set of firms and encourages vertical integration. As compared with the retail sales tax, the VAT avoids concentrating entirely on retailers, who often operate on a small scale and lack adequate accounts. Where retail activities are entirely dominated by small-scale venders with hardly any records, there is a case for confining the sales tax to the manufacturing level or taking it up to the wholesale level. An important advantage of the value-added tax is that it facilitates exemption or rebate for exports.

On the whole, however, the chapter emphasizes the importance of universality and simplicity in administering the VAT. The exceptions should be kept to a minimum, with the temptation to exempt government activities, for example, being resisted. The chapter considers the forfait system of determining the tax liability of small firms objectionable, because the arbitrarily agreed-upon assessment by tax inspectors may lead to bribery. It is also not clear where the tax burden falls.

This brings into prominence the important relationship between administrative considerations and the entire rationale of the tax. Considerable space is thus devoted to arrangements and procedures for the implementation and enforcement of the tax.

Chapter 3 relates to export taxes. It is a complete revision and summary of the essential arguments of an earlier study prepared for the United Nations by Albert G. Hart. While export taxes can be regarded as a form of sales tax, Chapter 3 concentrates on their use to strengthen international commodity agreements. The basic argument is that commodity agreements tend to generate excess supply and redistribute income in favor of profit takers who may not use the proceeds for development. The imposition of an export tax on the commodity will, however, eliminate the excess supply and permit the redistribution of income in favor of development.

The proposition is demonstrated by a conventional microeconomic tax incidence model, which, as is well known, rests on a number of restrictive assumptions. The question is whether these assumptions are sufficiently good approximations to reality.

The chapter recognizes that the case for commodity agreements will be exploded if demand for the commodity is more elastic than supposed and if substitutes are abundant or easy to develop. Even in such cases, however, it is argued that the risk of commodity agreements is reduced if they are accompanied by export taxes, since the tax rates can be adjusted to the cost structure for producers when market conditions change. Moreover, a short-term gain, which succeeds in generating significant development and diversification of the economy, may serve as a springboard for long-term development, which will not be nullified even if the tax rates and the price of commodities cannot be sustained in the long run.

The proposal is supplemented by a back-up program in the form of a uniform import tax, at the same rate as the export tax, to be imposed by the importing countries, with an arrangement for the exemption of import tax if export tax has been paid. The main purpose of the program is to reduce the incentive for exporting countries to refuse to enter into the agreement, since by doing so they would lose revenue to the importing countries without gaining a competitive advantage over other exporters.

It should be pointed out, however, that a crucial question remains as to the relative share of each producer's export. Even if it is granted that there is sufficient exporter solidarity, plus international-mindedness among the importers, to enable the scheme to be established, the difficulty can be illustrated by the example in which the export enterprises in question are state-owned, as is the case with petroleum and copper in virtually all the main exporting countries, so that the profit accrues to the fiscal authority just as export taxes do. Then, total profit, not to speak of foreign exchange proceeds, will increase with an increased share of the market. Restrictions on market shares would, therefore, continue to be required, but it is precisely these restrictions that are inherently divisive and demand a degree of exporter solidarity that is not usually present in primary commodities. The chapter does suggest, on the other hand, that the scheme can be combined with others, including buffer stocks. There will then continue to be an incentive for each exporter to secure a larger share of the market under the favorable price conditions established by the agreement.

On a more speculative ground, the chapter suggests a possible link with the commodity-currency scheme. While the need for the reform of the existing international monetary system is evident, especially the need to introduce discipline, the basic difficulties of the commodity-currency scheme are formidable.* Nevertheless, the suggestion is timely and

---

*In addition to the problems mentioned in the chapter, such as the cost of maintaining commodity stocks and the unsuitability of many commodities for the purpose, among the fundamental difficulties are (1) the asymmetry that exists

provocative, in connection with both the current discussion of
new initiatives in international monetary reform and international commodity agreements, including the long-neglected
Keynes plan on buffer stocks, which is more flexible than the
commodity-currency scheme.

Chapter 4, contributed by Richard E. Slitor, deals with
the use of taxes for pollution control.  Although the
environmental concern has attracted great attention both at
the national and international levels, the tax approach has so
far been neglected or regarded as less appropriate than the
regulatory approach.  This probably reflects the dominance of
viewpoints of those who are not especially interested in trade-
offs and tend to think in absolute terms.  The recent energy
crisis has, however, given rise to renewed interest in tax
measures that make use of incentives and disincentives in the
market system.

The main theme of the chapter is that pollution taxes can
be designed to internalize the social cost of pollution so that
environmental damages will be reflected in the market mechanism.
This includes the elimination of existing biases in the tax
system that contribute to the pollution problem.  The chapter
identifies specific areas of application of fiscal devices to
cope with a broad range of problems, including air pollution,
water pollution, solid waste pollution, development of clean
energy, thermal pollution, noise pollution, and cultural
aspects.  The chapter also examines the international aspects.
Issues concerning the export of pollution and effects on
competitive advantages are of special interest to developing
countries.  The chapter emphasizes the complementary role of
fiscal devices and direct regulation.  In particular, tax
measures can be used to support and strengthen regulatory
measures.  They have the added advantage of flexibility, and
they also permit more time for experimentation and adjustment.

---

between currency creation and commodity creation, so that a
run on commodities may develop like a run on gold under the
gold standard, (2) the problem of violent fluctuations of
individual commodities produced by an individual country,
which is not tackled at all, and (3) the fact that some
countries will be able to extract a monopoly profit by virtue
of the fact that the commodities under their control are
included in the commodity unit.

# Taxation and Development

# PROPERTY TAXATION
# AND DEVELOPMENT
### C. Lowell Harriss

## INTRODUCTION

Property taxes are much more important as sources of revenue than is often recognized. As they are often local taxes, figures for them may not appear in studies of national tax systems, which are chiefly concerned with central governments.

Types of property taxation vary tremendously in developing and developed countries. Similar names may be employed for taxes that are quite different, and differing names may be used for taxes that are similar.

Social, cultural, political, legal, and economic conditions differ from one country to another. The influences they exert, some subtle and intangible, inevitably affect the operation of a tax that applies to something so important as land. Moreover, the results achieved by a tax depend upon its actual administration, and the quality of administration can also vary widely and in ways not immediately apparent.

In seeking to learn at first hand about the actual operation of property taxation in many countries, the author has found that large gaps exist between what seems to be called for by the legal systems and what in fact takes place. This is true, for example, of the United States. Throughout most of its history (in fact, until World War II), property taxation was the largest source of revenue and is still highly important. Yet it has been, and in many cases is still, administered in ways that stray very far from the apparent requirements of the statute books. In 1972-73, the average statewide burden per $1,000 of personal income ranged from $14 in Alabama to $74 in Massachusetts, while

within those states, and in others, the variations from one
locality to another were substantial.[1]

A property tax may be designed, moreover, for purposes
in addition to revenue--for example, to assist in land
reform, rural or urban, or to supplement urban land-use
planning.  In such cases, identification of the results is
complicated and their evaluation hazardous indeed for the
outsider.  What actually occurs on either the urban or the
rural scene is the result of many forces.  A responsible
scholar may well conclude that it is impossible to attribute
a particular result with any certainty to the tax feature.
Econometric analysis may eventually yield reliable conclusions, and less complicated statistical studies and case
investigation may be able to throw light on experience, but
great caution needs to be exercised in making international
comparisons.

## Three Bases of Taxation

Using the same term for taxes with different
characteristics can give rise to imprecision and confusion.
Certain concepts, therefore, need to be clarified.

All taxes fall on people.  In other words, every amount
collected in taxes is ultimately subtracted from some human
being's economic power.  Some taxes fall on people directly
while others do so indirectly.  The distinction is not
always clear, and so property taxes may be classed as direct
taxes by some and indirect by others.

There are three general bases that governments can
utilize for imposing taxes:

1.   Income produced and received (or as it might be
received if a business were not required to pay a tax on its
earnings or operations).

2.   Expenditure (consumption), as people use income,
borrowed funds, and proceeds from former savings and other
sources (such as transfer payments from government).

3.   Wealth or property or capital: The first two
bases apply to a "flow."  A part of the flow of funds,
either as received or as used, is diverted to pay for the
government's activities.  The third is a stock or source,
and the base of tax may be the existence or possession of
wealth or its transfer (gratuitous gift or bequest or
exchange).

The three bases are not clearly distinguishable. It may not be plain, for example, whether a tax imposed on property reaches people in the form of a reduction of the flow of income received, higher prices for consumption, a reduction in the value of capital owned, or some combination of these. In any case, people are affected, and not merely such inanimate things as land or consumer products or such entities as corporations, which may seem separate from their members (employees and shareholders and consumers of the products).

The effects of taxes, per dollar or other unit of revenue, can differ, not merely as regards the distribution of the burden--by income group or age, rural or urban residence--but also as regards the impact upon the ways in which people act. For example, a property tax can exert a greater influence on the way in which land is used or on the types of structure built and their location than an income or consumption tax having an equal yield.

## Methods of Taxing Property

Before sketching the types of property taxation that will be considered in this chapter, we should note two that do not properly fall within its scope.

In some places in Europe, an annual tax is imposed on personal net worth. This type of taxation rates well according to several of the most widely accepted criteria for judging a revenue source, provided it can be well administered. However, it requires a more advanced and effective administrative effort than can be expected in the foreseeable future as far as most economies are concerned. Practical realities therefore exclude it from consideration here.

A capital levy would presumably reach all or most types of property. However, the few cases in which attempts have been made to utilize such a tax have been one-time affairs. A capital levy is not a continuing source of revenue. Good administration presents formidable difficulties, and the circumstances that would make a capital levy deserving of serious consideration are highly exceptional.

While inflation will not be dealt with as a tax on property, the relations of inflation to the issues discussed will be noted where appropriate.

Five types of property tax can be identified, each of which will be discussed more fully later.

1.    Tax can be based on <u>capital value</u> or worth--a
money amount--as determined in some way for each unit of
property identified.  Ordinarily, the money amount figure
used will not be one that is known in a definite and
objective sense.  The best value figure for a property would
presumably be a price determined in a free market transaction,
the true terms of which can be ascertained by the
administrative staff.  The number of such sales in any
period, say one year, will usually be no more than a small
fraction of the total to be taxed.  They may provide
satisfactory indications of the value of a range of
properties, but it is more probable that market tests will
be incomplete and inadequate.

2.    Tax may be based upon <u>income</u> from a particular
property, using either the actual income or some presumptive
figure.  The standard may be either the gross or the net
yield.  In such cases, the tax would probably be more
nearly an income than a property tax.  However, the tax may
relate not so much to the owner (as in the typical personal
income tax) as to the property considered as an economic
entity.

3.    Annual tax may be based on <u>size</u>, <u>location</u>, or other
<u>physical factor</u>, rather than a value figure as such.  Some
or all of the costs of governmental outlays benefiting the
property as such--for example, streets--may be covered by
taxes in the form of <u>special assessments</u>, levies to pay for
particular betterments.

4.    A special tax may be based upon <u>increments</u> in
value.

5.    Tax can rest upon the <u>transfer</u> of property.  Sales
of land and buildings (and possibly of securities other than
the bearer type) may require some kind of official recording
that makes the collection of a special tax feasible.  Tax
may also be imposed at death or upon transfer by gift.  This
type of tax differs from more or less regular annual taxes.

### Tangible and Intangible Property

The term "property" may apply to physical, <u>tangible</u>
things such as land, buildings, machinery, furniture,
animals and growing crops, and to <u>intangibles</u> such as
instruments of debt and shares of stock in a corporation.
The intangibles represent rights to and control over the
tangible things, or claims on income from them.  A building
constitutes property, and so does a piece of paper proving
title or ownership to it or evidence of a debt supported by

the building.  More than one layer of these paper rights--
debt and ownership--may be superimposed on a single body of
tangible things.  Depositors in a bank, for example, possess
intangible claims, which are supported by debts (notes) of
businesses or housing mortgages, which are in turn supported
by tangible assets.

A person's wealth may consist, in small or large part,
of securities--that is, intangibles rather than physical
things.  Debts, which are also intangibles, may reduce his
net worth.  In order for individuals to be taxed
systematically according to their wealth, the base must
include intangibles, both assets and debts.  The various
tangible properties underlying the securities do not always
accord with individual property ownership.

Trying to tax both the tangible things--for example,
land--and the securities that get their worth from being a
claim on the real assets gives rise to problems.  Problems
may also arise if it is possible to use different types of
ownership, perhaps complex and scrambled forms, in order to
escape taxation.  Unintended escape can be prevented by the
exercise of care by lawmakers in planning the tax.  It may
also be possible to correct the structure of a tax at a
later stage, but it will not be done automatically.  Defects
will not be self-correcting.  In each country, the legal
system, traditions of family relations, methods of conducting
business, and other conditions will help to determine the
kind of property taxes most likely to be effective.  Where
land is held in communal ownership, for example, a property
tax must be adapted accordingly if it is to have any
prospect of success.

## Capital as Distinguished from Income

Property--thought of for the sake of clarity in terms
of tangible things--is a corpus or stock.  It corresponds to
physical capital.  It is distinguished from income, which is
a flow of amounts during a period of time.  Capital is a
source--a farm, a tree, a factory--that provides benefits--
products or services--through time.  The worth of the source
or capital depends upon the total (net) benefits it is
expected to produce and on the time pattern in which the
benefits are to occur.  The tax on either, capital or
income, has effects on the worth and the use of the other.

Each month or year, the capital, along with inputs of
such things as materials and labor, will produce goods or
services.  These are real income.  Ordinarily, the output is
sold, and the money received is thought of as the income.
Thus, income is a flow, though not necessarily smooth or

regular.  Income is thought of as net if the source remains
unchanged after expenses have been covered.

Various attempts have been made to learn whether there
is some general relation between capital and labor and
output, in the sense that some amount of capital is
generally associated with some continuing flow of income.
Can we say, for example, that, as a rule, about two units of
capital ($2) are needed to support each unit of flow of
income ($1)?  No fixed relation has been found.

Taxation can rest on the capital value--that is to say,
on the property regarded as a source or stock.  On the other
hand, it may be based on the product or income, or on both.
A tax of 2 percent on the capital value may equal a tax of
20 or 30 percent or even more on the income.  Governments
often do impose both a property tax on the source and a tax
on the flow of income that it helps to produce.  Double
taxation may exist without recognition of the total burden.
More will be said later about the relationship between these
two types of tax, which, while differing, can, in an economic
sense, be closely related.  Decisions in regard to one can be
taken without adequate recognition of what is being done in
respect of the other.  The best results will come from careful
efforts first to distinguish between the two elements and then
to act in recognition of what is really involved.  (An income
tax, let us assume, applies to income from all sources.
Labor--that is, human beings--will not be taxed as such.
Thus, the source of wage income is not taxed.  But property,
which is a source of income, may be taxed in addition to the
income it produces; for example, both a building and the rent
received for it by the owner may be taxed.)

Tangible property, except for the "pure" land element,
results from the investment of savings out of income.  In
other words, a portion of the flow of income is saved, or not
consumed, and used to finance the production of assets.
These capital goods then add to the flow of income.  They
enlarge the total productive power of the economy.

The kind of tax that is applied to the flow of income
from property and from human services will influence the
growth of the capital base.  A tax on the property itself, or
capital, can affect the ability of the property to maintain
the output.  A tax on capital can reduce the net income at a
later stage.

The value of an asset depends heavily on the net flow of
benefits it yields and is expected to yield in the future--
net after taxes.  (Social standing and prestige may be
associated with the ownership of land, thus forming part of

the net benefits that affect the worth assigned by some
persons to the possession of an asset.  Expected protection
against inflation can also influence values assigned to
land and other property.)  The total value of a farm or house
or business establishment may not be owned by any one person.
Obligations can limit the rights attaching to the collection
of the assets of a business, or to any specific capital good
or piece of property.  The value of the physical assets may
be distributed in various ways.  Ownership is frequently
reduced by debts.  These, and the requirement to pay interest
annually, will influence the ability of the owners, users,
and others to pay taxes.  Rental and lease obligations also
affect the way in which the flow of income is shared.  As
noted earlier, levying property tax on tangible assets and
then on the intangibles whose value rests on the tangibles
may lead to burdens that could be inappropriate and produce
undesirable nonrevenue results.

Planners of tax systems should take account of the many
realities that exist.  The legal influences on the ownership
and use of property and on flows of income will obviously
affect what is possible.  In advanced planning, preparations
should be made to circumvent arrangements aimed at escaping
whatever taxes the government sees fit to impose.

## Differences between Land and Man-Made Property

A distinction of potentially far-reaching significance
between types of tangible property should be noted here.
Land, in a basic sense, is the product of nature.  Soils,
minerals, and other resources and such related factors as
rivers and climate that affect the desirability or value of
the land exist as a result of nature.  (For purposes of
simplicity, "land" is used hereafter to cover the broader
range of natural resources.)  To a large extent, they would
exist even if man had done nothing.  In some cases, the
continued existence of land in its present form will depend
not at all on the kind of taxes imposed; in others, it will
depend only slightly on taxation.  High taxes will not
reduce the supply or induce land to move to another area.
But the use that is made of land may be influenced strongly
by the kind of tax imposed, or not imposed, on ownership
pure and simple, on forms of operation, or on transfer.

Human activities, however, produce other productive
facilities--buildings and machinery, business inventory,
and other forms of tangible property.  Taxes will often
influence the amount and nature of these man-made assets,
the quantity and quality created, and the amount made
available for use.  The location of buildings, productive
equipment, and similar man-made property can depend in part
on differences in taxation among communities or nations.

In fact, parcels of rural or urban land, in the basic
physical sense, ordinarily represent, in part, the results of
what has been done by present and past owners.  More broadly,
some of the various elements that affect the usefulness of
land represent inputs of capital.  Draining, clearing,
fencing, fertilization, and so on are inputs made after
nature has finished its job.

Often it is difficult, even impossible, to make a clear-
cut distinction between land's original and present form.
For example, the attempt in New Zealand to base property tax
on "unimproved value" led to increasing difficulties in
trying to judge the present-day value of land restored in
concept to its original state.

It is beyond question, however, that throughout much of
the world, and especially in and near cities, the present
value of land far exceeds anything that can be attributed to
the inputs or capital investment made by past and present
owners in order to alter the characteristics of the land.
Some of these values of location reflect the presence of
streets, schools, sewers, and other facilities, often built
and paid for by the government.  Property taxation can be
devised that will pay for some of the governmental costs
that create land values and possibly even contribute to the
costs of utility and other services that are essential to
the survival of the modern city.

Nevertheless, although relatively heavy taxes on land
values may seem desirable, governments, in imposing them,
should take care to distinguish between what is really land
value, in a strict sense, and that portion of worth that
has resulted from inputs of capital, in order not to
discourage future investments to improve the land.


## ECONOMIC EFFECTS OF PROPERTY TAXATION

### Shifting and Incidence of the Tax Burden

Where does the ultimate burden of property taxation
really fall?  The processes of shifting and the probable
final incidence are more complex than can be dealt with in
detail here.  The general conclusions stated, however, are
such as would receive the widespread endorsement of
economists.  In specific situations, the results are
affected by many factors.  Some countries, for example, are
more susceptible than others to the loss of capital (or
failure to attract the full potential) and must, therefore,
expect somewhat different results in the shifting of a tax
on property.  The time required for the results of a tax

change to work out will vary.  The longer-run effects may
differ significantly from the immediate impact.  Businesses
and individuals may adjust their positions as new bargaining
is entered into and new construction is gradually put in
place.

Sometimes when taxes are shifted--as where rental
contracts stipulate a pass-through, for example--the process
may seem to be demonstrated rather clearly.  But how
different might the rental terms have been if the tax had
been expected to be greater or less?  The process is often
both obscure and slow.

## Two Taxes, Not One

In economic terms, property taxation of the annual type
(on capital value or income) consists of two different
levies, one on pure site or location value, and another on
buildings and other improvements and, possibly, business
machinery and inventory.

Land viewed as a productive resource resembles, in some
respects, labor and capital, but in others it differs
crucially.  The similarities include the fact that parcels of
land vary greatly in desirability, as do human skills and
machines.  A crucial difference, however, lies in mobility
versus immobility.  Space is immobile, while other things are
mobile.  Land is the one thing that a local or central
government can tax heavily without fear that it will move to
a lower tax area.  And, whereas a low tax on buildings, or a
complete exemption, will tend to attract capital funds
(perhaps from abroad) and encourage construction, a low tax
on land will not increase the amount of land in the area,
nor will a high tax cause land to disappear, whereas a high
tax on improvements may prevent buildings from being built
or lead to the deterioration and even abandonment of
existing structures.

Property values, moreover, come into existence by
different means.  For example, the worth of labor and
capital--the vigor of human endeavor, entrepreneurship, the
amount of machinery and structures--depends in part upon
what individuals expect to receive in compensation for their
efforts and their savings.  To get buildings, machinery, and
other productive capacity of these types, society must pay,
and what will count most will be after-tax income.  The
extent to which society tries to take back through taxes (as
in product prices) what it has paid to obtain the services
of capital and labor will affect the future supply.

Nature created land in the physical sense, but society has created much of the demand that makes some locations highly desirable. Some improvements that become embodied in land--drainage, clearing, leveling, and so on--represent the investment of capital and labor. In general, however, the amount of land in existence will depend scarcely at all upon the money paid for its use.

Because parcels of land, especially regarding space and location, differ immensely, something that will help to allocate use efficiently is of the utmost importance. In this respect, payments for the use of land perform a function of outstanding significance. But payments do not, as in the case of man-made productive capacity, also perform the function of inducing the creation of land. They may induce private owners to alter the land form by leveling, fencing, and so on or to provide facilities such as sewers or water pipes. Property taxes may be used to cover the costs incurred by the community for facilities that affect the desirability of locations. (On the outskirts of large American cities, from $15,000 to over $20,000 of governmental spending on streets, schools, water and sewage, and other facilities will often be needed for each new house. As population grows and incomes rise, land prices go up. Owners receive unearned increments, values above anything they have paid to have created.)

## Capitalization

One factor in the shifting and incidence of property taxation is derived from the permanent nature of land (space on the earth's surface) and the long life of some buildings.

An annual tax on the value of land, or on the income from it, affects the price a buyer will pay for it. The higher the tax, the lower the price. The capital value, or price, will be the expected net income, broadly conceived to include nonmoney benefits such as prestige, security, and hope for protection against inflation, related to the yields that are obtainable from other assets adjusted for quality. Let us assume, for example, that for the foreseeable future, the gross income from a piece of land, after all expenses except property tax have been paid, will be $1,200 a year. The owner has bargained as effectively as he can to get the best income possible. The tax on the land is $200 a year. Investments of comparable quality are yielding 5 percent a year. The simple formula for determining the price of the land is then as follows:

$$\text{Price} = \frac{\text{Gross income } \$1,200 \text{ minus tax } \$200 = \$1,000}{\text{Yields of comparable properties} = 5 \text{ percent}}$$

$$= \frac{\$1,000}{5/100} = \$20,000$$

The price, $20,000, is the capital sum that will bring the net income expected from this property. If there were no tax, the price of the land would be $24,000.

Assume, then, that the tax goes up by $100 a year but that this in itself does nothing to raise the gross income, nothing to make the land more attractive to a user. Then:

$$\text{Price} = \frac{\$1,200 \text{ minus } \$300 = \$900}{5/100}$$

$$= \$18,000$$

The rise in tax has been capitalized into a $2,000 decline in capital value. The person buying later is no worse off because the tax is $300 a year instead of $200, since he took the extra $100 a year into account in his purchase price. Much as the prior owner might have wished to charge a higher price after the tax went up, nothing enabled him to do so. Neither the $200 in the first case nor the $300 in the second would be a burden on a new buyer as compared with what he would have had to pay (land plus tax) if the tax at the time of purchase had been lower. The person or business firm that buys a piece of land allows for the tax on it in the price offered.

The principles of supply and demand operate, save that the quantity of land is not subject to change in the way that supplies of manufactured products can be expanded or restricted. The owner tries presumably to get as high a price as possible. He can not reduce the supply of land (space on the earth's surface) in order to get a higher price. As far as demand for a parcel of land is concerned, nothing will offset the effect of higher annual tax in lowering the price. To be sure, if the extra $100 is spent in ways that add to the attractiveness of the locality, the gross income is in some meaningful sense higher—for example, benefits of better streets and government services. Conceivably, there might be no drop in the price of the land. A new buyer might be willing to pay $20,000 because he would get more in services each year.

The underlying economic processes follow from inherent considerations that would seem to apply wherever market

forces have room to exert their influence.  In some developing
countries, conditions may differ significantly from those in
which the market forces operate effectively.  But the basic
realities would operate on a sufficiently general scale for
the results indicated above to serve as a foundation for
public policy.  Developing economies have a longer-run
potential for utilizing the probable rise in rural, and more
particularly urban, land values as a basis for financing
government expenditures.

Part of an existing tax, therefore, constitutes no
current burden on the present owner or user.  To the extent
that the owner has allowed for it in the price he has paid,
the annual payment of this portion of the tax constitutes no
true burden on him.  This conclusion of economic analysis
will not be evident to many owners of property.  Nevertheless,
part of what an owner pays to a government treasury each year
does not really leave him worse off, compared with what his
situation would have been if the tax had not applied when he
bought the property.

In some respects at least, "an old tax is a good tax".
Where property taxation is old, it has worked its way through
the economy, particularly as regards that portion represented
by tax rates other than the most recent increases.  Some
elements have been capitalized and other adjustments have
been made.  Even substantial inequalities and crudities in
the assessment process will have been capitalized and have
lost much of their sting as the economy has adjusted over
the years.

Instituting a new tax on property of long life, or
raising the rates of an existing tax, will impose burdens on
the current owner greater than the annual tax payment.
Owners will incur drops in the prices of assets equal to the
capitalized amount of the increase in tax, if the new tax is
expected to continue.  Sudden and large changes, therefore,
can impose greater burdens than may be apparent.

## Tax on Buildings, Machinery, and Other Man-Made Property

Initially, an increase in tax on improvements will fall
on the owner or user.  Both contract provisions and market
conditions will determine the immediate impact.  In the very
short run, presumably nothing about the tax will increase
the demand for housing or for the output of a business.  The
supply of buildings and other facilities will be so largely
fixed that little opportunity will exist to make a new bargain
in order to get better terms for the supplier.  The net return
to the owner--the supplier of capital--will go down because
of the higher tax.  If he had been netting 6.5 percent after

tax and now gets 6 percent, he may be "stuck" with the capital
invested in the building.  But, as he allocates new funds, he
will seek out projects where tax has not increased and where
returns of 6.5 percent net are still available.

As depreciation funds become available, representing the
wearing out of the plant facilities or housing in which he had
invested, he will not put such funds back into improvements
in the taxed area.  Gradually, therefore, the supply of
output from the more highly taxed plants or housing goes
down.  With a smaller supply being offered, producers can get
a higher price of rental.  In this way, the tax increase is
shifted to the consumer, though perhaps only slowly.  The
essential element is the flow of new capital funds.  These
funds will move to take account of new tax realities.
Consumers will not get the productive capacity needed to
supply them until investors can expect an adequate after-tax
income.

This reasoning assumes that savers have places in which
to invest where property taxes have not been increased.  The
assumption is valid insofar as decisions on property taxes
are made locally or regionally.  If the tax increase applies
to the whole economy, and if no export of savings is
permitted, however, savers may perforce have to be satisfied
with lower net yields.  (Imports of capital will tend to be
less than otherwise.  Over time, therefore, supplies of
output in the economy will be less than if the tax had not
gone up.  Prices to consumers will thus be higher, so that
buyers and renters will, in effect, bear some of the tax.
Identifying such forces will be difficult at best, and
measurement will be impossible, because no one can know how
much capital imports have fallen short of what they would
have been.)

If one community raises its property tax rate, the
effect is likely to be predominantly an increase in housing
rents and in the price of locally produced and distributed
goods and services rather than a reduction in net after-tax
yields.  The suppliers of capital bear some or all of the
increase in tax.  Because of lower income, or lower yield,
they may save less, thus reducing capital supplies and
permitting (some) shifting of the tax burden to consumers.
Under a truly universal property tax increase, personal and
business saving--the total supplies of new capital throughout
the economy--may be relatively unresponsive to changes in
after-tax yields.  If so, then a universal property tax would
rest (to a large extent) on the owners of capital.

The process would work by adjusting net yields; returns of various types of investment would bear about the same relations after tax as before but at lower levels. Property taxation would thus become a generalized burden on capital, even on types not directly affected by tax changes. Some of the effects would tend to be felt in land prices, though not necessarily all in the same direction. Increased tax rates on improvements might discourage costly improvement in city centers.

A summary of this argument would run as follows: Some, perhaps much, of a global tax on man-made properties falls on the owners of capital generally, while local tax rates above the general average of the economy will be reflected in higher prices to consumers for local goods and services. Effects on land values are likely to be uneven. Other irregular effects must be expected, and, during the time required for adjustment, changes in taxes will be distributed in ways rather different from those that will prevail after full adjustment has been made.

## Regressivity, Proportionality, and Progressivity

Estimates of the probable distribution of the burden of property taxation are heavily dependent upon assumptions about shifting. Estimating the probable final incidence according to income classes, or other social groups, will therefore be tentative at best.

A portion of the tax on land will rest on past owners (and their heirs) and present owners. Although there is no way to measure how the amounts involved are shared among income classes, it can be generally concluded that the lowest income groups own little or no land. Higher in the income scale, however, ownership of land will be relatively greater.

The part of the tax on housing and other man-made capital that rests on consumers will have some elements of regressivity relative to income--that is, it will be above average in relation to income at the bottom of the income scale and below average at the top. For most families over a period of years, however, the distribution of this tax may be roughly proportional with both income and consumption.

The portion of tax on man-made capital that remains on suppliers of capital will, in general, be small for the lowest-income groups. But the burden will tend to fall relatively heavily on those with large incomes and property holdings. Thus, the tax may be progressive, not smoothly but perhaps significantly so.

Much depends, therefore, upon the extent to which the tax on man-made capital is embodied in prices, as compared with the extent to which it burdens the suppliers of capital.

Moreover, estimates of burden distribution should take into consideration the fact that, more often than not, the property taxes as actually administered do not meet reasonable standards of horizontal equity as among comparable properties. Both land and buildings that are largely similar may not be taxed alike. In some cases, considerable property does not appear on the tax rolls. Errors--and corruption--in the making of original surveys and failures to list new buildings exist and go uncorrected.

In addition, revaluations do not reflect general price inflation or the changing relative values of different properties. New construction may be valued in relation to current costs, while little or no attempt is made to raise the valuations of existing buildings. Such practices will reduce the relative attractiveness of new capital investment in building, especially if property tax rates are high enough to have an important revenue potential.

## The Influence of Property Taxation

Taxation, of course, affects what people do--as regards production, savings and investment, and consumption. The method of imposing tax as well as the amount to be paid thus have nonrevenue results. The higher the rate of tax and the larger the revenue it brings, the greater the pressure it will exert in other ways.

We may assume that higher real income is a goal of public policy. If it falls more heavily on capital, as contrasted with income and consumption, property taxation may not conform with the objectives for capital formation (and its preservation), which are called for by policies for economic progress. The distinction between taxes on land and those on man-made capital bears crucially on this issue.

In devising taxes, legislatures should make an effort to reduce the conflict between the need to raise revenue, on the one hand, and, on the other, the conditions required for the best use of existing property and for an increase in productive capacity. Hopefully, a tax can be devised so that the incentives it creates can be directed toward actions that exert a constructive influence.

## Property Taxation and Ability to Pay

Most forms of property taxation are <u>in rem</u>--imposed on a thing and related to its characteristics--rather than <u>in personam</u>--imposed on a person and related to his situation or personal characteristics. The discussion of incidence and shifting has indicated that the actual burdens may not rest where it is assumed they do or even where they are identifiable. Nevertheless, some advocates of property taxation support it in part as a means of putting the costs of government on persons with above-average ability to pay. At the extreme, these advocates may assume that the tax will not be shifted (in any significant amount) to consumers, renters of housing, or others and that the property tax will burden only persons who own the kind of property taxed. In this case, it may be argued, the very poor will be freed of any obligation to pay a portion of the costs of government, and only property owners will pay. Property taxation may then appear as being at least roughly related to some concept of ability to pay. Even if the above assumption is not entirely true, the burdens on property owners may be larger relative to income or consumption than those on the propertyless.

## Rate Discrimination

Can property taxation employ discriminatory rates or even forms of graduation? Can the burden be adjusted according to concepts of ability to pay that rest upon rate progression? Annual net worth taxes may embody some rate graduation, but they do not fall within the scope of this study. Taxes at death or on gifts may be applied by means of graduated rates. The result may be what some members of society at least believe is desirable on grounds of equity in sharing the costs of government--there may be considerable progression, even though it may not necessarily be smooth on any basis (income, wealth, or consumption).* True, the concepts of "equity," "justice," and "fairness" in taxation are not subject to

---

*Unless there is allowance for debts outstanding, the tax base can fail to represent personal net worth or the relative taxpaying capacities of different owners of taxed property. Only net worth taxes can adjust burdens according to a refined concept of ability to pay based on wealth. Succession taxes as actually applied have extremely erratic impacts owing to variations in the frequency with which the tax is imposed and the wide range of devices by which tax-payers can circumvent the tax or mitigate its burden.

definitions that will receive complete endorsement.  Tax
progression, however, does enjoy widespread support as a means
of achieving equity.

Although the actual results after shifting may differ from
what these advocates expect, some objectives may be realized.
For example, little of the burden may fall on the poor--perhaps
less per dollar of revenue than in the case of other tax sources.
Even though persons of equal total wealth may not bear equal
burdens, and the amounts of tax from one wealth or income level
to another may differ in quite unsystematic ways, the
distributive aspects of the tax burden may be broadly and
justifiably endorsed.  Particularly if a revenue system has
some regressive elements, a tax that is progressive, albeit
imperfectly so, can serve as something of an offsetting
mechanism.

## Reduction of Large Holdings of Property as an Objective

A separate objective in addition to revenue may be the
reduction of large holdings of wealth.  A larger number of
small holdings may seem better in some ways than large
holdings.  Moreover, the ownership of wealth, it can be
argued, will tend to build upon itself in the "normal" course
of events as income from existing holdings permits the
acquisition of more wealth.  Taxes, notably those on transfers
at death, may be devised to reduce the tendency of the concentration of property to be cumulative.  But the growth of
productive capacity requires savings and investment.  Policies
that bear heavily on owners of relatively large amounts of
property will probably lead to a situation whereby, over the
years, productive capacity will be kept below what would
otherwise develop.

In Australia, annual taxes on land were graduated to
induce the subdivision of large holdings of rural land.
Observers report that the tax did exert an influence to this
end.  In some other cases, progressive rates have been applied
to urban property.  But the practical difficulties of breaking
up large holdings are not readily overcome.  Furthermore, a
policy of breaking up holdings of urban land will run counter
to some economic objectives of consolidating parcels for the
most economic use in modern ways and for conformity with the
goals of urban planning.

Achieving the desired results will depend upon such
things as the opportunities for using separate legal entities--
for example, corporations--to divide ownership, upon the
quality of tax administration, upon the number of separate
taxing jurisdictions, and upon the export of capital.

## Differential Rates and Exemptions

Land values, in the author's view, may "properly" be subjected to much higher tax rates than apply to man-made capital. The reasons for advocating especially high land taxes, however, do not depend upon the wealth or income of the owners.

Some types of property may also be favored. Developing countries, for example, may grant exemptions for certain types of investment. Home ownership may be encouraged. The United Kingdom favors agricultural property. Virtually throughout the United States, special exemptions have recently been provided for elderly persons with low incomes.

Almost as a general rule, property owned by government is fully exempt. Such treatment, although understandable, tends to distort comparisons of types of ownership and operation. The allocation of resources will be less likely to give an accurate reflection of the underlying economic realities and alternatives when governmental (or other) uses are exempt from taxes which apply to businesses and to most nongovern- mental activities. As long as tax rates are low, the exemption of governmental property will usually have only a slight effect on competitive positions. But a property tax high enough to be of considerable importance from the point of view of revenue will alter the factors that affect resource allocation. Forces that hamper the private sector will be created, for reasons that do not grow out of inherent factors of efficiency in production and the apparent relative desir- ability of products and services.

Although the prospect of governments, and even governmental enterprise-type organizations, paying taxes on the property that they own and use may seem illogical--money out of one pocket into another--there are persuasive economic arguments in favor of it. Resource allocation and efficiency in use will benefit by ready comparison between governmental and private use of property. Failure to subject governmental housing to the taxes payable by private suppliers will, among other things, add to the latter's competitive disadvantages.

## TYPES OF PROPERTY TAXATION

### Tax Related to Capital Value

One way of levying an annual tax on property is to base it upon the (estimated) capital value. This is the basis used in Canada, the Philippines, the United States, and, to a varying extent, numerous other countries.

U.S. tax rates are set by local governments and are often
2 percent or more of the full current worth.  In some
communities, the annual rates are over 4 percent of actual
capital value.  In relation to annual yields, of course, such
burdens are substantial.  Canadian rates are also locally set
and in some places about as high as in the United States.

The capital value basis for property taxation is usually
preferable to the income alternative, yet the arguments are
not overwhelmingly in favor.  Much will depend upon practices
of land ownership, transfer, and use--the ways in which the
society arranges its economic affairs as regards land and
buildings.  When the property tax applies to machinery and
business inventory--and possibly to furniture, automobiles,
jewelry, and other personal property--the use of value
rather than annual income seems essential, as no direct
income measure is normally available.

## Setting Capital Values to Use for Taxation (Assessments)

Someone, of course, must designate the value figures to
be used for tax purposes.  Various terms are used to modify
"value" as applied to property taxation--"normal," "fair,"
"in use," "owner's," and so on.  In most cases, the figures
are estimates, and making them presents formidable
administrative problems if the job is to be done well.
Experience testifies to great difficulty in achieving high
quality in administration in this respect.

Presumably, the standard of valuation--that is, the
general criterion or goal--will be market price as applied to
all property.  Some fraction, such as 50 percent, may be used.
This can serve reasonably well, provided it is uniform for
all properties.  Reliance upon market tests is of great
practical importance.

Current market prices are to be preferred to those of
some past date.  Today's prices will generally give a better
reflection of relative abilities to pay than market prices of
the past.  Present values should also give the best guide to
the forces that taxes exert for the allocation of property
among possible uses.  Valuations used for tax purposes may
not be changed for years on end.  Such practice may be
intentional or may come by default because of the inadequacy
of administrative facilities.  Changes in urban patterns have
made cadastral systems that were once reasonably accurate (by
some standards) grossly out of date as regards valuation.
The Federal Republic of Germany is a case in point.

## Rates

As regards land values--site or location values--alone,
the tax rate as a percentage of capital value can be very
high in relation to the amount after the tax itself has been
capitalized into lower land prices.  Rates of tax on structures
and other man-made capital cannot by any means be so high,
except perhaps for a very brief time.  Flows of capital will
respond to the incentive to seek locations of lower burden.
The revenue effects--the net yields--of differences in tax
rates depend not only upon the rates themselves but also upon
the effects of the rates on the tax base.

The higher the tax rate, the greater the importance
attached to the assessment.  The money amount of tax--the
revenue--will depend on the assessed valuation.  Owners have
strong incentives to try to have values fixed low;
administrative officials, therefore, must expect to secure
and retain low tax valuations.  In addition, the fairness of
burdens as among taxpayers will be affected by errors in
valuation.  The economic effects, as property owners take
account of the tax, and their desire to adjust to it, will
also be greater when tax rates are high.

## Effects in Addition to Those of Revenue

A tax based on current capital value of land on the
market can be supported as desirable in order to bring the
land into the most economically productive use.  The price
that land would bring in the market is often significantly
higher than that which would be justified by the use to which
it is currently put.  If a tax is based on the value of land
in its current use, as is often advocated on the grounds that
otherwise the tax levied will be out of line with the revenues
available to pay it, this will introduce a bias into decisions
as to when to develop the property for a new use.  Since
development now involves an increase in the tax to be paid,
it is likely to be postponed.  If the tax is levied on the
basis of full market value rather than on the lower value
involved in the current use, the higher "cost" of holding
the land may induce development.  This is not necessarily
desirable since the socially optimum procedure may well be
a slower pace of development of land.  If, however, the owner
of the lot is able to finance the tax payments at the market
interest costs, or sell it at a fair price, the options open
to him will have the same relative yield as they would in the
absence of any tax.  His decision would, in principle, be the
same.  Conceivably, therefore, some compromise might help
matters.  One solution is deferment of that part of the tax
obligation that corresponds to the excess of market value
over current use value, with a suitable rate of interest

charged; the deferred tax would become a lien on the property. In this way, the impact of the tax on the timing of development will be neutralized, and the decision on the timing of development can be made as though there were no tax involved.

If the tax is applied to improvements as well as to the land, however, this neutrality is lost, and development is discouraged, deferred, or diverted to less efficient, less intensive forms. When more is invested in a property in order to improve it, the amount of tax due will increase. New capital investment, mostly in buildings, will enlarge the base on which the owner must pay tax. By some standards--for example, in certain views regarding ability to pay--such a result may seem desirable. Someone does possess more property than existed in the area before, and this may seem a good basis for taxation. When an old and obsolete structure is replaced by a new and better one, the tax will go up. Will the owner who has added new capital, and will the renters using the property, get more government services for the added tax? Perhaps, but more probably the revenues added to the government's coffers will bring no discernible benefits to those who pay. The heavier tax then constitutes an incentive against capital investment.

Is the creation of such an incentive desirable? Is not new construction almost always desired, especially in developing countries? If the tax rate is low, the effects of the tax in discouraging progress will be correspondingly small. If the tax rate is high, any proposal to exempt buildings and other man-made property will perhaps conflict with widely accepted concepts of ability to pay. In general, a tax that introduces or reinforces a tendency to discourage building would seem to be unwise if better alternatives for raising revenue can be devised.

If the jurisdictions using the property tax are small, with each locality having considerable independence with regard to its tax rate, as is the situation in the United States, the adverse pressure of a tax disincentive can be serious for localities with above-average tax rates (unless expenditure levels benefit the owners and users of the property to an equal extent). Less new capital will find its way into the specific areas of high taxes if other places with lower rates are available as locations for investment.

A property tax might, of course, cover the whole economy at about the same rate. Such a tax would leave fewer opportunities for shifting new investment funds in order to keep tax lower than local taxes utilizing rates which differ widely from one place to another. However, some of the potential advantages of local freedom and autonomy would be lost.

Neither the income from the property nor the actual current use will directly determine the amount of tax when capital value is the base. In generaly, the value of a piece of property is the capitalization of the net benefits (income) it is expected to bring in the future.


## Tax Based on Income

Tax on land and buildings may be based upon the income produced (rent) rather than the (estimated) capital value. The United Kingdom and parts of the British Commonwealth utilize this method. In the United Kingdom, the tax falls on the occupier; land is not taxed.

## The Income Concept Used as the Tax Base

The base used may be the actual income, gross or net, subject to various provisions regarding calculation. Or it may be some past income figure, actual or assumed. The lag may be a year or two only, or much longer. Some presumption or estimate of the amount of income currently produced by the property may also be used. Finally, tax may rest upon an estimate of the potential income, on what could be obtained, when the current use of the property is not the best. Where rental values are expected to be stable over time, a tax based on income might not differ much from one based on capital value.

The income (rent) actually received can differ materially from the full potential--that is from what could be obtained--where land is vacant or much underutilized. Where this is the case, the tax can differ significantly from one based on capital value, unless the government insists upon using a presumptive rental figure that takes full account of the potential. In Singapore, for example, land deemed to be vacant can be assessed on the basis of an imputed rental of 5 percent of capital value.

In India, where the income basis of taxation has been used in some places since 1793, rent controls in many localities have for many years, along with other factors, depressed revenues. What might be a normally growing revenue source has been held back by rent freezes. Nevertheless, the tax provides a considerable portion of the revenue raised by local governments.

In France, the French-speaking countries of West Africa, and Indochina, urban property and land improvements both are taxed on a net rental basis. For maintenance, depreciation, insurance, and other such expenses, standard percentages are

deducted from the gross rent.   Numerous Arab countries also use
some form of net rental basis.

## Rates

Tax rates are difficult to express in meaningful terms.
Nominal rates--as high as 36 percent of annual rental value in
Singapore and 33 percent in some places in India--are misleading.
The valuations on which the taxes actually rest are far below
the true current income, but by amounts that cannot be determined from the evidence available.   In the United Kingdom,
rates are payable by the occupant and may exceed the net for
the owner.

## Economic Effects

Tax based on actual realized income may be criticized for
failing to put pressure on owners to make the best use of
property.   It is, of course, appealing to the speculator.   As
long as the actual use does not bring much income of the type
that forms the basis for tax, this tax costs him little.   Most
of what he gets or hopes to get ("income" in a broad sense)
will consist of rising capital value, but this rise does not
enter into the income calculation used in computing the
property tax base.   The inducement to "higher and better use"
is much less than would result from a tax based on market value.

A property tax of this type may conform rather closely to
an income tax as such, at least as regards computation of the
tax base, for income from one source.   The tax may thus seem
to conform to an in personam levy, which meets standards of
ability to pay, although a more complete analysis would reveal
weaknesses in any such conclusion.   Only a portion of the
income of families would be reached and then usually at a flat
rate.

Such a tax as it falls on output or income could influence
incentives significantly.   In an agricultural area, for example,
if the government were to take a considerable portion of the
crop as the property tax, the operator might produce less than
if the tax rate were negligible or zero, especially if the tax
were on increments of output.   Taxes at rates high enough to
produce substantial revenue could exert appreciable influence
as a marginal force on property income.   The results will
depend upon factors that may be quite special to a particular
economy.   In principle, adverse incentive effects could be
drastically reduced while revenue remained substantial by
structuring a tax to have high average but low marginal rates
on the output attributable to capital and labor (and the
opposite on land).   The practical obstacles to devising such
a tax, however, seem to rule it out, except perhaps in special
situations.

## Administration

Problems of administration differ from those encountered
in the case of tax based on capital value. In some respects,
the rental basis seems simpler. In many economies, far more
properties are under rental agreements than are sold each
year; therefore, more market tests of current conditions would
seem to be potentially available. More tax determinations can
actually rest on valuations as made in the market. In choosing
between the two bases (capital value and rental), the relative
frequency of various forms of ownership and lease arrangements
should be taken into account. Is use by owners more common
than rental? Are complicated arrangements for splitting and
dividing various rights permitted and customary--for example,
as in superimposed levels of tenancy and subtenancy?

In the case of property occupied by the owner--housing,
for example--no money income as such may be received. In such
cases, presumptive amounts must be estimated. In extreme
cases, rental transactions may be even scarcer than sales so
that rental may be even harder to determine from the market
than capital value. If business and residential properties
are generally on a rental basis, it might seem that the
annual income will be rather clearly indicated for perhaps a
majority of properties. But where a business is conducted on
the property--farming or retailing, for example--income
figures and rentals may mix business receipts and expenditures
with those of the taxable element per se. Getting an estimate
of what is really desired for tax purposes may require a
complicated separation of elements.

Problems will also arise in deciding the degree of net
value as against a gross rental basis. For example, what
figure is appropriate for building depreciation? Gross rents
can be used, with arbitrary deductions for expenses. Other
possible complications will ensue from subleasing, the
inclusion of varying combinations of services provided by
landlords in the rental, and payments in kind.

### Taxes Based on Some Objective Characteristics

A tax on property, presumably an annual tax, could be
imposed according to more or less objective factors, such as
size, location, usage, or governmental facilities provided--
that is, elements that do not directly involve valuation.
Such a tax could bring in revenue without being the only one
related to property; in other words, it could be used to
supplement other property taxes. It would be more suitable
for urban than for rural areas. This type of tax has certain
potential merits. It might well be simpler to administer than

taxes on value.  If each year's tax, or a part of it, rested
upon the number of square meters in a plot of ground or on the
cubic contents of a building, determining the amount due could
be easier than attempting to value a capital amount or income.
Subjective factors, which can be so important in valuations,
would be largely eliminated.  The base could be unchanged from
year to year, while the tax rate, so much per square meter of
land surface, could be altered.  Adjustments could be made for
location, one part of a city offering more government
facilities than another, or for the type as well as the size
of structure.  The greater the attempt to refine the adjustments, the less the merit of simplicity.

The costs of some government services and the worth of
services received by owners and users of land and buildings,
may be more closely related to physical characteristics than
to value.  Resource allocation could tend to benefit somewhat
from such tying of tax to service costs, if the figures were
set with such an objective in mind.  Decision makers in local
government might perhaps be subjected to more effective
pressure to assure the provision of services, while having a
rather more than normally good prospect of getting funds to
help cover the cost.  The worth of services provided by
government will, of course, influence property values and
income.

Less bias against investment in new buildings and in
improvements would result from a tax of this kind than from a
tax on value.  However, criticism might arise if deteriorated
(slum) buildings were taxed about the same as buildings of
much better quality.  In fact, poor structures might be taxed
even more heavily per room if the tax was designed to penalize
buildings subject to fire hazard and to encourage those of
high quality, which cost government less and are presumably
better for the community.

Adjusting the tax partially to the governmental services
received may have merit on grounds of fairness.  Those users
and owners of property getting more benefits from expenditures--
streets, sewers, water supply, lighting, and so on--would pay
more, while owners and users of properties receiving fewer
services would incur less tax.  At least one aspect of fairness and equity would tend to be achieved.  Care must be taken,
however, not to construe the notion of benefit too narrowly.
For example, a stonemason  may consider that his establishment
has no need for fire protection.  Nevertheless, if he is using
land that is provided with fire protection, his use is
displacing others who might build structures on the property
that would benefit from the protection and he should in
principle be prepared to pay for the protection service even
though he makes no direct use of it.  Indeed, the location of

the stonemasonry within the area provided with fire protection
would be justifiable only if the patrons of the masonry were
prepared to pay sufficiently for the convenience of having the
masonry nearby so that, in effect, they compensate for the
exclusion of the potential tenants of the building that might
be built on the site. The mason benefits from the presence of
the firehouse in that it protects his patrons who without the
fire protection would live further away and not be willing to
pay him so much.

The cost of the fire protection is to be assessed against
the property to which the protection service is extended,
independently of the presence of any combustible structure on
the property, if efficient use of the land is to be promoted.
Limiting charges for the cost of the fire protection to the
combustible structures that benefit directly in a naive sense
will result in uneconomical stinting in the erection of such
structures within the area protected by the firehouse.

For financing a limited range of governmental services, a
tax of this sort might well be appropriate, not only as being
relatively easy to administer and as encouraging efficiency in
resource allocation, but also as being fair. This base would
relate to the benefit principle of taxation, which has merit
for some purposes. Problems would arise in setting up dividing
lines between services appropriately financed on a benefit
basis as compared with ability to pay, for example. Funds for
financing the more general services of government--national,
provincial, and local--would presumably have to come from
other sources--income and consumption taxes. But if these
sources were freed from responsibility for financing specific
functions such as streets, lighting, water supply, sewers,
and garbage collection, general benefits would, in a sense,
flow from the specific taxes. The choice need not rest upon
such conclusions, however, for the more direct and limited
considerations may seem adequate for a decision.

In some respects, however, the use of physical factors
would not correspond to what might be considered fair
according to ability to pay as it is often envisaged. Two
properties of the same size but significantly different
capital value, or that produced significantly different
income, might be taxed the same. The tax actually borne by
different persons would not conform to their wealth, income,
or consumption.

If revenue from the tax were considerable, the grounds for
criticizing such a form of taxation as failing to conform to
ability to pay might be serious. Rather large differences in
burden might derive from factors that seem to bear little
rational relation to important considerations of tax policy.

### Increments in Value as a Base for Special Taxes

Land prices, especially in urban and nearby areas, often rise because of general increases in population and income and through movement to the cities. In addition, the rise in demand can make existing buildings worth more. Owners receive increases in wealth, "unearned increments," vastly above anything that is due to their additions of capital to enhance the worth of the property.

### Unearned Increment as a Basis for Property Taxation

Such socially created increases in wealth are true economic surpluses. Taxes to capture a sizable portion of them for government have great appeal in principle. The arguments in favor of taxes on such increments are very persuasive, and the process of urbanization adds to their force.

Numerous efforts have been made to impose special taxes on increments in land and other property values, but the practical difficulties are formidable. They depend, among other things, upon the features of the particular tax, the nature of the economic system and its methods of conducting business, the laws regarding property ownership and transactions, and the quality of tax administration.

Decrements in the value of land and other property can also result from general social forces, including the results of governmental actions. The risks of such loss will be considered by owners. Tax refunds or offsets where decrements occur are unlikely even if they are coupled with a tax on increments, Yet, for reasons of fairness, recognition of such losses would seem to be necessary. A tax on increments alone would add to the risks of ownership. The amount of land would not be reduced, but demand for it (and thus prices) would be lessened.

An annual tax either on capital value or on the income that could be obtained will, if the tax is kept (moderately) up-to-date, impose increasing burdens as properties become more valuable and reduce tax where values drop. The results may fall short of the ideal of an increment tax but may be about as much as is practically obtainable. Resources for administering taxes are likely to continue to be seriously limited in most of the world. In the circumstances, concentrating on a basic annual tax would probably be wiser than allocating part of the available manpower to administer a tax on increments in value. As a practical matter, the continuing annual tax will have far greater revenue significance. Despite the appeal of heavy taxes on increments, the practical possibilities of getting revenues are limited compared with the potentialities of an annual tax.

## Income and Death Taxes as Means of Reaching Some Increments

If a government has an income tax, and most do, it might
be made to apply to capital gains and losses generally.
Increases in land and other property values would in some
cases be taxed.  (Usually, only realized changes in value,
not accruals, are taxed.)  Influential pressures against
taxing capital gains have kept them largely free from income
tax in most countries.

The arguments against taxing gains, to the extent that
they may have merit, do not, in the author's view, apply to
increments in land prices.  For example, one may question
the desirability of taxing the growth in the worth of interests
in businesses when they represent the plowing-back of earnings
that have to some degree been taxed already.  But there do
exist unearned increments in tax values resulting from public
investments and general development and not from the
reinvestment of owner's income that has already been taxed.

Limited resources for tax administration would, in the
author's opinion, be used to better advantage in making a
general income tax effective, and by including capital gains
in full in the income tax base than by a special tax on
increments in value.  Such a procedure is all the more
advisable in that full inclusion of gains can be made a key
step in substantial simplification of the income tax law
through eliminating the often capricious, detailed, and
arbitrary provisions needed to draw the final legal
distinctions between ordinary income and capital gains when
these are treated differently.  Some of the revenue might be
assigned to the local government where the property is
located, on the grounds that expenditures on infrastructure
had produced some of the increment, or that the funds were
needed there for new projects, though this would probably be
more tedious and less in line with relative local needs than
other bases for the distribution of such funds.

Another somewhat indirect approach to the taxation of
increments falls within the more traditional pattern of
government finance, at least in more developed countries.
Taxes on wealth transferred at death (supplemented by a tax
on lifetime gifts of capital to heirs) will apply to
increments in property values as they pass from one
generation to the next.  A death tax would presumably not
single out such increments for heavier taxes than are applied
to property acquired from savings out of income.  Thus, normal
death taxation does not achieve a special form of tax equity
in the form of extra burdens on unearned increments as
contrasted with property acquired from constructive efforts
and thrift.  We live in an imperfect world, however, in which

taxation is one of the elements furthest from perfection.
Perhaps most countries would do better to concentrate on
making a general system of death taxation operate as well as
possible, rather than on trying to enforce in addition a tax
on increments in property values.

## Possible Rates

A high rate might be considered--60 percent of the
increment or even more, or less extreme rates of 25 to
40 percent--if the tax were really limited to unearned
increments and excluded the results of the owner's use of
capital and effort to improve the land.  The higher the tax
rate, of course, the greater the effect of the tax on
incentives and behavior, the greater the inducements to
avoidance and evasion, and the larger the problems of good
administration.

In terms of fairness, high rates on such a base can
survive much criticism.  How can the owners of land with
large-value increments who are forced to pay complain that
they are being deprived of something of their own creation?
What is being taken away is presumably not any reward for
their effort and investment.  To assure this result, however,
provision must be made for the cases in which the owner has in
fact made investments to enhance the worth of the land-drainage,
clearing, and so on.  Sellers of land could complain, of
course, that they were being discriminated against as compared
with owners with gains who do not sell.

## Practical Issues

A serious stumbling block is the absence of reliable data
on values as of some base period.  Unless an accurate set of
values has been established in the past, as by a good property
cadaster, it might be a long time before much increment could
be taxed.  Nevertheless, societies might now begin to
establish records of values in order to permit future taxation
of increments.

Inflation also presents problems.  Should owners be
allowed to adjust the money amount of gain in order to take
some account of the loss in the purchasing power of money?
If so, on what basis?  Israel's land appreciation tax adjusts
for the length of time the land is held, a 0.5 percent
reduction of tax being permitted for each month owned through
15 years, then followed by 1 percent a year until tax
disappears after 37 years.  The higher the rate of tax, the
greater is the need to make allowance for issues growing out
of inflation.

On most urban and suburban land, there will be one or more buildings or other improvements, and sales figures will apply to land and buildings combined. The separation of value elements between the two can raise difficulties. To include increments in building values would require depreciation to be taken into account and outlays for current maintenance and for improvements to be separated. If a very high rate of tax is involved, controversy would be lively. The strains on administration could be serious. To ignore the nonland elements would require skill and good records in order to overcome the effects of incentives to distort the figures.

Another problem would arise out of the possibility of using methods of land transfer, which would enable the tax to be avoided, perhaps legally, perhaps illegally. Greater use of leases for longer terms would need to be taken into account. Concealing transactions, as well as misreporting the terms of sale, may be used to save tax. It must be assumed that the society includes landowners who are quite as ingenious as the persons who devise the law. Incentives to escape a tax at very high rates will be strong. One indirect but potentially effective device is to keep the administrative organization inadequately provided with funds for enforcement.

If the rates of tax are progressive according to the percentage of gain--for example, 20 percent on the first 100 percent of gain and 50 percent on gains over 400 percent-- owners may have an incentive to engage in artificial transactions in order to multiply the number of separate events rather than utilize only one.

The incentives to avoid or delay sale could also be strong. As a result, actions to put land to better use would encounter an adverse tax factor. Holding land off from more socially desirable uses would be a normal result tending to raise prices. Such a result runs directly counter to one objective of the tax--to discourage (undesirable) speculation and induce improvements in the use of land. On the other hand, to assess the tax at a high rate on the basis of appraised increments would put a heavy strain on the appraisal process.

On the whole, there are persuasive reasons in favor of a serious effort to examine the possibilities of taxing increments in land value, especially if capital gains are not subject to effective income taxation.

## Experience with Increment Taxes

The United Kingdom has made various attempts to tax increments, starting before World War I. None would be classed as a success, and all have been abandoned (the latest in 1971). The most recent, the Betterment Levy, was a limited tax requiring highly sophisticated administrative effort. It applied, in effect, to the increase in value of land through certain governmental actions that permitted more productive use. The levy did not apply to the more general rises in value from expanding population and income, or even to the results from government spending on new facilities. Whether or not it might, within its narrow terms, eventually have been judged successful, it would not be a model for the kind of increment levies generally proposed. It did have a dampening effect on the conversion of property to new uses.

Johannesburg and various other localities of the Republic of South Africa apply essentially the same sort of levy on increments of value resulting from governmental grants for more profitable use. The revenues are used to pay for certain urban development functions. These levies, too, put heavy demands upon the skilled valuation of properties before and just after official action. Administrative capacity of such a high order is especially scarce in developing countries, and what is available will probably be used to better advantage on taxes of more general application and with greater revenue potential.

Some years ago, Japan reduced its capital gains tax as applied to suburban land in order to encourage sales. The objective was to make land available, particularly for housing. In 1970, New South Wales (Australia) began to develop and implement plans for a Development Contribution. A tax (contribution) of 30 percent applies to increases in the value of nonurban land in the Sydney area. The tax applies to increments after August 1969 (values as fixed by the Valuer General) adjusted upward by 2 percent a year. Tax is due if land is sold or if a new "development consent" is granted. The statutes of some countries in Latin America provide for taxes on value increments, but the administration does not, apparently, tax many gains, except as part of general taxes on capital gains under income tax legislation.

## Taxation of Transfers of Property

Changes of property ownership may be made the occasion for a transfer tax. Some kind of official recording may be required for purposes quite independent of tax considerations. Records of property titles and changes in ownership may be

desirable for reasons of economic policy, to serve as a basis
for claims, or for other purposes. Requirements may be so
exacting that one if not both parties has a compelling self-
interest in recording and, perhaps, even accurate reporting
of the terms. To attach a tax where there is such a recorded
change of ownership may seem easy.* Sometimes, however,
learning the true price will be difficult. Transfers of
securities may be taxed--but not bearer issues--and the
existence of bearer securities can go far to frustrate such a
tax.

Presumably the tax rate would be uniform (flat rate).
Attempts to make the tax progressive--X percent for values up
to 100X, then 2X percent on the next 100X, and so on--would
greatly complicate matters. Incentives to split ownership
and parcel transfers would exert an influence.

If the transfer is a sale, enough cash may be involved
to make the payment of a tax relatively simple. In effect,
the government can take a part of the funds changing hands.
If the transfer is by gift or exchange, however, cash for
payment may not be so naturally available. Complex
transactions, and leases long enough to be virtually sales,
would present problems.

The tax would not reduce the quantity of land. It might,
however, discourage new construction and investment in
buildings, because the net attractiveness would be reduced by
the tax on any transfer. Marketability and liquidity would
suffer to the extent that the net return expected would be
lessened.

There is not much economic logic for basing tax on the
transfer of ownership. In other words, change of ownership
of property is not so obviously a sensible basis for taxation
as ownership (use) year by year. An intermittent and
irregular tax, once every 2 or 3 years in some cases, once in
10 years in some, once a generation or longer in others, can
hardly be justified on accepted criteria of tax fairness.
There is also reason to criticize such a tax on economic
grounds.

If the amount of tax is other than nominal--large enough
to bring significant revenue--the prospective burden will
deter transfers. It will tend to distort planning and

---

*By tax, of course, is meant an amount considerably in
excess of recording fees, which are in line with the
governmental costs of performing the service.

decisions by introducing a tax elements foreign to the
inherent economic merits of choices.  A tax that will be owing
if a transaction occurs--and not payable if there is no
transfer--will reduce the attractiveness of transfers.

A good market in property serves a useful economic
purpose.  It aids in the allocation of resources for better
results.  Shifting from one use to another will affect the
efficiency and productivity with which properties are used.
Consolidation and division of land and other property are
elements of the economic process that can be expected to aid
in improving productivity.  (Sales of securities are an
indication of the relative attractiveness of different
investments.  A capital market serves a valuable purpose and
can play a useful role in economic development.)  Of course,
property transfers are not always constructive.  In general,
however, owners will try for changes that have the promise of
better uses.  Buyers will pay more only if they expect to
make the new use justify the terms offered.

A tax high enough to yield appreciable revenue will
discourage transfers and thus hamper shifts to better use.
Some sales will be delayed, and tax-induced delays will do
nothing constructive to improve the economy.  Governments
must have revenue but the nonrevenue results (fewer transfers)
would be a social cost of the tax.  An "excess burden" element
occurs in the shape of costs to the economy that bring no
benefit to the treasury.

Ownership by corporations (and by personal trusts in
countries such as the United Kingdom and the United States,
where the legal system permits it) could be used to avoid
taxable transfers of tangible property while at the same time
permitting changes of economic benefit.  Subterfuges and
inefficiencies can result, which distort the system of
property ownership.

A low-rate tax could, of course, bring in some funds
without introducing substantial inhibitions on transfer.  It
could be used for obtaining information about terms of sale.
For many years, the U.S. government imposed a stamp tax of
0.1 percent of the sale price of real estate and thereby
obtained useful data, which became matters of public record.

## Levies to Pay for Facilities

Some government expenditure goes to things that are to a large extent localized--construction projects of various kinds, such as streets, sewers, lighting and water supply systems, and services such as garbage collection (as well as housing, in some places). Most of the benefits are obtained by users in the area and, therefore, differ to some degree from the more fundamentally general and collective benefits. Property owners benefit directly if they are also the users; if they rent the property to others, they will presumably be able to get higher rentals when lease rentals are renegotiated.* Although some general public benefit extends to people beyond the particular area, the element of localization is clear enough to make possible the use of special financing devices. Various names may be given to such financing--in the United States, the term is "special assessment." Use of this means of raising revenue increased gradually during the nineteenth century and assumed considerable importance by the 1920s, after which it declined markedly. Since World War II, use has varied from community to community. (Bogota and some other cities of Colombia utilize a "valorization" system, which collects the costs of major street and some other urban projects from the owners of land in the areas affected.)

Some or all of the cost of the project can be covered by taxes on nearby properties. Owners can be given the opportunity to join together to initiate undertakings they are willing to pay for. The normal processes of government decision making can be supplemented--and in a way that has some merit. There are facilities that people usually rely upon government rather than the private sector to supply. Groups smaller than the total community that are able and willing to pay for such facilities can get what they want and need not be held back by other groups in the city or some larger area. Where such financing is available, economic development ought to be more rapid, and more in line with the preferences of those directly concerned, than when decisions rest entirely upon the processes of government in larger units.

Answers to the practical problems require careful preparation and continuing administrative effort. For example, to what extent, if any, will the owners of property be given a voice in the selection and planning of projects? Will property

---

*Long-term leases and various complex arrangements for subleasing and erecting superstructures of interests exist. They will affect the actual incidence of benefits from government services and the ability of owners and subtenants to alter the rental charges to capture some of the worth of changes in government programs.

owners (or users) have an opportunity to take the initiative?
How will the costs be allocated among the various properties?
If benefits do not equal the costs that are assigned, will
owners have the right to appeal and get redress?  How will
adjustments be made?  If benefits are greater for some
properties than the charges originally assigned, will government
demand some of the excess?  How will owners get cash to pay?

### Taxes on Property Passing at Death and by Gift

Property taxes as generally conceived, and as described
so far, are in rem rather than in personam levies.  Ultimately
they rest on people.  But in their final incidence the burdens
do not necessarily amount to what would seem desirable by one
criterion or another as regards the distribution of taxes.  We
refer again, therefore, to the possibility of supplementing
annual in rem property taxes by taxes at death, which may be
somewhat more rationally adjusted to personal ability to pay.

Inheritance, legacy, estate, accession, and gift taxes
take various forms.  The amount due can be related to the size
of the amount passed from the decedent or to those received by
the individual heirs.  The taxes can also be imposed at
graduated rates.  Thus, they can be designed to further what
may be felt as objectives of equity among individuals in
sharing the costs of government.

Whereas annual property taxes may, in some cases, be
shifted from the point of initial impact to other persons who
have no awareness of the burden--and who may not be the
persons who ought to bear the tax in the amounts involved--
taxes on capital values passing at death or by gift can rest,
unshifted, on the persons originally burdened.  Some
observers would attach importance to the use of death and gift
taxes to achieve certain goals of fairness.  These taxes can
perhaps make up for some of the weaknesses of property taxes
as far as sharing the cost of government is concerned.
Persons who do not have much wealth, and some who do, may
believe that justice can be served by coming down heavily on
transfers at death or by gift.

The net effects of a lifetime's activities may be a
particularly suitable basis for taxation. (However, the person
whose affairs are considered is the one passing from the scene,
not the person securing the property.)  Death taxes can apply
to net worth after allowing for debts in a way that annual
property taxes do not take into account logically and
systematically.  Intangible property (securities) can be
reached, along with the tangible forms to which annual
property taxes apply.  Unearned increments can be taxed if they
are retained until death (or become taxable as a gift).

Some observers, for egalitarian or other reasons, favor taxes that reduce large holdings of property. This concern may be closely related to land reform--rural or urban--and the objective may be less the reduction of total wealth holdings per family than the breakup of landed estates or large holdings of urban land. Redistribution that may not be achievable by tax or other means in the normal course of events, from year to year, may be forced by taxes at death.

The issues raised in discussions of the redistribution of capital by taxation at death are exceedingly difficult to deal with in a responsible manner, in making recommendations for public policy--especially in general terms not related to specific countries and their social and economic systems or their systems of general values. With or without much real basis for solid assurance, writers may express considerable agreement on the principle of reducing the perpetuation of major economic inequalities by inheritance and gift. New generations, they may argue, should not have so unequal a start as would be the case if all the property of parents were passed to their heirs. Death taxes can play a role in reducing holdings of wealth as well as in raising revenue.

Yet generalities are not enough for actual provisions of tax law. How can agreement be reached on the specific features that are essential for concrete action? The precise numbers-- actual death rates--that will further the achievement of such objectives, for example, as offsetting weaknesses in annual property taxes do not follow from general theory. Moreover, actual taxes on capital may hamper the realization of other goals, such as capital accumulation and economic progress. The ability to save and the incentive to do so will be affected by actual and prospective taxes.

Advocates of use of death taxes for purposes of redistribution may be tempted to go too far in supporting rates that are high and steeply graduated. Incentives for evasion multiply under such conditions. Death taxes, being based on the accident of death, are often capricious in their impact. Undesirable economic effects are not prevented by good intentions.

One problem of death taxation in the United States involves forced liquidation of business firms as a result of the tax. Developing countries will have to face similar issues to the extent that their enterprises are privately owned. In many cases, business firms are built up as a result of efforts and investments by one or a few individuals and their families. A significant amount of the growth of the economy may derive from such closely owned companies. Some- times the result is an establishment in which the owner has

enough wealth to be subject to heavy death tax.  The tax may
amount to a sizable fraction of the worth of the business
itself.  Government will usually insist upon payment, perhaps
soon after death, in liquid funds--money or perhaps government
bonds.  But the estate may have difficulty in making such
payments.  The firm will probably have needed all the liquid
funds available to it in order to finance its operations.  The
accumulation of excess cash before death in order to prepare
for the payment of inheritance tax would be a costly, and
almost certainly for the business firm wasteful, use of
resources.  Success in the company's own operations will
ordinarily take more and more financing as the firm expands.
A shortage of cash for growth, rather than an excess of funds,
is frequently the case, at least in the United States.
Inadequate capital, liquid funds in particular, restrains the
expansion of output and employment, and progress in the
reduction of costs and improvement of quality, through the
acquisition and use of better equipment.  (Each year's taxes
will seem to the owner to impair the company's ability to
grow.)

How can the owner before death, and the executor of his
estate after it, accumulate cash without hurting the business?
Insurance on the life of the owner may be proposed as a way out,
but the payment of premiums on life insurance takes funds that
would be helpful in the enterprise, while the value of the
policy itself will often be included in the taxable estate.
Inevitably, the company's finances will be strained at
precisely the time when the business is also undergoing
stresses associated with changes in ownership.

In the case of land, some payment "in kind" might be
possible.  The government might accept a fraction of the land
in payment of tax due.  Such a possibility might also be in
conformity with nonrevenue purposes, for example, if the
breaking up of land holdings were itself an objective.  But
practical problems, such as actual procedures of government
ownership, management, and possibly distribution, might create
complexities.

Possibilities may exist for tax avoidance through the use
of trusts, generation-skipping transfers, arranging transfers
so as to escape the jurisdiction of high tax countries, as by
purchase, gift, and sale of tax-haven real estate, or, as a
last resort, by emigration prior to transfer.

Devising a good system of death and gift taxes presents
more difficulties than are appreciated save by a few experts.
The conclusion to be drawn is not that the task is too
difficult to undertake, but that it calls for both skill and
effort, plus recognition of the positive role a good system of

death taxation can play. Special care must be taken to fit
the tax into the legal, social, and economic traditions and
realities of the country. Administrative problems can be
greater than foreseen, and extreme rates can be counterproductive.

## ADMINISTRATION

Administration of property taxation has often been poor.
In fact, high-quality enforcement, frequently achieved for
other taxes, is rare, even in the more developed areas. If
the various requirements for good administration are
recognized, however, efforts can be made to employ methods
that have been used with success elsewhere. Improvements can
also be developed. The United Nations' Manual of Land Tax
Administration provides an excellent foundation. Only a few
points of special importance will be noted here. Property
taxes present special difficulties of administration which
account for some of the failure of these taxes to become more
important sources of revenue.

## ASSESSMENT

### Absence of Direct Tie to Market Transactions

One source of difficulty is that an annual property tax
is not imposed coincident with a market transaction.
Enforcement must be accomplished without the active
cooperation of a disinterested party, as exists in the
administration of other important taxes. Income taxes can be
largely withheld by the employer, while consumption taxes must
generally be paid before a buyer receives his purchase. These
two groups of taxes, therefore, are closely bound up with
decisions and actions determined by nontax considerations.
Enforcement can thus center on economic transactions. The
terms of transaction--a wage payment or a conscious purchase--
and hence the amount of tax will be fixed by market forces.
This objective determination of the amount of the tax is not
generally possible with the property tax.

### Physical Identification and Valuation

Efforts must be made in designing the structure of a
property tax to take account of local and national conditions.
Given the structure of the tax, the conditions needed to make
the tax effective can be set down as guidelines for effective
administration.

1.    The first requirement  is the listing of properties
to be taxed.  Mapping requires care--for example, in making
accurate records of plot size, shape, and location.  Building
characteristics must be discovered and recorded.  A thorough
cadastral survey by traditional methods can be expensive, and
perhaps beyond what is of practical use in the circumstances.
Aerial mapping, however, can be relatively inexpensive and
quite effective as a base for use in preparing the tax rates.
Keeping the information up to date presents demands that can
be met--provided staff and other resources are adequate.  A
system of building permits will help here.

The total job of physical identification and description
requires various skills, considerable time to amass a complete
starting inventory, and continuing efforts to keep up-to-date.

2.    Under most types of property tax, the listing and
description of the physical features will usually be only a
starting point.  The next step is a value figure (capital or
income).  Property tax ordinarily rests upon a judgment or
determination (assertion) by an official.  Almost always,
the official can place the estimate higher or lower over a
considerable range.  His decision, therefore, can have much to
do with the amount of tax payable.

Owners (or occupants if they are responsible for payment)
obviously have an inducement to seek to have values set low
for property tax purposes.  When tax rates are high enough to
produce substantial revenue, the incentive to try to influence
valuation is powerful.

A bias against the government results, because no
personal interest of equal force exists in favor of high
assessment.  No one on the other side of the valuation
process--the government side--has the same direct personal
interest.  Pressure for poor valuation--understatement--can
be sustained and effective.  Substantial evidence from all
over the world shows that the forces in favor of low
valuations will succeed in being effective even when needs
for government revenue are serious and pressing.  Automatic
checks by market processes cannot be expected to protect the
government's revenue interest.

Moreover, inequalities of valuation, and of tax, can
produce considerable inequity.  Some owners will be more
successful than others in pressing for low valuations.  For
this and other reasons, inequalities produce inequitable
differences in tax.

## Land Alone Easier to Value Than Land Plus Buildings and Machinery

The mapping and valuation of land will be less difficult than the work needed in the case of a tax that includes additional types of property. One of the arguments in favor of confining tax to land is simpler administration. Generally speaking, lots in the same neighborhood can be assessed equitably at closely similar values per unit of acre; substantial discrepancies will be apparent even to relatively unsophisticated taxpayers. Comparison of values inclusive of improvements, which are likely to lack such a patent common denominator, will be more difficult; inequities are more likely to arise and go unchallenged. Experts in developing countries report that many of the most difficult problems arise in connection with the identification and valuation of buildings, in all their vast diversity, machinery, goods in process, and other types of property. Where administrative resources are very limited, a realistic facing of conditions will include frank recognition of the advantages of not attempting to tax those types of asset that are most difficult to value effectively.

## Self-Assessment

One course that may be considered is self-assessment. Government might reserve the right to acquire properties at the owner's declared value or that value plus a certain percentage. Some land will be needed for streets, schools, parks, government buildings, possibly housing, and other purposes. Owners could be made responsible for setting the property value to be used as the base for taxation. In that case, undervaluation to save annual tax would involve the risk of forced sale to government at less than the true worth. (If the tax rests upon annual income rather than capital value, the government's right to acquire properties would be at a multiple of the declared income--perhaps 20 times the income, or the equivalent of an annual yield of 5 percent.) The basis for computing the amount of capital gains upon sales might be the valuation by the owner approved for property taxation. In countries where such self-assessment is used for land values, it is usually a supplement to carefully made initial governmental valuations.

Conceivably, any private person or business, not merely government itself, might be given the opportunity to acquire the property at a price related to the figure set by the owner for tax purposes. Such a possibility, however, would give rise to many problems. For example, it would weaken confidence in the security of property. Even with careful planning and many precautions, enough popular approval for

adoption seems unlikely.  In an inflationary economy, moreover,
much uncertainty and injustice might result.  Owners could be
caught unaware as rising market prices made a figure they had
approved for annual taxation so low as to be attractive to a
private purchaser.  Automatic adjustments based on a price
index could reduce this particular defect.

Group efforts at valuation might be attempted in some
places.  Owners in an area might be required to set values for
land, or for all their taxed properties, on a cooperative basis.
Where types are relatively similar and the general information
as to types, uses, and worth is spread over the community, such
a procedure offers some promise of achieving more uniformity
and acceptability than could be obtained by other feasible
methods.

## Shortcuts and Arbitrary Rules

Deliberate efforts to structure the tax in light of
administrative requirements can help achieve better results.
Over the world, a variety of shortcut devices have been
developed.  For example, a city may be divided into sections,
and a value for a typical unit of land--for example, a square
meter--may be assigned to each section.  Formulas may be used
to adjust for such factors as corner location.  Once the basic
figures have been computed, possibly with the direct
participation of real estate dealers and owners, assessments
of individual parcels can then be made as a matter of routine.
Building valuations can rest largely on the applications of
formulas; costs of various types of construction may rest on
present or recent actual figures; with adjustments for age
and other factors, estimates of the worth of existing
buildings can then be computed with relative ease.

Arbitrary elements in lieu of values--such as presumptive
income from farm lands (or types of operations)--can also
reduce the practical problems.  The benefits are obtained,
however, at the sacrifice of some potential equity of treatment.
Such a trade-off will probably be wise in many cases.  The use
of objective factors such as size, location, and type of
operation can substitute for more complicated requirements.
Relating some of the tax to the services provided, with so
much for streets or lighting or sewers, can be simpler than
value determination.

Extensive price changes, such as occur during inflation,
complicate the problems of valuation for tax purposes,
including those of equality among owners of property.
Certainly, if real efforts are made to employ a refined tax,
especially at high rates, the practical problems take on a
significance that cannot in fact be handled well by the staff

generally available in a developing country, unless vigorous
action is taken by policy officials to support the development
of good administration.

Relatively few actual market transactions occur in any
year (as a percentage of the total). Even for these cases,
the true price figures may not be matters of public record.

The qualifications needed for good assessors will depend
in part upon the kind of tax. The ability to train personnel,
and to get the kinds of evidence needed, will vary from place
to place. Once developed, these skills will be in demand for
purposes other than taxation. The loss of qualified personnel
must be expected unless, somehow, special provisions are made.

## Collection

Collecting the tax that becomes due requires special
provisions. Once again, account must be taken of the fact
that the tax does not follow as an incidental part of a market
transaction. The association of payment with harvest, with
income from crops or animals, will be appropriate in
agricultural areas, perhaps as part of a marketing system. In
urban regions, provision for frequent payment in small amounts
is generally to be preferred over annual or semiannual payments
of large sums. The taxpayer's convenience should receive
deliberate attention.

Assuming that the tax rests on property, the seizure of
the asset for nonpayment of tax provides a means of ultimate
enforcement. This sanction may, or may not, serve well in
practice. While the security of the asset exists, utilizing
it can be difficult. Taking away what may be a family's
source of livelihood will inevitably be unpopular. Political,
economic, and administrative problems can be large. For
example, sale may not in fact be feasible.

Various governments have developed requirements for
proof of payment of tax as a condition for the approval of
some desired action--the transfer of property by sale or gift
or bequest, the issuing of building permits, foreign exchange
transactions, or the receipt of some payment or service from
government. Such aids to enforcement may be useful in other
countries as well.

## EXPERIENCE IN SELECTED COUNTRIES

Evaluation of the effects of property taxation is faced with great difficulties due to lack of basic facts. Data on revenue yields in various countries are seriously inadequate. Figures for local government finances are often even less complete than those for national government. Taxes with similar names may be quite different. Nevertheless, it is fairly clear that nowhere does property taxation play a role as a constructive force in economic development commensurate with its underlying economic potential.

In countries where revenue yields are now about as high as would seem desirable (if such a conclusion can be reached for a locality, a larger area, or a whole economy), the structure of the tax frequently has defects. Adverse nonrevenue results that might have been avoided must then occur.

Moreover, administration rarely meets reasonably acceptable standards of achievable quality, and is in general seriously deficient. The staff and procedures needed for moderately satisfactory administration can be developed, but only with sustained determination and effort.

### Revenue

Table 1.1 shows the relative contribution of taxes on net wealth and immovable property to total tax revenue in nine developed countries. In a majority of these countries, as shown in Table 1.2, the taxes in question are largely property taxes. Canada, the United States, and the United Kingdom clearly make more intensive use of property taxes than the other countries listed. These countries show a relatively high figure for property taxes as a proportion of GNP, as shown in Table 1.3.

Table 1.4 indicates share of property taxes in total tax revenue in selected developing countries. The range is as wide as among the developed countries shown in Table 1.1. Table 1.5 shows that, in relation to GNP, however, none of the developing countries have attained the same proportion as Canada, the United States, or the United Kingdom. This reflects the low share of total tax revenues in GNP in the developing countries.

Evidence from a longer sweep of history provides additional insights. During the period from 1870 to 1913, when the United States was developing at an impressive, though uneven, rate, property taxation was much the largest source

TABLE 1.1

Tax Structure in Selected Developed Countries, 1972
(percentage)

| Country[a] | Taxes on Goods and Services | Taxes on Individual Income | Taxes on Corporate Income | Social Security Contribution | Taxes on Employers Based on Payroll or Manpower | Taxes on Net Wealth and Immovable Property | Taxes and Stamp Duties on Gifts, Inheritances, and Corporate and Financial Transactions | Other Taxes | Total[b] |
|---|---|---|---|---|---|---|---|---|---|
| Italy | 34.0 | 12.7 | 7.4 | 39.1 | -- | 1.0 | 5.6 | 0.2 | 100.0 |
| Japan | 21.8 | 25.5 | 18.2 | 19.4 | -- | 4.9 | 4.3 | 5.9 | 100.0 |
| United Kingdom | 28.6 | 32.1 | 7.1 | 15.6 | 2.1 | 11.1 | 3.3 | 0.1 | 100.0 |
| Netherlands | 26.7 | 27.9 | 6.6 | 35.2 | -- | 1.8 | 1.4 | 0.3 | 100.0 |
| France | 36.2 | 11.1 | 5.9 | 40.5 | 0.8 | 1.3 | 2.0 | 2.2 | 100.0 |
| Federal Republic of Germany | 28.7 | 28.1 | 4.7 | 33.7 | 0.7 | 2.5 | 0.9 | 0.8 | 100.0 |
| Canada | 32.5 | 34.5 | 10.8 | 8.7 | 0.3 | 10.5 | 0.7 | 1.9 | 100.0 |
| Sweden | 30.1 | 42.1 | 3.9 | 20.3 | 2.3 | 0.6 | 0.7 | -- | 100.0 |
| United States | 19.3 | 33.6 | 11.2 | 20.5 | -- | 13.2 | 2.2 | -- | 100.0 |

[a]Countries are arranged in ascending order of per capita income in 1972.

[b]Figures may not add due to rounding.

Source: Organisation for Economic Cooperation and Development, Revenue Statistics of OECD Member Countries, 1965-1972 (Paris: OECD, 1975), pp. 89-112.

44

TABLE 1.2

Revenue from Taxes on Net Wealth and Immovable Property
as a Percentage of Property Tax Revenue in
Selected Developed Countries, 1972

| Country[a] | Total[b] | Net Wealth | Immovable Property | Nonrecurring Taxes |
|---|---|---|---|---|
| Italy | 100.0 | -- | 100.0 | -- |
| Japan | 100.0 | -- | 100.0 | -- |
| United Kingdom | 100.0 | -- | 99.6 | 0.1 |
| Netherlands | 100.0 | 31.8 | 69.1 | -- |
| France | 100.0 | -- | 89.1 | 10.9 |
| Federal Republic of Germany | 100.0 | 59.3 | 40.7 | -- |
| Canada | 100.0 | -- | 95.1 | 4.9 |
| Sweden | 100.0 | 97.8 | 2.2 | -- |
| United States | 100.0 | -- | 100.0 | -- |

[a]Countries are arranged in ascending order of per capita GNP in 1972.

[b]Figures may not add due to rounding.

Source: Organisation for Economic Cooperation and Development, Revenue Statistics of OECD Member Countries, 1965-1972 (Paris: OECD, 1975), pp. 89-112.

TABLE 1.3

Revenue from Taxes on Net Wealth and Immovable Property
as a Percentage of Gross National Product in
Selected Developed Countries, 1972

| Country* | Percentage |
|---|---|
| Italy | 0.32 |
| Japan | 1.03 |
| United Kingdom | 3.87 |
| Netherlands | 0.77 |
| France | 0.47 |
| Federal Republic of Germany | 0.89 |
| Canada | 3.53 |
| Sweden | 0.25 |
| United States | 3.71 |

*Countries are arranged in ascending order of per capita GNP in 1972.

Source: Organisation for Economic Cooperation and Development, Revenue Statistics of OECD Member Countries, 1965-1972 (Paris: OECD, 1975), pp. 89-112.

of total governmental--national, state, and local--revenue.
Intensity of use (according to various measures) differed
considerably from one place to another. The nationwide average
yield appears to have been from 3.2 to 3.7 percent of GNP. The
annual revenue yield was apparently from 0.7 to 1.2 percent of
the estimated value of privately owned wealth.

In the 1920s, another period of economic progress in the
United States, property taxation was about 4.5 percent of GNP,
at times somewhat more. In some localities the tax was
relatively much heavier. During the depression of the 1930s
and the years of World War II, many changes took place that
altered the relative importance of property taxation. In the
1950s, property tax yields went up substantially, but other
taxes and GNP rose relatively more. Nevertheless, property
tax revenues were about the same percentage of GNP as before
World War I.

Local rates in the United Kingdom (taxes on the annual
rental value of property) played a prominent part in government
finance during the decades of growth in the nineteenth century.
In these years, when Great Britain was a leader in economic
development, property taxation brought in more than 90 percent of
local government revenue, until near the end of the century.
Although grants from the national government grew somewhat,
locally raised rates yielded more than three-fourths of total
local revenue at the outbreak of World War I.

The figures presented indicate that property taxes of
3.5 percent or more of GNP (higher, of course, in relation to
national income) are consistent with rates of economic
development judged good by historical standards. To be sure,
development might have been even better if property taxes had
been at a different level or structured differently, but at
least their effect was not disastrous.

These figures do not indicate that any upper limit has
been reached. The concept of an upper limit is not clear, but
we have in mind a point beyond which improvement in levels of
living and fairness in sharing the costs of government are
impaired. The practical top figure may have been what has
been recorded, but it may be higher, depending on the nature
of the tax, what other taxes are imposed, the expenditure of
funds, the degree of urbanization, the prevalence of exempt
economic activities, the quality of administration, and
other factors.

The practical limits in many areas are now, and will
continue to be probably for a long time, administrative
rather than economic. Moreover, much will depend on how well
the revenues are spent and on the consent of the taxpayers.

TABLE 1.4

Tax Structure in Selected Developing Countries, 1953-55 and 1969-71
(Percentage)

| Country[a] | | Total[b] | Income Taxes | Taxes on Property | Poll and Personal Taxes | Taxes on International Trade | Import Taxes | Export Taxes and Other | Taxes on Production and Internal Transactions | Other[c] Taxes |
|---|---|---|---|---|---|---|---|---|---|---|
| Chile | I | 100.0 | 39.0 | 5.8 | -- | 17.0 | -- | -- | 34.9 | 3.3 |
|  | II | 100.0 | 32.7 | 4.9 | -- | 11.0 | 11.0 | -- | 50.7 | 0.7 |
| Costa Rica | I | 100.0 | 16.2 | 3.7 | -- | 59.7 | 53.4 | 6.3 | 17.8 | 2.6 |
|  | II | 100.0 | 20.8 | 1.7 | -- | 32.7 | 27.9 | 4.9 | 42.1 | 2.6 |
| Brazil | I | 100.0 | 16.2 | 2.9 | -- | 12.6 | 2.1 | 10.5 | 50.1 | 18.2[d] |
|  | II | 100.0 | 13.2 | 0.4 | -- | 7.4 | 3.4 | 4.0 | 67.1 | 11.8 |
| Guatemala | I | 100.0 | 7.5 | 8.8 | -- | 53.3 | 24.2 | 29.1 | 28.5 | 1.9 |
|  | II | 100.0 | 12.8 | 5.4 | -- | 30.6 | 25.6 | 5.0 | 51.2 | -- |
| Tunisia | I | 100.0 | 12.7 | 6.1 | 4.0 | 9.1 | 7.6 | 1.5 | 60.0 | 8.2 |
|  | II | 100.0 | 29.9 | 3.6 | 1.7 | 9.6 | 6.1 | 3.5 | 52.4 | 2.8 |
| Korea | I | 100.0 | 28.6 | 5.5 | -- | 15.4 | 15.4 | -- | 50.5 | -- |
|  | II | 100.0 | 33.7[e] | 3.8 | -- | 12.3 | 12.3 | -- | 49.8 | 0.4 |
| Honduras | I | 100.0 | 18.4 | 1.1 | -- | 63.9 | 59.6 | 4.3 | 16.2 | 0.5 |
|  | II | 100.0 | 27.1 | 3.1 | -- | 32.1 | 23.8 | 8.2 | 37.7 | -- |
| Paraguay | I | 100.0 | 19.4 | 5.9 | -- | 35.8 | -- | -- | 38.9 | -- |
|  | II | 100.0 | 10.2 | 5.8 | -- | 37.6 | 34.9 | 2.9 | 45.8 | 0.6 |
| Ghana | I | 100.0 | 15.6 | -- | -- | 82.6 | 22.4 | 60.2 | 1.8 | -- |
|  | II | 100.0 | 21.4 | 1.8 | -- | 46.7 | 15.1 | 31.6 | 30.2 | -- |

48

| Country | Period | | | | | | | | | |
|---|---|---|---|---|---|---|---|---|---|---|
| Ecuador | I | 100.0 | 16.6 | 7.5 | -- | 55.1 | 40.3 | 14.8 | 18.5 | 2.4 |
| | II | 100.0 | 13.0 | 9.0 | -- | 50.6 | 40.2 | 10.4 | 26.9 | 0.5 |
| Morocco | I | 100.0 | 18.3 | 9.8 | 1.0 | 33.8 | 29.7 | 4.1 | 25.1 | 2.0 |
| | II | 100.0 | 22.6 | 4.6 | -- | 18.0 | 16.1 | 1.9 | 52.5 | 2.3 |
| Egypt | I | 100.0 | 14.2 | 14.2 | -- | 34.7 | 25.1 | 9.6 | 33.5 | 0.1 |
| | II | 100.0 | 23.1 | 3.2 | -- | 31.3 | 31.3 | -- | 34.9 | 7.5 |
| Philippines | I | 100.0 | 21.1 | 11.8 | 0.8 | 7.4 | 6.5 | 0.9 | 56.4 | 2.6 |
| | II | 100.0 | 28.6 | 4.4 | -- | 24.4 | 19.5 | 4.8 | 41.3 | 1.3 |
| Thailand | I | 100.0 | 8.4 | 0.1 | -- | 47.8 | 30.3 | 17.5 | 42.2 | 1.5 |
| | II | 100.0 | 15.0 | 3.0 | -- | 37.4 | 29.7 | 7.6 | 44.1 | 0.1 |
| Kenya | I | 100.0 | 37.6 | 0.7 | 5.7 | 38.4 | 35.2 | 3.2 | 17.5 | -- |
| | II | 100.0 | 39.0 | 0.5 | 2.8 | 32.5 | 31.8 | 0.7 | 20.1 | 5.1 |
| Indonesia | I | 100.0 | 36.1 | 0.9 | -- | 28.6 | 16.5 | 12.1 | 34.4 | -- |
| | II | 100.0 | 40.6 | -- | -- | 32.5 | 25.4 | 7.1 | 26.9 | -- |
| India | I | 100.0 | 25.1 | 16.0 | -- | 25.0 | 18.2 | 6.8 | 33.8 | 0.4 |
| | II | 100.0 | 18.7 | 7.8 | -- | 11.3 | 8.9 | 2.4 | 66.2 | -- |

[a] Countries arranged in descending order of 1971 GNP in U.S. dollars per capita.
[b] Excludes social security contributions.
[c] Unclassified because of lack of information.
[d] Mostly internal indirect taxes.
[e] Includes land tax.

Note: I signifies the first period (1953-55), and II the second period (1969-71).

Sources: Rajah Chelliah, "Trends in Taxation in Developing Countries," International Monetary Fund Staff Papers 18, no. 2 (July 1971): 270-71; and Rajah Chelliah, Hessel J. Bass, and Margaret R. Kelly, "Tax Ratios and Tax Effort in Developing Countries," in ibid. 22, no. 1 (March 1975), Table 3.

## TABLE 1.5

Revenue from Major Categories of Taxes as a Percentage of Gross National Product, Selected Developing Countries, 1969-71

| Country[a] | Total Taxes Including Social Security Contribution | Social Security Contribution | Income Taxes[b] | Taxes on Property | Poll and Personal Taxes | Taxes on International Trade | Taxes on Production and Internal Transactions | Other | Per Capita GNP (U.S.$) 1971 |
|---|---|---|---|---|---|---|---|---|---|
| Chile | 27.2 | 7.6 | 6.4 | 1.0 | -- | 2.2 | 9.9 | 0.1 | 1,057.0 |
| Costa Rica | 15.4 | 2.2 | 2.8 | 0.2 | -- | 4.3 | 5.6 | 0.4 | 578.0 |
| Brazil | 28.7 | 5.8 | 3.0 | 0.1 | -- | 1.7 | 15.3 | 2.7 | 466.0 |
| Guatemala | 8.9 | 1.0 | 1.0 | 0.4 | -- | 2.4 | 4.1 | -- | 356.0 |
| Tunisia | 24.7 | 3.0 | 6.5 | 0.8 | 0.4 | 2.1 | 11.4 | 0.6 | 308.0 |
| Korea | 15.4 | -- | 5.2 | 0.6 | -- | 1.9 | 7.7 | 0.1 | 291.0 |
| Honduras | 11.7 | 0.4 | 3.1 | 0.4 | -- | 3.6 | 4.3 | -- | 278.0 |
| Paraguay | 13.3 | 2.4 | 1.1 | 0.6 | -- | 4.1 | 5.0 | 0.1 | 278.0 |
| Ghana | 17.0 | 1.2 | 3.4 | 0.3 | -- | 7.4 | 4.8 | -- | 269.0 |
| Ecuador | 17.5 | 4.1 | 1.7 | 1.2 | -- | 6.8 | 3.6 | 0.1 | 261.0 |
| Morocco | ... | ... | 4.0 | 0.8 | -- | 3.2 | 9.4 | 0.4 | 240.0 |
| Egypt | ... | ... | 4.4 | 0.6 | ... | 6.0 | 6.7 | 1.4 | 220.0 |
| Philippines | 10.2 | 1.0 | 2.6 | 0.4 | -- | 2.2 | 3.8 | 0.1 | 201.0 |
| Thailand | 12.4 | -- | 1.9 | 0.4 | -- | 4.6 | 5.5 | -- | 187.0 |
| Kenya | 14.5 | 0.1 | 5.6 | 0.1 | 0.4 | 4.6 | 2.9 | 0.7 | 153.0 |
| Indonesia | 10.1 | -- | 4.1 | -- | -- | 3.3 | 2.7 | -- | 112.0 |
| India | ... | -- | 2.5 | 1.0 | -- | 1.5 | 8.3 | -- | 99.0 |

[a]Countries arranged in descending order of 1971 GNP per capita in U.S. dollars. A dash (--) indicates that the figure is zero or less than half the final digit shown, or that the item does not exist. Dots (...) indicate that data are not available.

[b]Includes royalties on minerals.

Source: Rajah Chelliah, "Trends in Taxation in Developing Countries," International Monetary Fund Staff Papers 18, no. 2 (July 1971): 270-71; and Rajah Chelliah, Hessel J. Bass, and Margaret R. Kelly, "Tax Ratios and Tax Effort in Developing Countries," in ibid. 22, no. 1 (March 1975), Table 3.

In some developing countries, a major obstacle to effective
taxation of property improvements, on the scale long utilized
in Canada, the United Kingdom, and the United States, may be
the flight of capital. Where the government cannot tie a tax
to benefits from spending received by the property owner,
export of wealth can present problems. Fear of excessive
rates can also be a factor. Once tax has become established,
will governments raise rates above the level the owners of
wealth believe acceptable? In the United States, some state
constitutions put ceilings on property tax rates. Investors
can thus have some assurance that burdens are not likely to
go above a top figure.

In the United States, approximately half of property tax
revenues come from residences. Where government provides as
large a proportion of housing as may be the goal of some
developing nations, at least in newer urban areas, inclusion
of a property tax element in the rental price may seem to run
counter to a policy of subsidizing such housing.

## Role of Local Government

To a certain extent, discussion of the role of property
taxation can involve issues of centralization of government as
against decentralization. More can be involved than a revenue
source alone.

In most cases, property taxation serves local governments.
There is enough logic in this practice to suggest that it
should generally be considered as useful for decentralization
and local autonomy. The type of property taxed is essentially
local and relatively immobile; in the case of land, and to a
lesser extent other property, intercommunity rivalry in
attracting business establishments through differences in
local tax rates has only a limited likelihood of altering the
location of the tax base. While movements of new capital may
take account of relative tax burdens from one place to
another, especially those on improvements, differences in the
local expenditures financed by the tax will have a counter-
balancing influence on investment decisions and the value of
the land. Thus, there is an element of fairness--on a
geographical basis--in property taxation for local government
spending. High burdens tend to exist where the spendings
bring large benefits. Property values will reflect the
combined effects of tax costs on the one hand and the fruits
of the expenditures, on the other.

Communities that use this tax have some scope for
adjusting the expenditure on local services to what they are
willing and able to pay for, as contrasted with dependence

upon government decision making at more remote levels.  The
importance attached to this feature will, of course, differ.
Where factories or other large units serve people over a wide
area, or where natural features create high land values in a
particular area, there may be considerable injustice in letting
a few local governments have exclusive use of such property
spending in the fortunate communities (except as needed to pay
for services to the businesses).

In the United States, it has been argued as another merit
of property taxation that, for most of the tax base, it is
possible to achieve good administration locally, whereas other
taxes require enforcement on a larger scale.  That local
administration of property taxation has been poor does not
mean that the potentials are more promising for other local
revenues.  In any case, nothing makes property taxation
inherently a solely local revenue source.  Certainly, narrowly
local administration is not essential.  In fact, good
administration will require more expert capacity than local
governments, even of considerable size, may be able to afford
on a permanent basis.  Also, provincial or national
administration may be freer from personal influences than
the local officials.  Reliance on staffs in larger units of
government, therefore, may result in higher standards of
integrity than are achievable locally.  Be that as it may,
property taxation can provide a basis for a degree of local
independence.  Any separation of the decision making as to
expenditure from the decision making as to tax rates and
financing methods is fraught with dangers of irresponsibility.
If freedom to act on the basis of some financial independence
is lacking, potentials, for local innovation, initiatives, and
leadership will be lost.

## Some Current Practices

The introduction to the U.N.'s Manual of Land Tax
Administration[2] reads as follows:

Interest in the land tax has been flagging for some time
owing to the low productivity of the tax (which in turn
resulted from the difficulty of revaluation in a generally
inflationary climate) and to the rise of major new tax
sources (especially income and profits taxes).  Recently,
however, more and more tax authorities have been turning
their attention to the potentialities....The ever-
increasing population pressure combined with the
expansion of infra-structure facilities and general
economic development have pushed land values constantly
upward;...recent technical innovations in survey and

valuation methods and tax procedures make it much more
feasible than before, also for a developing country, to
install a modern land tax and keep assessments up to
date, and thus obtain worth-while tax revenues at a
reasonable cost.

Land taxes as set up currently present serious
problems in equity and administration, which have
become exacerbated in many countries where the base
or even the amount has remained unchanged for decades
and has failed to reflect changing price levels, land
uses and revenue needs.  The principal difficulty has...
been to obtain and maintain a reasonably accurate and
current valuation of each property at a reasonable
cost.  Another difficulty...is the influence exercised
in many Governments and legislatures by the owners of
much of the potential taxable real estate.  In both
respects the present situation is much more favourable
to land tax reform in many countries than it has been
in the past.  This change...is a result of urban growth,
economic diversification and the tendency of Governments
to seek wider bases of popular support.


Land taxation today is seldom very important in
the total of government revenue.  It may, however, loom
very large in the revenue of local (municipal or state)
governments....


Existing land taxes in many developing countries
often produce too little revenue....Effective tax rates,
in relation to land market values or to the income from
land, are so low in some cases that tax administrations
and taxpayers alike do not take the tax too seriously....
Exemptions...frequently given by developing countries as
an incentive to certain kinds of investment, are
ineffective because the tax is too small to make any
real difference in the calculations of potential
investors.


Some use of property taxation is found in most countries,
but the actual amounts collected differ greatly in relation to
other magnitudes.  Moreover, actual yields clearly differ by
more than a reading of descriptions of laws would lead one to
expect, and the effectiveness of administration varies substantially.

## Taxing Farm Property

Taxing the farm sector presents formidable problems.  In
their efforts to do so, several countries tax agricultural
income in ways that resemble property taxation of the income
variety.  At one extreme, the tax may be based on net income,
as determined by standard accounting.  In that case, the
departure from a property tax can be substantial, because of
the weight of factors other than land and other property in
determining income and thus tax.  Building a satisfactory
(land) tax system upon such existing income taxes would require
changes both in government operations (administration) and in
the attitudes and practices of farmers.

In practice, the use of accounting concepts of income as
a basis for taxing farmers and farm property must be expected
to fail, except for relatively large commercial farms.  As a
substitute, several governments have developed presumptive
standards for use in estimating income, yield, or value.  In
a number of French-speaking developing countries, the system
of presumptions--forfaits--is used, as practiced in France for
determining the income of farmers.  In France itself, where
the system is advanced, standards are set for different regions
and types of crops.  Average gross yields per hectare are
announced, and production costs are estimated with allowances
for special factors such as unusual weather and damage.  The
tenant then pays tax on this basis, and the owner is taxed
the rental income he receives.

Some of the states of India use presumptive incomes for
taxing farmers, but the revenue obtained is overshadowed by
other taxes; as a practical matter, agricultural property
escapes effective taxation in India.

Several countries exempt farm income from the national
income tax, either explicitly or through personal exemptions,
but then tax agricultural income on some basis of notional
land yield.  Morocco and Uruguay have such taxes, which
function parallel with the income tax of the general government.
Ethiopia, Indonesia, the Republic of Korea (South Korea),
Malawi, Nigeria, and Uganda have local taxes on farm income,
which utilize the notional principle.

Morocco's present system replaced in 1961 a proportional
tax based on the gross value of output as presumed on the
basis of productivity.  The present tax rests on estimates of
standard income per head of cattle per hectare.

In 1951, the Republic of Korea introduced as a wartime
measure a new system of taxing agriculture.  The tax was
based on estimated standard yields and was payable in kind.

A cadastral system, including detailed information on the
location, size, ownership, and other aspects of each plot of
land, was drawn up.  Prior average harvests provide the basis
for setting the standard yields.  Local farmers serve on a
board, which has a role in determining standards and making
adjustments when hardship is claimed.  Farmers are not taxed
on production above the standard output.  This provision
serves to stimulate production.  Gradually, it is true,
improved yields will enter the base used to compute the
standard, but, for the most part, the farmer knows that efforts
to produce better results and greater efficiency will not
raise his tax in the current year.  Actual crop prices are used
to value standard outputs; in a time of inflation, therefore,
government revenues would, in principle, tend to rise.  In
practice, price-fixing by government and other factors have
prevented the tax revenue from rising as rapidly as the
increase in the money value of agricultural output.

## Taxing Urban Property

     Among selected Asian nations studied in the 1960s,
Indonesia, the Republic of Korea, Laos, and Thailand made only
small use of urban property taxation.  The taxes noted below
are chiefly local; those of Indonesia and Laos are levied and
collected by the national government.  The tax in the
Philippines is imposed by the central government and used
locally.  In terms of yield as a percentage of local government
revenue, property taxes are most important in India, whereas,
in Malaysia, Pakistan, and the Philippines, they yield less
than 20 percent of local revenue.  In the Philippines, the
property tax burden has been undergoing revisions since the
imposition of martial law.  The prior situation left much to
be desired, as property was assessed at much less than the
basis that the law called for (true and full value in the
competitive market).  Real property values were put on the
assessment books at an average of about 45 percent of actual
value 15 or more years ago.  The subsequent increases in
value were not added to the tax base.  Property owners
naturally objected to raising the assessments, and assessors
did not want to antagonize owners, many of whom were
prominent leaders.  In urban areas, long delays in valuing
meant that big increases in land prices were not brought into
the tax base.  Actual taxes were reported at about 0.5 percent
of market prices in the late 1960s.  Also, the collection
process was not effective.  Interest charged on unpaid tax
at 12 percent a year was not high enough to put great pressure
on owners, and legal processes for seizing and selling
property were not adequate.

     In most Indian states, urban property tax is a
substantial source of local government revenue.  The tax rests

on annual rental value.  Rent controls, however, have been in
effect for many years and have frozen values used for tax
purposes.  Therefore, the tax has been less responsive to
revenue needs than might have been expected since, partly
because of inflation, the price of property has risen markedly.
The legal restrictions on rents are not the only reason for
the lag in the growth of yield.  Local governments do not
possess sufficient staff and other resources needed to revise
the assessment rolls promptly and fully at the five-year
intervals generally called for by law.  Owners of property
have reason to use their influence to delay the updating of
assessments.  In addition, tax collection has suffered from
deficiencies of administration.

In Indonesia, tax is assessed on the basis of detailed
classifications.  In urban areas, the tax reflects location,
the community facilities available, and the class of property.
However, actual burdens are low.

In the Republic of Korea, taxes on urban land lagged far
behind the rise in land prices.  Capital values--the base of
the tax--are not accurately redetermined for tax purposes.
Buildings are assessed and taxed on a basis different from
that which applies to land.  A penalty levy on idle land was
apparently not effective in reducing tendencies toward
speculation and was removed in 1967.  There is a national tax
on the registration of property and local taxes on acquisition.
A low (0.3 percent) inheritance tax applies to land.

In Latin America, the tax laws embody a richness of
ingenuity and imagination and, though probably not often
translated into practice, deserve attention as providing
possible models for adoption elsewhere.

In Argentina, local governments levy an in rem tax, which
applies to urban and rural land and improvements on the
official value.  The general rate is 0.1 percent.  Buenos Aires,
however, applies progressive rates with a maximum of 1.6
percent.  Various local governments have taxes and charges for
special services and to pay for improvements, such as paving.
The income tax has special provisions applying to land rent
in some cases.  There are also taxes on the transfer of
property.

Bolivia has no national land tax, but the income tax
applies to actual or presumed income from urban and rural
lands.  Local governments tax rural land.

The national government of Brazil has power to impose a
tax on rural land to ensure uniformity throughout the
country, since local governments tax urban land at rates that
can vary from 0.5 to 10 percent.

In Chile, a national government tax on real property has existed since 1927. The rate of 2 percent applies to the total value (including land and improvements) as set for tax purposes for each taxpayer. Local governments receive part of the revenue. A net wealth tax to be computed by the taxpayers (individuals or corporations) includes land.

In Colombia, tax at rates of about 0.4 percent of the cadastral value is administered and collected by municipalities. There is a national surcharge of 10 percent of the municipal tax. A national net wealth tax on individuals was approved in 1960.

Costa Rica levies a national tax on the total official value of the property owned by a taxpayer (including land and improvements), as officially determined. The rates range from 0.3 to 1.5 percent. A 1961 law establishing a tax on uncultivated lands has not become effective.

The property tax in Ecuador consists of one levy on rural and one on urban properties. They apply throughout the country but are administered by the municipalities. Both taxes are applied on the total value of the real property of a single owner located in the same jurisdiction. In the taxation of rural property, the tax is applied on the commercial or real value of the property, including land, equipment, animals, improvements, and other installations. A deduction of approximately U.S. $430 plus debts is allowed. In some cases, tax rates are progressive, and special taxes apply to help pay for improvements. An annual tax of 10 percent of the estimated value applies to sites not built upon. Capital gains on property transfers are taxed, but no allowance is made for monetary inflation. A tax of 1.2 percent applies to transfers of ownership. Valuations are to be made by municipalities at 60 percent of market value at five-year intervals. In fact, it is reported, tax valuations can be much below what the law apparently requires. Plans have been made for the national office of valuation to assess rural property.

No property tax as such exists in El Salvador, but real property is included in the national net wealth tax. A national tax on uncultivated lands is of little significance. A law approved in 1970 establishes an annual tax on real property, but implementation has lagged.

In Guatemala, a municipal tax on urban property is based on actual or presumed income. There is also a national tax on real property, levied on a personal basis on the total official value of the real property of each taxpayer (including improvements). The rates range from 0.3 to 0.6 percent. A national tax on uncultivated lands is not actually in effect.

The property tax in Honduras rests on a national law but is administered and collected by the municipalities.

The real property tax in Mexico is administered by the states. In addition, municipal governments impose several taxes. In Mexico City, the real property tax applies on two bases: income and capital value (including land and improvements).

The Nicaraguan national real property tax is levied on the total value of all properties owned by each taxpayer, with mortgages and debts being deducted under certain conditions. There are two classifications of real estate: urban residences and up to 10 hectares in rural zones, and all remaining properties. A national tax on uncultivated lands is of little significance.

The real estate tax of Panama applies at progressive rates on the cadastral value of each property (including land and improvements). A national tax on uncultivated lands has little significance.

The law of Paraguay imposes a national real property tax along with other contributions based on land. The rate is 1 percent; the taxable amount is the figure for both land and improvements as officially determined.

In Peru, the land tax system was restructured in 1968. The real property income tax was left to the local governments. An annual tax on the value of real property is to be administered by the national government, which will also receive the revenue. The new tax is applied separately on the total value of urban and rural property, including land and improvements. The value is self-assessed by the taxpayer but will be checked by the tax administration.

In Uruguay, a uniform rate of 2 percent falls on rural property as valued by the national office. A municipal tax applies on land and improvements. On urban lands, the tax rests on the cadastral value fixed by the national office, with different rates for each municipality. There is also a national tax on minimum agricultural production in order to reach the potential income of agricultural land. There are other national taxes that affect real property, including one on net wealth, which rests upon the official valuations of land and improvements.

Each municipality of Venezuela applies a tax on land according to the actual or presumed income of the urban property. Rural lands are taxed by local governments.

## FUTURE DIRECTIONS FOR PROPERTY TAXATION

High and rising land prices, especially in cities, could provide more funds for needed government services. In all parts of the world, urban land prices have risen and seem likely to continue to do so, not necessarily regularly but from decade to decade. Speculation plays a part, as does general inflation, but fundamental economic forces of rising population and real income are also at work. Governments need more and more money to pay both for physical infrastructure and for the operating expenses of growing populations that demand better services. Taxes on land could supply money without reducing the quantity of land area. At the same time, taxes would bring down the price of land and encourage better use. The opportunities are promising indeed, but there are problems that are not easily solved.

All around the world, city populations are multiplying. In developing countries especially, the demands for governmental services are rising faster than the available funds can pay for--in many cases by a large amount. The quality of life for the increasing millions who live in cities suffers because funds are not adequate for the streets and water supplies and sewage and educational facilities that governments are expected to provide.

People pay heavily for living and working space in the city. But not all who come to the cities of developing countries pay for the land on which they live. Around many cities of Latin America, Asia, and Africa, squatters are numbered in the tens of thousands. Other occupants may pay some rent but not enough to provide the landowner with significant taxpaying capacity.

Generally, however, in cities, there is a growth in the effective demand for the use of space, which sends land prices up. And the increasing amounts that urban residents pay to use land for housing and business go primarily to private owners, while the money that goes to provide better public services lags far behind. Expectations of further rises in land prices create competition and inspire speculation, which bids prices up still more. In both developed and developing countries, present owners can withhold land from better use because the hope of further price increases seems to make any commitment to a currently more productive use unnecessary and unattractive.

Nevertheless, the massing of people in cities, which multiplies the need for governmental services, also creates a potential source of funds for meeting some of the costs. This revenue can be obtained without making the users of land as such worse off on the whole and without reducing the supply of

land.  A tax that brings about this result can also exert
pressure to put land to better use and to make more land
available at lower prices.

The responsibilities of city governments for providing
services and capital facilities vary from one country to
another.  National governments assume differing service
obligations, as do the private sectors.  Occasionally, only
one level of government exists--as in the case of Hong Kong
and Singapore.

Traditions, systems of land titles and ownership, methods
of financing the purchase and leasing and the use of land and
buildings, the governmental use of zoning and eminent domain
(compulsory acquisition), all have many effects.  Old
traditions, new developments, and a host of special conditions
make intergovernmental comparisons hazardous.  But the needs
for revenue are universally high, and, as more people with
more purchasing power seek to utilize the limited space of
cities, the amount they are prepared to pay per unit of surface
space of land rises, and by more than the general level.

What the user pays for a house or a pair of shoes or
other products and services is necessary in order to get them
produced.  Land, however, is created by nature rather than by
the owner.  Some of what the user pays could go to finance
urban services without reducing the space in the city.  Of
course, inputs of material and labor must be recognized as
being beyond the product of nature.

Labor and capital are man-made.  The quantity and quality
of training, the vigor of human endeavor, the amount of
machinery and structures, all depend in large part upon what
individuals receive by way of compensation.  Land is
essentially different.  In the sense of space, the amount of
surface area in existence will depend scarcely at all upon
the amount paid for its use.  The area of a city block will
be the same whether the payment per year is X or 10X.

However, the way improvements are taxed will make a
difference in whether an area becomes available, instead
perhaps of being held essentially idle, possibly as a
speculation for a further rise in price before the commitment
of capital for construction.  A need to pay tax in cash will
increase pressure to secure money income.  The amount paid for
use of land will govern the particular use to be made of a
plot of land in an urban area.  Payments for land--rental or
purchase price--thus perform a vital function.  These payments
facilitate the transition of use to more intensive forms.
But payments do not, as in the case of man-made productive
capacity, also perform the function of inducing the creation of

resource.  Tax land heavily, and it will not move elsewhere.
Tax it lightly, and the favorable tax situation will not create
more space in the city.  As far as attracting capital from
outside the country and providing incentives to local
investors is concerned, leaders in a developing economy should
recognize that land possesses characteristics that differ
significantly from those of man-made capital.

Another aspect that deserves attention is equity in
sharing the costs of government.  A widely held principle ties
economic justice to rewards based on what a person accomplishes
and on the productivity of capital facilities that his saving
and investment have made possible.  But this principle does
not lead to justification for large rewards based on the
ownership of land in its natural form.  Differences in payments
for human services or for the use of capital can rest, and
rest fairly, on what the recipient has done.  For the owner of
urban land, however, the same kind of justification cannot be
found to the same extent.  Purely passive owners, doing
nothing creative, may enjoy unearned increments which can be
very great.

Land price increases in and around cities have made rich
men out of owners of nearby farm land.  More than one owner of
a few acres of rice land near an Asian city has reaped handsome
gains because of the pressure of population.  In many countries,
enrichment has come to the passive owners of land who have done
little or nothing to create the increase in value.  Urban
growth has brought them good fortune.  Some of the rise in the
worth of urban land results from government expenditure on
public facilities.  The owners of land as such, however, have
contributed relatively little in taxes to defray the cost of
the infrastructure that has helped elevate the price of land.

The moral justification for private ownership of such
increments of property values seems weak.  The owner's
contribution may have been nil.  From time to time, there may
have been some managerial effort involved in getting land put
to better use or some payments in taxes.  Compared with labor
and capital, however, land offers much greater possibilities
for the enhancement of private wealth without regard to the
creative contribution of the person benefiting.

Nevertheless, private ownership of land can serve an
important purpose for the general good.  An owner has an
incentive to direct land use into better rather than poorer
alternatives.  The scarcer the land and the higher the price
it can command, the more important it is for the general
public that it should be used well.  As urban congestion
grows, so does the need for the efficient use of space.
Private ownership can help to bring about this result by

allowing the owner to reap a personal benefit from seeking out
and realizing a form of land use that yields a higher return.

Extensive governmental ownership of land might be defended
as a means of ensuring the public receipt of increments in
value.  The cost of acquisition, however, rules this out as a
realistic alternative except in most unusual cases.  Most
cities have more pressing and promising uses for available
funds than the purchase of land as an investment against a
rise in price.  Critics may argue that governmental ownership,
rather than private, will be less productive as far as land
use is concerned.  Political bodies and processes, it is
feared, will tend to be less effective in developing and taking
prompt advantage of possible improvements in land use.

Although cities may be essentially immortal, so that in
principle a city government may be thought of as taking the
"long view," in practice the time horizon of individual policy-
making individuals may be the next election.  While private
property owners often have a longer horizon than the next
election, it probably tends to be short of a socially desirable
time span.  Moreover, broader community interests will not be
fully recognized by any but quite exceptional private owners.
Some form of urban land planning, and the related execution
and implementation of such plans, would seem to be desirable,
even essential, both in government's management of its own
land and its direction of the use of privately owned land.

In any case, governments must somehow acquire considerable
land, for streets, parks, schools, fire stations, and other
uses.  Urban growth will require reservation or acquisition of
land for public use.  High land taxes will help keep land
prices and the costs of future acquisitions lower than they
would otherwise be.  A growing city might deliberately form
its policy with such considerations in mind.  Present-day
private owners have an interest in lower land taxes and higher
prices--to get more from future buyers, who will thereby suffer
somewhat from a failure now to impose higher taxes on land
values.

Failures to make the best use of privately owned urban
land do occur, even aside from the influence of distorting
taxes.  They are most likely to result on a significant scale
when the owners are under no financial pressure to search out
the best opportunities.  Inertia and lassitude often result
in undue postponement of development, especially if the costs
of delay are slight and the requirements for cash outlays
small.  If government taxes capital gains only when realized,
without increasing the tax according to the period held, the
owner may delay a change in land use because the immediate
sale of his land would result in a heavier tax burden.

Although tax pressure can exert influences toward better use, matters are not simple, nor are the guidelines clear. Development of land can be premature and harmful, not only to the owner but also to his neighbors and the broader community. While the general lines of desirable policy action are plain, great caution is called for and the realities of administrative capacity must be taken fully into account.

## NOTES

1.    Practices in the United States are discussed, and the economic, administrative, and other aspects examined more extensively  in C. Lowell Harriss, Property Taxation in Government Finance (New York:  Tax Foundation, Inc., 1974). An annotated bibliography on property taxation is also available from the Tax Foundation.  Valuable references to additional sources may be found in two studies by George E. Lent, "The Taxation of Land Value," International Monetary Fund Staff Paper 14 (1967): 89-121, and "The Urban Property Tax in Developing Countries," Finanzarchiv 33 (1974): 45-72.

2.    E.68. XVI.  3;6 (New York, 1968).

# 2

## VALUE-ADDED TAXATION IN DEVELOPING ECONOMIES

John F. Due

NATURE, TYPES, AND USE OF VALUE-ADDED TAXES

The value-added tax (VAT)* is a tax imposed upon the value that the activities of a business firm add to the goods and services it purchases from other firms--that is, upon the excess of sales during a period over the amounts paid for goods and services acquired from other business firms during that period. For example, a retail store buys $6,000 of bread during a month from a bakery and acquires $1,000 of wrapping paper and supplies for handling the bread. It receives a total of $9,000 from the sale of the bread. It has therefore added $2,000 to the value of the bread that it has handled. Some of this $2,000 will be paid out as wages to employees; some will be paid as interest; some will cover miscellaneous items; and the remainder will constitute profits for the owners.

### Historical Development

Early reference to a VAT occurred in Germany immediately after World War I, when such a tax was proposed by Carl F. von Siemens to replace the multistage turnover tax. Shortly thereafter, proposals for such a tax were made in the United States, as a substitute for the corporation income tax. Through the 1920s and 1930s, occasional reference was made, in the United States and Germany, and probably elsewhere as well, to this form of tax.

---

*The initials VAT are used in the United States and the United Kingdom, TVA in Europe.

In 1953, the state of Michigan enacted a form of VAT as a compromise between groups seeking and opposing a state corporation income tax.  This levy, imposed in addition to the state retail sales tax, was essentially regarded as a levy on business firms, per se, as a charge for the privilege of doing business.  Firms were required to calculate value-added and apply the rate to this figure, rather than use the tax credit method described below.  There were numerous exemptions. Ultimately, the tax was replaced by a corporate income tax.[1]

A value-added tax was proposed by the Shoup mission for the prefectures in Japan, but the tax was never implemented.

Meanwhile, as early as 1935, the manufacturers' sales taxes of several countries gained value-added features; manufacturers were required to pay tax on the excess of sales over purchases of produced goods.  This rule was introduced in Argentina in 1935 and in France in 1948.

The modern trend toward VAT began in 1954 with modifications in the French production tax, following the work of Maurice Lauré and the application of the name "value-added tax" to the reformed levy.  The change involved two elements: the extension of the tax through wholesale distribution (not until 1968 through the retail level), and the exclusion from tax of capital equipment on a current basis, instead of materials and parts alone.  The success of the French levy and the realization that the existing cascade multiple-stage taxes were incompatible with the European Common Market led the Fiscal and Financial Committee of the European Economic Community to recommend in 1962 that all member countries shift to the value-added form.  This was approved by the EEC Council of Ministers, and gradually implemented, commencing with the Federal Republic of Germany in 1968 and culminating with Italy in 1973.  Ireland (1972) and the United Kingdom (1973) imposed the tax as they became members of the EEC.  The three Scandinavian countries,[*] seeking to exclude all producers' goods from their sales taxes because of competitive relations in world markets with the EEC countries, and believing that this was most easily accomplished with the VAT, made the change between 1967 and 1970.  Austria followed in 1973.  In recent years, VAT yield as a percentage of total tax yield has been roughly 32 percent in Belgium, 16 percent in Denmark, 42 percent in France, 23 percent in the Federal Republic of Germany, 27 percent in the Netherlands, 9 percent in the United Kingdom and 17 percent in Ireland.

---

[*] Finland has not yet changed to a general VAT, but the tax has long had value-added features.

In the last decade, use of the tax has spread to the
developing economies.  In Africa, the countries that were
formerly French colonies have followed the French precedent
in moving to a levy designated as a VAT, although it is almost
entirely limited to the import and manufacturing sector.
Senegal (1966), the Ivory Coast (1960), and the Malagasy
Republic (1969), in tropical Africa, and Algeria, Morocco
(1961), and Tunisia (1955), in North Africa, now use the tax.
In Latin America, the tax was adopted for the states of Brazil
in 1967; Uruguay established the tax in 1968, Ecuador in 1970,
Bolivia in 1973,* and Argentina in 1975.  Draft proposals have
been developed in Chile and Mexico but have not yet been
implemented.  There has been substantial discussion in Asian
countries, including Singapore and Malaysia; the Republic of
Vietnam imposed the tax in the summer of 1973.  Table 2.1
presents a summary of VAT in use as of 1 January 1975.  The
table does not include those taxes using the value-added
principle in the manufacturing sector (the Philippines,
Colombia, and Brazil /federal/) but usually classified as
manufacturers' sales taxes.  (These taxes are basically the
same as those in Francophone West African countries
designated as value-added taxes.)

Major differences among the levies are summarized below:

1.    Rate complexity.  Several of the taxes, including
those of Norway, Denmark, and the United Kingdom, use a single
rate.  At the other extreme, France, Italy, and Belgium use
four or more rates, the low rates being on items regarded as
necessities, the top on luxury items.  The African countries
typically use three rates, although Tunisia has a single rate.
The Latin American countries use two rates, except Uruguay,
which has a single rate.

2.    The level of the taxes.  The basic level ranges from
20 percent down to the 4 percent figure in Ecuador.

3.    Inclusion of the retail level.  In general, all the
European and Latin American levies extend through the retail
level.  Those in the African countries do not go beyond the
wholesaler and primarily affect the manufacturing and import
sectors.

4.    Exemption of farmers.  The Federal Republic of
Germany, Denmark, Sweden, and some states in Brazil include

---

*The levy has value-added features, but the application
of the value-added technique is limited.

### TABLE 2.1

Value-Added Taxes, as of January 1, 1975

| Country | Year Introduced | Rates, 1974[a] | Features |
|---|---|---|---|
| **EEC countries** | | | |
| France | 1955 | 20; 7, 17.6, 33.3 | Through retail level since 1963 |
| Germany, Federal Republic of | 1968 | 11; 5.5 | Through retail level since 1963 |
| Netherlands[b] | 1969 | 16; 4 | Through retail level since 1963 |
| Luxembourg[b] | 1970 | 10; 2; 5 | Through retail level since 1963 |
| Belgium[b] | 1971 | 18; 6, 14, 25 | Through retail level since 1963 |
| Italy | 1973 | 6; 12, 18 | Through retail level since 1963 |
| Ireland | 1972 | 6.75; 11.11; 19.5; 36.75 | Through retail level since 1963 |
| United Kingdom | 1973 | 8 | Through retail level since 1963 |
| Denmark | 1967 | 15 | Through retail level since 1963 |
| **Other European countries** | | | |
| Sweden | 1969 | 17.65, 3.09, 9.89 | Through retail level since 1963 |
| Norway | 1970 | 20 | Through retail level since 1963 |
| Austria | 1973 | 16; 8 | |
| **Latin America** | | | |
| Brazil[c] (state) | 1967 | 16.3 to 19 | Through retail level since 1963 |
| Uruguay | 1968 | 10 | Through retail level since 1963 |
| Ecuador | 1970 | 4; 9 | Through retail level since 1963 |
| Argentina | 1975 | 13; 21 | |
| Bolivia (partial) | 1973 | 5 | |
| **Africa (levies known as VAT, but primarily limited to the manufacturing sector)** | | | |
| Senegal | 1966 | 10; 4.25; 33 | Primarily on manufacturers |
| Malagasy Republic | 1969 | 13.6; 6.4 | Through wholesale |
| Ivory Coast | 1960 | 10; 20-23.9 | Optional beyond manufacturing |
| Algeria | -- | 25; 42.9 | Primarily on manufacturers |
| Morocco | 1961 | 14.6; 18.6; 25 | Primarily on manufacturers |
| Tunisia | 1955 | 17.8 | Primarily on manufacturers |

[a]Basic rate given first.

[b]The Benelux countries agreed in 1973 on a uniform base rate of 16 percent, with a 4 percent reduced rate on necessities.

[c]The federal tax has value-added features but is confined to the manufacturing sector.

Note: Rates shown are effective rates, adjusted to a tax-exclusive basis if imposed on a tax-inclusive basis. Changes occur rather frequently.

Source: Compiled by the author.

farmers within the scope of the tax, while the other countries
do not. Even in some of those named, many farmers are in fact
excluded through the exemption of small vendors.

5.  Exclusion of small firms. All jurisdictions provide
for some form of exclusion from tax liability for small
vendors or for the application of a _forfait_ system to them.
In Norway, Denmark, and Sweden, which have few very small
venders, the exemption figures are low. In Denmark, for
example, only firms with annual sales under K 5,000 (about
$900) are exempt. The figures are much higher in other
countries--those with annual sales under £5,000 (about
$12,000) are exempt in the United Kingdom, for example.

6.  Commodity exemptions. The Federal Republic of
Germany has virtually no exemptions; all the others exempt
basic foods and some additional items regarded as necessities.

7.  Inclusion of services. Some taxes, especially in
the EEC, have very broad coverage. At the other extreme, the
taxes in Brazil and Ecuador apply only to commodities.


Types of VAT

There are several bases for classifying value-added taxes.
Of particular importance are the extent of vertical coverage
through production and distribution stages; the treatment of
amounts paid for producers goods, particularly durable capital
equipment; and the method used for calculating tax liability.

Extent of Vertical Coverage Forward from Manufacturing

The value-added principle may be used within the
manufacturing sector only, with tax applying to each
manufacturer on his value added but not to wholesalers or
retailers, except to a limited degree. Such a levy is
designated as a variety of VAT in former French areas in
Africa. In other parts of the world, however, largely for
historical reasons, such a tax is usually designated as a
form of production tax or manufacturers' sales tax (for
example, Colombia, Philippines, Argentina prior to 1975), and
not as a VAT. This form of manufacturers' sales tax is a
substitute for the suspension, or Canadian, type, under which
the tax is applied only to the sale by the manufacturer of
the finished product. With this form, the tax applies of
course to the full selling price of the final manufacturer,
not merely to his value added.

Secondly, the tax may extend through the last wholesale
transaction--that is, down to the retailer. This was the
original form of the French VAT from 1954 to 1968.

Thirdly, the VAT may extend through the retail level, encompassing either all retailers or only those with sales in excess of certain figures, as do the present taxes in the EEC countries.

## Extent of Vertical Coverage Backward from Manufacturer

A value-added tax may encompass all producers of basic materials, including farmers. Frequently, however, farmers are excluded from liability from tax in order to avoid the difficulties of taxing a large number of small establishments and scattered units.

## Treatment of Producers' Goods

Another basic classification of the VAT relates to the treatment accorded to producers' goods--that is, to goods purchased for use in production rather than for personal use. Universally, the value of articles purchased for resale or for incorporation into the finished product as materials or parts, plus fuel, is deductible in ascertaining tax liability. If this were not so, the tax would become a multistage turnover tax of the cascade variety. But practice with respect to other purchases by business firms differs. Conceptually, there are three types of VAT on the basis of treatment of producers' goods:

Consumption Type of Tax. With the type of VAT used in Western Europe, all purchases (with minor exceptions) for use in production, including purchases of durable capital goods, are deductible in determining tax liability in the period in which they are purchased. Thus, the tax actually applies only to purchases for personal household use, with all purchases for use in production by taxpaying firms being excluded from tax. No distinction is made between parts and materials physically incorporated into the product, supplies and fuel, and durable capital goods. Thus the term "consumption type" is used; the tax is limited to purchases for personal consumption purposes, and, if there are no exemptions, the total tax base is equal to total personal consumption expenditures during the period. The base of such a tax is also equal to that of a retail sales tax confined to sales for final personal consumption, including consumption of services, since sales to final consumers and personal consumption expenditures are merely alternative ways of looking at the same magnitude.

Since this type of VAT is the most common, and since a major feature of the change in the French sales tax in 1954 to a levy labeled a value-added tax, instead of a production tax, involved extending the exclusion from tax to cover inputs

of capital equipment and other durable producers' goods, there
is a tendency to regard this type of VAT as the only kind.
But there is no necessity for capital goods inputs to be
excluded in calculating value added.

Income Type. A second type of VAT is one that does not permit
deduction of the purchase price of durable capital goods in
the period of purchase but instead allows the deduction of an
annual depreciation charge arising from such purchases. The
proposed VAT in Mexico takes this form. The term "income
type" is given to this version because the total base of the
tax is equal to total personal income (for the determination
of which, depreciation during the period, rather than current
outlays on capital equipment, is deductible) and therefore
to the base of a personal income tax without exemptions.

Product Type. The third possible type makes no provision for
deductions on durable capital equipment. The tax is therefore
equivalent in coverage to a retail sales tax, which includes
in its base durable capital goods. The measure of the tax is
the same (with complete coverage) as gross national product.
While there are no good examples at present, this form of tax
has received serious consideration in various countries,
including Chile.

## Classification on the Basis of Method of Calculation

The procedure used almost universally for assessing VAT,
following the original French example, involves indirect
calculation. The firm deducts the amount of tax paid on its
purchases during the period from the figure calculated by
applying the tax rate to its figure of taxable sales for the
period. Thus, value added, as such, is never calculated at
all, but the effect is exactly the same as if the figure were
calculated and the tax rate applied.

As an example, let us use the same figures as in the
first paragraph of this section. A retailer pays $6,000 for
bread during the period, and $1,000 for supplies. He sells
the bread for $9,000. He has borne (assuming a 10 percent tax
rate) a total of $700 tax on his purchases. The figure
obtained by applying the 10 percent tax rate to his sales is
$900. He therefore pays to the government $200 ($900 - $700).
If he had calculated value added, $2,000 ($9,000 - $7,000) and
applied the 10 percent tax rate to this figure, the answer
would be the same--$200.

The other two approaches both involve direct calculation
of value added. Under the first, the subtraction method,
purchases of produced goods are subtracted from the figure of
sales during the period, as suggested in the initial definition

of VAT. This procedure was used in the Michigan VAT. The second, the addition method, involves the summation of all the elements that constitute value added--wages and salaries, interest, profit, and the like. So far as is known, this last approach has never been utilized.

The tax credit method is so superior to the other methods in terms of application and enforcement, as well as adaptability to various rate modifications, that it is now universally employed and will be regarded in the remainder of the chapter as the standard method.

## Other Features

Coverage of Services. A VAT may be limited to transactions in physical commodities, or it may be extended to include some or all services. In this respect, VAT resembles other sales taxes.

Exemptions of Commodities. A VAT may be universal in its coverage of commodities or it may exempt particular types, such as food. In a developing economy, unprocessed food used by the producing families or purchased in local markets from small venders is not likely to be reached, in practice, under any circumstances.

Exemptions and Zero Rates on Certain Types of Businesses. Distinct from commodity exemption is exemption of, or application of zero rates to, certain types of establishments. If particular enterprises are exempted, the tax applies to their purchases, and they receive no credit for or refund of this tax since they are not taxpayers. In effect their purchases are treated as consumption expenditures. If they are granted zero rates, they receive refund of tax paid on their purchases.

Zero Rating of Classes of Sales. Zero rating may be applied to classes of sales such as exports or sales to government agencies, correspondingly reducing the tax payable by the seller or, where his sales are predominantly zero rated, entitling him to a credit or refund.

Separate Quotation. With the usual tax credit method of calculation, VAT is usually required to be quoted separately on invoices for sales among business firms, so that the purchasing firm will know how much tax to deduct in calculating its own tax liability. On sales to final consumers, the tax may be quoted separately, as with the retail sales taxes in the United States and Canada, or it may, as is typical in Europe, be hidden in the prices of the products. Some countries require concealment; in others, concealment is not required but is the common practice.

### The Shifting and Incidence of VAT

The question of the shifting of any tax, and thus the final incidence or impact upon the distribution of real income, is always a difficult one to answer, and relatively little attention has been given to this aspect of the VAT.

As far as the consumption type of tax is concerned, under the usual concept of differential incidence, with the assumption that the use of VAT in lieu of other taxes does not alter aggregate demand for factors and thus the level of national income, the basic conclusion is reached that VAT will raise the prices of consumption goods relative to those of capital goods and incomes. Therefore the burden will be distributed in relation to consumer expenditures--that is, will be on consumers. In the typical manufacturing, wholesale, and retail markets, shifting will take the form of direct additions of the tax to the prices, either as separately quoted supplements or through a revision of prices. The fact that the firm shows the tax as a supplement to the price is not in itself conclusive evidence that the tax is shifted forward, since the net-of-tax price might be reduced. But given usual pricing methods in these markets, actual shifting may be regarded as likely, at least in the short run. In the markets for basic agricultural products, however, characterized by a high degree of perfect competition, individual sellers have no direct control over price, and the addition of a separate element may be impossible. In such markets, actual shifting will not occur until supply falls off sufficiently, relative to what it would be under whatever tax the VAT is supplanting.

There are undoubtedly some exceptions to shifting. The higher prices, including tax, will affect the sales of some products more than others, and some changes in relative outputs will occur. Thus, relative prices and factor incomes will be altered somewhat, except when constant cost conditions prevail in all the affected lines of production--that is, the cost of production is not affected by changes in the total output of the product.

Likewise, differences in the extent of price competition may affect forward shifting in some instances.

On the whole, however, the assumption of forward shifting is a reasonable one to make as a first approximation.[2] With this assumption, the distribution of burden by income class will be determined by the pattern of consumer spending relative to income, by income class. In a typical developing economy, the lowest-income groups will depend primarily on subsistence farm products and unprocessed foods bought in

local markets and almost certainly not taxed.  For the wage-
earning groups, the tax is likely to be regressive relative
to income because consumption probably does not rise as
rapidly as income.  The exemption of widely used food products
and other items of basic necessity will make the tax less
regressive.

As regards the income and product type of tax, the
distributional effects are much less clear.  There are two
conflicting approaches.  According to one approach, since the
income type includes in its base the interest on funds
invested in capital goods, it affects both consumption and the
return from saving.  Therefore it is equivalent to a tax on
income--with distributional patterns the same as those of a
proportional income tax without exemptions.  A product type of
VAT will likewise be distributed in a fashion somewhat
comparable to that of an income tax, since the prices of both
consumption goods and capital goods are increased.

The alternative approach is based upon the assumption
that business firms will treat the tax element on capital goods
as an element in the cost of the capital goods, and with usual
depreciation and pricing methods will include this tax element
in the prices of the consumption goods made with them.  Thus,
ultimately, this element also will be borne in relation to
consumer expenditures, but in a somewhat haphazard and uneven
fashion on the consumption of various goods, since some goods
require more taxable capital goods in their production than
do others.  Thus, the return from savings will not be reduced,
except perhaps incidentally.

This is a very complex economic issue, and no attempt will
be made to resolve it here.  In the remaining sections, which
center on the consumption type of VAT, the assumption will be
made that the tax is distributed in relation to consumer
spending.  It will be recognized that the other two types may
to some extent reduce the return to savings and thus may be
somewhat less regressively distributed, but they are likely to
be distributed in a highly haphazard fashion relative to
consumption or income.

## What Type of Tax is the VAT?

The analysis of incidence suggests that VAT, in its usual
consumption form, should be regarded as a sales tax, since the
burden is distributed in relation to consumer spending.  As
noted above, the total base, other things being the same, is
the same as that of a retail sales tax.  The retail tax is
collected entirely from the retailer, on the retail price.
VAT is collected, piecemeal, from all units in the production

and distribution system, on their respective values added.  The
yield of the two taxes will be the same, at a given tax rate.
VAT is universally regarded as a sales tax in Western Europe,
and in all European countries was introduced to replace an
existing sales tax (in the United Kingdom, known as the
purchase tax).[*]  There are, it is true, a few dissenters from
this classification, but they are in a very small minority.[3]
With the income and product versions of the tax, the appropriate
classification is less clear, but for purposes of this study,
these versions will also be regarded as sales taxes, following
general practice.  The mere fact that the bases of the income
form of the tax and a proportional rate personal income tax
are the same in no way demonstrates that the distributional
effects of the two taxes are the same.  This is a major issue
unanswerable with any assurance at the present time.

     VAT, like other sales taxes, is classified as an indirect
tax, because it is paid by business firms to the government
and shifted to the purchasers of the products, rather than
being collected directly by the government from the purchasers.

Summary

     VAT has come to play a major role in the tax structures
of many countries.  Universally regarded as a sales tax in
the countries in which it is used, even though in some forms
its distributional pattern may resemble more closely that of a
proportional income tax than a consumption-related tax, it has
replaced other forms of sales taxes in all countries of
Western Europe except Switzerland, Spain, Portugal, and
Finland (but the tax in Finland has value-added features).
Its use has been expanding in Latin America and Africa and
has been widely considered in Asia.

     The distinctive feature of the tax is that of "fractional"
impact without "cascade" features.  Under the single-stage
sales taxes, the entire amount of tax is collected at one
stage in production or distribution; VAT applies at more than
one stage in production and distribution, but only to the value
added.  Except in Africa, the term is applied only to those
taxes that apply beyond the manufacturing sector; taxes using
the value-added feature but confined to the manufacturing
sector are usually regarded as manufacturers' sales taxes.
VAT, however, does not necessarily apply to services; the
coverage is not necessarily broader than that of other forms

---

[*]The U.K. VAT also replaced a "selective employment tax."

of sales taxes.  Exclusion of producers' goods, particularly durable capital equipment, while common, is likewise not a necessary characteristic of VAT, nor is concealment of the tax from the final consumer.  The tax may or may not be quoted separately on the final sale.  Use of the tax credit method of calculation is likewise not essential but is almost universal and will be regarded as a standard feature.

For purposes of this chapter, the assumption will be made that VAT is shifted forward to consumers, raising prices of consumption goods relative to incomes and therefore distributed in relation to consumer spending.  It is recognized that there are likely to be exceptions to this rule, particularly with the income and product versions of the tax, and in the long run even with the consumption version.

## THE CASE FOR AND AGAINST VAT IN DEVELOPING COUNTRIES

The purpose of this section is to evaluate the use of VAT in a developing country.  The analysis is presented in three parts, involving evaluation of the use of indirect consumption-related taxes in developing economies, of the use of sales taxes in lieu of other forms of consumption-related taxes, and of VAT in lieu of other forms of sales tax.

### Criteria for Evaluation

Evaluation of a tax's use and structure must rest upon accepted criteria.  These criteria, in turn, must be based upon the goals or objectives regarded as preeminent in a particular society.  In a developing country, the following objectives are typically stressed, but with relative emphasis on the various objectives differing according to the general political, economic, and social philosophy of the government:

1.    Acceleration of economic growth:  in other words, a constant rise in per capita real income designed to move the level of real income as rapidly as possible to that of the highly developed countries.

2.    Optimal use of available resources, to allow maximum output and optimal resource allocation--that is, allocation of resources to the production of various goods in such a way as to satisfy most effectively the preferences of the people of the society.

3.    Attainment of an acceptable pattern of income distribution, requiring the elimination or prevention of extreme disparities in income and wealth distribution.

4.   Reasonable price stability.

5.   Avoidance of foreign domination of the economy.

6.   Political stability:  the avoidance of constant
overthrow of governments by force, on the one hand, or
stagnation and political indecision--failure to act--on the
other.

## Determinants of Growth

Given the stress placed in most developing countries on
economic growth, further attention to this objective is
needed.  Knowledge of the determinants of economic development
and growth is by no means adequate.  It would appear, however,
that major determinants of growth include the following:

1.   The rate of capital formation.  A basic cause of
low per capita income is an inadequate stock of capital goods;
hence, a higher rate of capital formation is essential for
growth.  This, in turn, requires the following:

(a) A higher rate of savings--that is, of total savings
    as a percentage of national income--or increased
    availability of capital from outside the country.
    Since the latter is limited in availability and may
    lead to foreign domination of the economy, the
    former--additional savings--is of primary importance.

(b) A higher rate of real investment--a willingness of
    private firms or government to translate the
    additional savings into real capital formation.  If
    this does not occur, additional attempted savings
    will tend to be negated by a fall in output
    accompanied by unemployment, as in a developed
    economy.

2.   Optimal capital allocation in terms of the incremental
capital output ratio (ICOR).  Not only is a higher rate of
capital formation required, but the capital formation must be
of such a nature as to make a maximum contribution to
development--that is, to allow the maximum increase in output
per unit of capital goods, or, in the terminology of
development theory, to allow the lowest possible incremental
capital output ratio--a minimum amount of capital goods to
obtain a given increase in output.

3.   Greater ability to import.  The optimal types of
capital goods and materials necessary for domestic production
require ability to import them.  Ability to import goods

essential for development, in turn, is determined by the ability to export, to restrain increases in imports of nonessentials as income rises, and to obtain foreign aid and loans.  Given the limitations on the ability to obtain aids and loans, primary reliance must be placed upon the first two determinants.

4.  Introduction of new technology.  Technology is, of course, available from the more developed countries, although not always of the type best suited for the developing countries.  Actual introduction usually requires real investment in equipment involved in the new technology.

5.  Increased availability, skill, and training of human resources.  Improvements in skill and training constitute a major source of higher per capita real incomes.

6.  Increased availability and utilization of natural resources.

Economic development, as distinguished from growth in a per capita real income sense, is primarily dependent upon the extent to which growth affects the population as a whole, not merely small segments of it and is, thus, largely dependent upon the distribution of income and wealth.

## Conflicts among Objectives

It is obvious that conflict may arise among the various objectives.  For example, a high degree of inequality of income may stimulate savings and real investment but will conflict with the objective of an equitable pattern of distribution of income and wealth.  Such conflicts can be resolved only on the basis of a weighing by the particular society of the various objectives.

## Criteria for Taxation in a Developing Economy

These objectives suggest the use of the following criteria to evaluate taxes in developing countries:

1.  Maximum net contribution to economic development, with maximum positive and minimum negative effects.  Among the various elements that affect this contribution are the following:

(a) The attainment of total revenue levels that allow maximum government contribution to economic development and optimal balance between private and governmental sectors.

(b) Maximum encouragement for persons to save more and
    spend less on consumption.

(c) Minimum adverse effects on real investment decisions.

(d) Guidance of capital formation to types that offer the
    maximum contribution to economic growth.

(e) Avoidance of adverse effects on exports; positive
    stimulation to exports if possible.

(f) Minimum adverse effect on the willingness of foreign
    countries and international organizations to provide
    aid and loans--to the extent that such aid and loans
    are sought.

(g) Maximum assistance for, rather than restriction of,
    the improvement of levels of skill and education.

(h) Maximization of labor hours available in the economy--
    subject to the society's preference ratio between
    work and leisure.

(i) Maximum encouragement of more effective utilization
    of natural resources.

2.    Minimum adverse effect on efficiency in the
utilization of resources and encouragement of greater
efficiency if possible.  Thus, taxes should not distort
production and distribution methods from the optimum and
should not alter consumer choice patterns except as
specifically desired for development or distributional goals.

3.    Ease of administration of the taxes.  The objective
is to minimize the use of resources in compliance with and in
the administration of taxes, so as to make more resources
available for production purposes, and at the same time
attain acceptable enforcement, to maximize revenue and
minimize evasion and inequity.

4.    Maximum contribution to the attainment of desired
patterns of distribution of income and wealth--in other words,
conformity with accepted standards of equity.  This requires,
under the usual standards of equity, avoiding any tax burden
on the lowest-income groups and imposing a relatively
progressive burden at the higher levels.  The exact optimal
patterns of distribution are determined by the consensus of
thought in the particular society on inequality in wealth
and income distribution.

5.   Revenue elasticity.  The automatic adjustment of tax revenues to rising national income, preferably at a more rapid rate than the latter, ensures that revenues keep pace with rising incomes without the need for politicaly difficult tax-rate changes or the addition of new taxes.

## The Role of Consumption-Related Taxes

There are two general approaches to consumption-related taxes.  Such levies may be directly on individuals, in the form of expenditure or spendings taxes, or they may be indirect, imposed upon production or sale and collected from the sellers, and presumably passed forward to the consumers of the product. The expenditure tax can be adapted to desired standards of equity more effectively than the indirect form, since it is a personal levy and exemptions and progressive rates can be provided.  With highly progressive rates it offers great potential for reducing consumption and increasing savings.[4] From an administrative standpoint, however, it encounters not only all the problems of income taxation in developing economies but additional problems as well, since net increases in savings must be ascertained and checked, as well as the various items entering into calculation of income.   Thus, except for limited experiments in India and Sri Lanka, it has not been attempted in developing economies, nor has it been implemented even in industrialized countries.  Stress, there-fore, will be placed on the indirect form, of which VAT is a subspecies.

## Merits of Consumption-Related Taxes

Indirect, or consumption-related, taxes offer several advantages in a developing economy, compared to greater use of direct income or wealth-related taxes.

Revenues.  Indirect taxes offer a greater revenue potential than sole reliance on direct taxes, thus providing the government with greater funds for expenditure on education, health, roads, and other purposes that aid economic development. The greater revenue yield is partly a matter of greater administrative effectiveness, as noted below, and partly a matter of political reactions--the typical resistance to high direct taxes in a society in which these taxes have been relatively low.

Effects on Consumption.  For a given revenue, consumption-related taxes have a greater effect in restricting consumption than income taxes and thus help to increase the portion of national income saved.  The consumption-related taxes strike

heavily on those families that spend high percentages of their
incomes, thus forcing a curtailment of consumption and giving
some incentive to save more.  Such a reaction may not be
entirely logical if the taxes are expected to continue, but
it may nevertheless occur.

Luxury Imports.  Consumption-related taxes constitute a more
effective means than direct taxes of discouraging the
consumption of "luxury" imported goods, thus lessening the
danger of foreign exchange crises and freeing foreign exchange
for the importation of goods essential for economic development.

Incentives.  Consumption taxes offer less interference than
progressive income taxes and corporate income taxes to the
development and expansion of business activity.  Export
duties, another source of revenue, may reduce production for
export and lessen the earnings of foreign exchange essential
for economic development.  Excessive use of direct taxes
could reduce the willingness of persons to obtain an education
or to enter the commercial labor market, though effects of
this type are unlikely, except possibly for wives of persons
with substantial incomes.

Ease of Administration.  On the whole, it is easier to
administer indirect consumption-related taxes than taxes on
income or wealth.  The tax is collected at the point of
importation and from a relatively small number of business
firms, instead of from large numbers of individuals, many
of them, in a developing economy, illiterate and lacking the
most elementary records.  While any form of sales tax
encounters problems with small artisans and traders, it is
easier to collect from these persons a tax based on their
sales than one based on their trading profits.  The greater
ease of administration allows more effective enforcement
with less use of resources, for both the taxpayers and the
government.

Equity.  While, as noted below, consumption taxes present
some defects from the standpoint of equity, nevertheless they
accord with usually accepted standards of equity to a greater
extent than similar taxes in highly developed economies.  The
lowest-income groups live primarily on subsistence production
and unprocessed foods, which are almost universally excluded
from any form of indirect tax in a developing economy, and
escape almost all tax.  While evidence is lacking, there is
reason to believe that consumption of taxed goods--largely
manufactured goods--is at least proportional to income and
possibly progressive, in a developing economy, over a
substantial range of income.  Only at the higher income
levels is the tax inadequate on distributional grounds, as
noted below.  Likewise, to the extent that sales taxes are

*middle to lower*

more effectively administered than income and wealth taxes, actual equity may be greater even though the latter taxes would be regarded as more equitable if they were effectively enforced.

Revenue Elasticity. While in theory an income tax should provide greater revenue elasticity, in practice, because of enforcement problems, the elasticity of sales and related taxes may be greater. This is borne out by empirical studies. One by Chelliah shows elasticity of revenue for sales and excises in developing economies to be 2.4 percent, that of income taxes 1.4 percent.[5] In part, however, the high figure for sales taxes reflects a shift away from imports to domestic production.

## Inadequacies of Consumption-Related Taxes

The principal deficiency of sales and other consumption-related taxes is their inability to lessen inequality of wealth and income, in view of their regressive or more or less proportional distributional patterns, particularly at high income levels. The importance of this inadequacy depends upon the distributional pattern regarded as optimal, the extent to which other taxes in the tax system work to reduce inequality, and the emphasis given in the society to lessening inequality of income and wealth. While attempts are made to mitigate the inadequacy of indirect taxes as regards equity by providing higher rates on luxury goods and exempting commodities primarily purchased by the poor, it appears virtually impossible to contribute substantially toward the desired goal without serious complications in the operation of the taxes.

Secondly, as will be explained below, the framing of a consumption-related tax that will not distort methods of production and consumer choice and thus lessen overall efficiency in the use of resources in an economy is very difficult. Since these taxes are collected from business firms, undesirable effects upon the choice of methods of doing business may be very difficult to avoid. There are also serious problems in adapting the structure of the tax in order to attain desired ends; there is, for example, an inherent conflict between the desire to strike luxury consumption more heavily and the objective of simple administration. Finally, the taxes do not offer a potential for guiding investment into optimal channels in the fashion permitted, albeit to a limited extent, by income taxes.

Sales Taxation in Lieu of Higher Customs Duties and Excises

Granted the strength of the argument in favor of using indirect consumption-related taxes in a developing economy, a choice must be made between sales taxation on the one hand and a greater use of customs duties and excises on the other. Typically, customs duties constitute the dominant form of tax in the least developed economies.[6] With little domestic production and the domination of domestic activity by subsistence agriculture and small-scale trading, there is little potential for sales (or excise) taxes. Customs duties can easily be enforced, as long as smuggling can be prevented. Since most imports consist of luxury goods, the system conforms reasonably well to standards of equity. But customs duties become progressively less satisfactory as the development of a country continues. First, the development of domestic production tends to reduce customs revenue, at least relative to national income, and perhaps even in absolute terms. To an increasing extent, as development continues, imports consist of capital goods and of materials for domestic production--unsuitable for import duties--rather than of finished luxury products. Customs duties likewise become progressively less equitable, as some luxury goods are produced domestically while others are not. If customs duty rates are pushed higher and higher to maintain revenue, unwanted protection of domestic industry will develop; new industries for which the country has no advantage and which are not sought under development plans will spring up behind high tariffs designed for revenue purposes--and, once they develop, employment and political considerations will make it very difficult to eliminate them.

As domestic production develops, the first step is usually to introduce excise taxes on domestic production, in order to compensate for the revenue lost at customs. As long as domestic production is confined to a few products, particularly items such as cigarettes, beer, motor fuel, and liquor, this is a relatively simple approach. But, as domestic production expands into wider fields, excises become progressively less satisfactory and more complicated. New products are not reached until the legislation is changed to include them. The government is faced with the administration of a large number of separate levies, and particular firms may be subject to a number of them. The point is ultimately reached at which a broad-based sales tax becomes far more satisfactory from the standpoints of revenue, compliance and administration, and equity. Because of the broader base, the tax yield is greater. With a single levy, administration is easier. The tax catches all commodities at a uniform rate, except those for which either exemption or a higher rate is desired, thus avoiding discrimination on the basis of personal

preferences.  When sales taxes are introduced, there is merit
in retaining a small number of excises, on liquor, beer,
tobacco products, and motor fuel, on which burdens much heavier
than that of the sales tax is desired.

## VAT Versus the Cascade Tax

Given the merits of sales taxation in developing economies,
there remains the decision on the choice of form of sales tax.
There are two general types of alternatives.  First, VAT may be
considered as an alternative to, or substitute for, a multistage cascade or turnover type of multiple sales tax, under
which the tax applies to the selling price at each point of
sale, from the initial production of materials to the final
sale to the consumer.  (The initial sale by the farmer and
the final sale by the retailer may be excluded.)  Alternatively,
the choice may be between VAT and a single-stage sales tax--
such as the manufacturers' sales tax, the wholesale tax
(applying to the last wholesale transaction through which a
commodity passes), or the retail sales tax, either in its pure
form, applying to all sales at retail, or with smaller
retailers exempted and tax applied to sales to these firms
rather than sales by them.

### Merits of VAT over Cascade Taxes

Most of the present value-added taxes have been
introduced to replace the cascade form of sales tax, and in
most of the few countries still using the latter form of tax,
VAT is under serious consideration as a substitute.  VAT offers
very significant advantages over the cascade tax.

First, VAT is entirely neutral among various systems of
organization of production and distribution, thus causing no
distortion or loss of economic efficiency, whereas the cascade
tax provides strong pressure toward vertical integration, both
within the production sector and in physical distribution.
(Both taxes are neutral with respect to financing.)  Given the
degree of vertical integration, the cascade tax discriminates
against goods with more than average value added at early
stages.  The cascade tax applies each time a product is sold,
from initial production to sale to final consumer (or at least
to the last stage covered, if the tax stops short of the final
retail sale).  The tax therefore offers a strong incentive
for integration; if a manufacturer produces his own materials
and parts, he escapes paying tax on them.  If he bypasses the
wholesaler and sells directly to the consumer, the tax is
reduced accordingly.  Thus, discrimination results against the
small, nonintegrated firm to the benefit of the integrated
firm, and integration is strongly encouraged.  There is

substantial evidence that this type of effect has occurred in
Chile, for example, where a cascade tax has been used for a
long period.  Integration is not per se objectionable when it
arises from economic forces.  However, it results in loss of
efficiency and lower output and growth rate if it is
artificially encouraged and may in any case lead to undesirable
concentrations of economic power and monopolistic tendencies.

VAT does not affect integration in any way, since the
total amount of tax on a product will be the same regardless
of the organization of the production and distribution system.
If a firm integrates forwards or backwards, it will be subject
to greater VAT, but overall no more or less tax than the total
paid by nonintegrated competitors.

As far as modifications to lessen discrimination are
concerned, the experience in most countries using the cascade
form of tax has been that strong complaints lead to special
concessions to various groups of firms, such as independent
wholesalers, and thus result in a series of different rates
that materially add to the complexity of the tax without
solving the basic problem of distortion noted above.

With VAT the amount of the tax relative to the final
selling price is known (apart from some deviations from
forward shifting noted in the first section).  This burden can
be adjusted in terms of the objectives of the tax; it is
uniform save when rates are deliberately varied for equity
reasons or in a desire to lessen consumption of certain types
of goods.  By contrast, with the cascade tax it is impossible
to determine in any routine manner how much tax is incorporated
in the final selling price of the product, because the tax
has entered into the final selling price from a variety of
sources, including the taxation of materials, machinery,
supplies, and the like, which affect the cost of the product.
The consequence is that the relative burden on consumption of
various commodities and services cannot be ascertained without
costly special investigation.

There is also the matter of an uneven burden on various
commodities.  While the exact burden on various commodities
cannot be ascertained, it is obvious that the burden will
vary with the typical number of transactions through which a
commodity passes on its way to the final consumer.  The
consequent distributional pattern will thus be haphazard, with
the burden falling more heavily on the consumption of certain
commodities than others without justification.  It is
impossible to remove all tax burden from food and other items
regarded as necessities, because of the taxation of items used
directly or indirectly in their production.

By contrast, apart from shifting irregularities, the
burden of VAT will be uniform on all commodities taxed at a
uniform rate and will vary according to the desired pattern
on others.

The cascade form of tax also tends to discriminate
against domestically produced goods as compared with imports,[*]
since the former pass through a larger number of taxable sales
transactions within the country than the latter.  This can be
offset in part, but by no means exactly, by a compensating tax
on imports, designed to reflect the average tax that is paid on
equivalent domestic production of these goods.  VAT avoids
this problem, since the imported goods will either bear tax on
their full value at the time of importation or (under the tax
credit method) have this value taxed at the first subsequent
sale, and then subsequent value added will be taxed in the
same fashion as with domestic goods.

The problem with exports under the cascade tax is that
the amount of tax incorporated into the prices of exported
goods is not readily ascertainable.  While the export
transaction is freed of tax, there is no practical way of
refunding the exact amount of tax accumulated on the product
up to the point of exportation.  Thus, underrefunding, with
consequent short-run harm to domestic producers selling in
world markets, or overrefunding, which constitutes a subsidy
on exports in violation of General Agreement on Trade and
Tariff (GATT) treaty rules, is inevitable.  By contrast, the
exact amount of VAT at the point of exportation can be
calculated and refunded to the exporter.  Tax must be shown
separately on invoices, and the cumulated amount of tax is
easily ascertained by applying the tax rate to the price at
the sale to the exporter.  In the long run, the overall
discrimination in favor of imports will be adjusted by changes
in exchange rates or relative price levels.

Lastly, there is the question of allocating sales tax
revenue in a common market area.  Harmonization of sales taxes
is essential in a common market area, or sales taxes will be
utilized as deliberate instruments of protection, and sales-
tax differences will place producers in some countries at a
disadvantage in competing with producers in others, once
tariff protection is eliminated.  It is generally recognized

---

[*] Except to the extent that imports have borne comparable
taxes in the exporting country.  But most countries relieve
their exports from taxation in one way or another on
mercantilist principles.

that satisfactory harmonization of cascade taxes is impossible,
and it was this consideration, more than others, that led the
EEC countries to accept VAT in lieu of the cascade form of tax.
With the turnover tax, the amount of tax on the export is not
known, as already indicated; producers in countries using the
cascade form would almost certainly find themselves at a
disadvantage in competing with firms in countries not having
the tax.  VAT, with its known zero impact on exports and its
ability to treat imports and domestic goods equally, is far
superior.  As noted below, VAT offers some advantages over
single-stage taxes with respect to common market harmonization.

## Merits of the Cascade Form of Tax

The cascade tax offers only limited advantages relative
to VAT.  The rate necessary for a given sum of revenue is less,
and the tax, as long as it is not complicated by concessions
to various types of firms, is somewhat simpler.  The cascade
tax applies to gross sales at all transactions; VAT applies to
value added, and thus requires one more step in calculation.
But this advantage of simplicity is lost once the cascade tax
is modified in an effort to lessen discrimination and to meet
the complaints of nonintegrated firms, as has commonly
occurred.

The low rate of the cascade tax is unfortunately an
obstacle to its elimination.  Governments have in practice
been reluctant to make the change from a cascade tax to other
forms because of the sharp increase necessary in the rate.

### VAT Versus Single-stage Levies

The disadvantages of turnover taxes have become so well
known that they remain in few countries today--despite their
widespread use a decade ago.  Spain, Mexico, Sri Lanka, and
some of the states of India are among the remaining users of
the cascade tax.  The issue in most countries today, therefore,
is, Shall VAT be chosen in preference to a single-stage tax,
either as regards the introduction of a new tax, the replacement of a cascade tax, or the replacement of a single-stage
tax?

## VAT Versus Manufacturers' Sales Tax

Since any of the single-stage taxes, properly designed,
will avoid the worst evils of the cascade tax, the case for VAT
is somewhat different and less clear-cut.  Its basic advantage
over the single-stage taxes is essentially that it avoids the
evils of the turnover tax without concentrating the impact of
the tax on any one layer of firms in the production and distri-

bution system.  At the same time, if carried through the retail
level, it avoids the inherent disadvantages of the manufacturers'
sales tax and the wholesale tax.

The manufacturers' sales tax, as experience in Canada,
Colombia, and elsewhere has shown, suffers from certain
disadvantages, although in significance they do not compare
with those of the cascade tax.

As regards the effect on forward integration, whereas a
cascade tax encourages vertical integration, a manufacturers'
sales tax artificially discourages it, leading firms to push
various functions beyond the point of impact of the tax in
order to reduce the amount of the tax due.  Thus, forward
integration of manufacturers is discouraged.  Canada has
attempted to meet this problem by allowing readjustments in
prices for tax purposes on direct sales to retailers or
consumers, but in doing so has materially complicated the
tax without providing complete neutrality.

Another difficulty is that it is virtually impossible for
domestic and imported goods to be treated uniformly, since the
extent of production and distribution activity subject to tax
will differ in the two cases.  There is a particular danger of
favoring imports, since advertising and other distributional
activities with respect to these goods may be performed after
the point of importation, whereas the costs of these activities
will be reflected in the manufacturers' prices of domestically
produced goods, if they are performed by manufacturers.

The burden on consumers is also not uniform.  As with the
cascade tax, the tax, assuming that there is forward shifting,
will constitute a varying percentage of final consumer
expenditures on the goods.  This variation results from the
variation in the magnitude of wholesale and retail margins on
various goods.  A 20 percent manufacturers' tax will constitute
a 13.3 percent burden on consumer spending (excluding tax) on
goods with a total wholesale-retail markup (on cost) of
50 percent, a 10 percent burden with a margin of 100 percent
(50 percent of retail price).  This variation is haphazard;
if anything, the burden will be greater on basic necessities,
which tend to have low margins, than on the most luxurious
goods (for example, expensive jewelry) on which the margins
tend to be high.

Further problems arise in freeing exports from tax
without frequent refunds, since the goods may be sold
domestically, subject to tax, prior to exportation.

In addition, since the tax applies only to the
manufacturer's price, the tax rate must be substantially higher
than that of a retail tax or VAT through the retail level.

There is also the question of pyramiding.  Whenever
percentage markups are used by merchants, as appears to be
common, the price increase to the consumer will be greater than
the tax received by the government.  Essentially, the markup
percentage is being applied to the tax element.  Competition
may eliminate pyramiding, by compelling an adjustment of markup
percentages, but only slowly.

These disadvantages apply equally to the Canadian form of
manufacturers' sales tax and to VAT confined to the manufacturing sector, as it exists in Senegal.  The principal advantages
over the manufacturers' sales tax are attained only if VAT
includes the retail sector.  There are advantages in this
limited-scope VAT over the suspension-type manufacturers' tax,
but they are somewhat limited:

First, the value-added technique avoids the concentration
of all the tax on the manufacturers of the finished product;
some is collected from materials and parts processors, thus
lessening somewhat the danger of evasion.

Secondly, since tax applies to imports of materials, the
danger that licensed manufacturers may import materials tax-
free and then resell them, or fail to pay tax on their entire
output produced with them, is avoided.  Tax will at least be
collected on the import value of the materials.

Third, the cross-audit feature, and the exclusion of
advantages for producers' goods noted below are attained.

The relative advantages of VAT over the wholesale sales
tax are comparable to those relative to a manufacturers' tax,
but to a lesser degree, since the wholesale tax is levied one
step closer to the final sale to the consumer.

The principal disadvantage of VAT compared with the
manufacturers' tax is the larger number of taxpayers involved,
especially if VAT is carried through the retail level.  If it
is carried only through the wholesale level, the number is no
greater than with a wholesale tax, other features being the
same, unless some manufacturers make no sales to final
purchasers or retailers, and thus are not subject to the
wholesale tax.  However, there are few such firms.

## VAT Versus the Retail Sales Tax

The retail sales tax avoids virtually all the problems
of a tax limited to the manufacturing sector because it is
imposed at the final sale to the consumer.  There is no
incentive to alter distribution systems; most imports and
domestic goods can be treated equally; pyramiding is avoided;

and the desired pattern of burden can be attained.  But
collection of a retail sales tax places the entire impact of
the sales tax upon retailers.  In contrast, much--half or more--
of VAT is collected at pre-retail levels.  Thus, particularly
in a developing economy, the danger of complete evasion is far
less with VAT, since any sales tax can be collected more
effectively from typical manufacturers and wholesalers than
from retailers.  Administration, generally, is easier, and
complaints from retailers will be far fewer.  In developing
economies, the typical retail trader is a small entrepreneur
with relatively inadequate records and a high propensity to
evade taxes.  He may also be less able to plan his cash flow
in such a way as to be able to meet his tax payments--that is,
he is more likely to be able to pay the wholesaler, including
the tax element in the wholesale tax, than to be foresighted
enough to set aside the money for paying a periodic tax bill.
With VAT, if evasion does occur in the form of failure to file
any return, only the tax on the retail margin will be lost.
Although evasion achieved by understating sales while claiming
full credit for the tax on purchases will result in loss of
tax on the full retail value of the sales not reported, this
can be prevented relatively easily through audit.

     Thus, basically, VAT offers the advantages of the retail
form of sales tax without the need to collect the entire
amount of the tax from the retailer.  VAT does not, however,
solve the problem of the very small shopkeeper without records.
This problem is equivalent with both types of taxes, other
features being the same, except that with the usual forms of
evasion, the revenue loss is less with VAT, if the firm's
suppliers can be reached by the tax.

Other Merits of VAT

     VAT has other advantages over the other forms of single-
stage sales taxes.

     First, there is the cross-audit feature.  With VAT, tax
reported to the government by one firm as being paid by it to
another firm, its supplier, and therefore a tax credit, should
appear as a tax payment by the supplier to the government.
Cross-checking of this kind greatly lessens the ability of
firms to overstate deductions of tax paid on purchases and to
underreport tax paid to the government.  Such cross-checking
is not automatic and requires a substantial portion of the
auditors' time, but it does offer some net gain in
administration.  Somewhat similar techniques are used with
retail sales taxes; an auditor will check the sales records of
the retailer's supplier when he suspects that sales by the
former are understated.  However, the cross-checking is more
clearly indicated with VAT.

A major argument for the value-added form, and one that influenced two of the Scandinavian countries to shift to this form of tax, is the possibility that producers' goods--goods purchased for use in further production--can be more easily excluded from tax with the value-added form with less danger of evasion. With a usual single-stage tax, any exemption of producers' goods involves two firms: the firm purchasing the goods for use, and its supplier, since the sale is made tax-free. Both firms must keep records or evidence of the tax-free nature of the sale. In case of doubt, an auditor must check both sets of records. With VAT, only the purchasing firm is affected; the supplier is not concerned with the use to which the goods are put. The purchasing firm simply claims credit for tax paid on the purchases, and, in the event of doubt, only its records must be checked. This difference simplifies checking, eases the tasks of the suppliers, and lessens the danger of evasion.

While there is probably some net advantage with VAT in this regard, the difference is not as great as might first appear. As with income taxes, some checking on reported use is necessary or firms will deduct tax paid on purchases made for the personal consumption of the owners. Furthermore, the same device can be, and to some extent is, used in single-stage sales taxes. For example, under the Argentinian version of a manufacturers' sales tax, manufacturers were taxable on all purchases but were allowed to deduct from their tax liability tax on purchases made for certain purposes. There is no need, therefore, to check on the supplier. Some states in the United States permit designated manufacturers to make all purchases free of retail sales tax, and then to account for the tax themselves on goods used for taxable purposes.

A final advantage of the value-added form is relevant in a Common Market area. The ideal approach to sales taxation in such an area, once all customs duties and frontier customs posts are eliminated, is application of the tax on the basis of origin. The jurisdiction of location of the seller would tax each sale to destinations within the common market area, without refund at export. No border checking, no import or export verification or control, would be needed. Each country in the Common Market would give credit for sales tax paid to another country in the market area. Administration of the tax would be far easier under such an approach, since each country would be concerned only with transactions made by sellers within its geographical jurisdiction. With the origin system, VAT provides for the allocation of sales tax revenues on intercountry transactions on the basis of where the particular economic activity creating the added value is located. In contrast, a manufacturers' tax attributes disproportionate revenue to the areas in which manufacturing is located, and the retail tax to the location of the consumer.

## Objections to the Value-Added Form

VAT gives rise to some difficulties as compared to single-stage taxes.

First, the tax is basically more complex than single-stage taxes. Firms must not only calculate taxable sales but must also keep records of tax paid on purchases as well, and both sets of figures must be subject to audit.

Second, there is the question of refunds. Large sums of tax would be collected and subsequently refunded, especially in a country in which exports are substantial. A single-stage tax would minimize refunding.

As contrasted with a manufacturers' sales tax, the use of several tax rates and exemptions would be made more complicated, since the different rates and exemptions would either apply throughout production and distribution, involving a large number of firms, or at the retail level alone, where the application of different rates is particularly difficult and where the evasion of tax on highly rated goods would be widespread. One major advantage of the manufacturers' form of tax is greater ease in applying different rates to different goods, since manufacturers work on a relatively large scale, keep better records, are more highly specialized by type of goods, and sell in relatively large transactions.

Because of the tax credit feature, the exemption of certain classes of firms, as, for example, farmers, creates a type of complication that does not arise with the other taxes Any class of firm exempted because of small size, such as farmers, would not be able to claim a refund of tax paid on their purchases, nor could the firms to which they sold obtain credit for tax elements that entered into prices. Therefore, an element of multiple taxation would arise; tax would apply to a portion of the farmer's costs, and then to the full selling price of the product after sale by the farmer. Various devices may be used to meet this problem, but they add complications and are somewhat arbitrary. Outright exemption of sales to farmers means losing the basic merit of VAT in taxing all sales.

## Summary

The case for substantial use of indirect consumption-related taxes is much stronger in a developing country than in highly developed countries, given the difficulties of operating broad-based income taxes there. Not only are indirect consumption-related taxes easier to operate, but they

offer positive advantages in reducing consumption relative to
savings and reducing imports of luxuries.  In addition, they
avoid possible adverse effects of income taxes on incentives
to work and to undertake real investment.  The sales tax
offers significant advantages over greater reliance on
customs duties and, beyond a certain level of development,
over excise taxes.  VAT is greatly preferable to the cascade
form of sales tax.  Basically, the great merit of the tax is
that it allows a country to avoid the disadvantages of the
cascade tax without concentrating the tax impact on one set
of firms.  If carried through to the retail level, it allows
most of the merits of the retail sales tax to be achieved
without the need to concentrate collection entirely on
retailers--the type of business most difficult to control.
On the other hand, it is clearly a more complex levy and, if
carried through the retail level, as is necessary to attain
the advantages of the retail tax, involves far more taxpaying
firms than the manufacturers' sales tax.

Final decision on the choice between VAT and other forms
of sales tax should be influenced primarily by the following
considerations:

First, the nature of wholesale and retail activity in
the country.  If these activities are carried on almost entirely
by small-scale venders with limited records, the case for
confining the sales tax to the manufacturing level is
particularly strong, despite the higher tax rate required and
the economic distortion that results.  If wholesale firms are
typically large, there is some merit in using VAT through the
wholesale level--a tax that does not differ greatly from the
Colombian form of manufacturers' sales tax.

Second, the amount of revenue sought from the tax is
also important.  If relatively small amounts of money are
required, it may be possible to use the retail sales tax
with small firms exempted, tax applying instead to their
purchases, since with the low rate the concentration of the
impact of tax at the retail level will be less serious, and
the complexities of VAT will be avoided.

A further consideration is the importance attached to
excluding producers' goods from tax.  The greater the
importance attached to exclusion, for foreign trade or other
purposes, the stronger the case for VAT.

There are two arguments advanced for VAT that are
spurious.  First, it is argued that the coverage of the tax
is broader than that of other sales taxes, since all services
are covered.  Actually, VAT may not cover services (for
example, Brazil), and single-stage taxes can be applied to

services as well as commodities, although with the
manufacturers' sales tax a separate supplemental services tax
is required.  This difference is not a product of the form of
tax but of other considerations.  Second, it is argued in
defense of VAT that the tax is hidden from the final consumer.
Whether such a result is desirable or not will be considered
later.  In any event, this is not an inherent characteristic.
Other sales taxes can be concealed in prices; this rule can be
made mandatory, as in Norway in the past.  Alternatively, VAT
can be shown separately at the final retail sale as well as
on earlier sales.

     In conclusion, VAT is an entirely acceptable form of
sales tax, avoiding the disadvantages of the turnover tax.  It
is, however, more complex than a single-stage levy.  Final
decision as to its choice must be made on the basis of
production and distribution conditions in the country concerned,
revenue needs, administrative qualifications, and other factors.


                         STRUCTURE OF VAT

     This section is devoted to questions of the structure of
VAT, including the method of calculating the tax, the extent
of coverage of all stages of production and distribution, the
tax treatment of producers' goods, the extent of coverage of
commodities and services, the use of multiple or single rates,
and the tax treatment of imports and exports.


                 Method of Calculation of the Tax

     As indicated in the first section, the tax may be
calculated in any of three ways.  First, with the addition
method, the various elements constituting value added are
added together, and the tax rate is applied to the sum.
Secondly, under the subtraction method, the firm calculates
its value added by subtracting from total receipts the cost of
produced goods purchased during the period.  The tax rate is
applied to this figure.  Thirdly, with the tax credit method,
the tax is calculated by subtracting the tax paid on purchases
from the figure calculated by applying the tax rate to the
figure of taxable sales.

Advantages of the Tax Credit Method

     The tax credit method offers very substantial
advantages over the other two approaches.

     Either of the other methods gives rise to numerous
questions about the inclusion or exclusion of certain items,

as, for example, under the addition method, gifts to charitable organizations.  These politically troublesome questions are obscured by the tax credit approach.

In addition, the tax credit method is much easier for most firms to comply with.  It is much easier to cumulate taxes and deduct this sum from the figure of tax times total sales than to add together a number of separate items that constitute value added or deduct various types of expenses from total sales.

The tax credit approach also greatly facilitates cross-audit.  For example, Firm A indicates on its tax return that it has paid $10,000 in VAT on purchases from supplier B.  When B's own VAT return is audited, a check will be made to see if B has actually reported and paid the $10,000 on its sales to firm A (less credits).  The addition method provides no means of cross-checking at all, and the subtraction method provides much less clear-cut guidance for cross-auditing.

The tax credit method also stresses the consumption nature of the tax, and lessens the danger of pyramiding.  This method necessitates separate itemization of the tax on all transactions between business firms and thus encourages the firms to regard the tax as an element distinct from the selling price, to be added as a supplement to the selling price.  This procedure greatly lessens the danger of pyramiding through application of percentage markups.  If the tax element is incorporated into the prices of the products, there is much greater danger of pyramiding in some instances and failure to shift in others, as firms follow different pricing policies.  Uniformity of treatment of a tax is highly important for tax shifting in the typically nonperfect competitive market.

Moreover, the tax credit method greatly facilitates the handling of exemptions and rate differentiation.  The other methods would require the firm to segregate its purchases of materials on the basis of their use in producing exempt or taxable goods.  With the tax credit method, the amount to deduct is indicated by the taxes shown on the purchase invoices, provided that tax paid on purchases to produce exempt or zero-rated goods is deductible.  (In the EEC countries, the task is complicated by the EEC directives denying the deduction of tax paid on purchases of goods to produce exempt, as distinct from zero-rated goods.)

If favored treatment is sought for a particular type of product, this result can be attained by applying the lower rate to the final product alone; with the tax credit, higher rates applied to previous transactions affecting the price of the product will be offset by the low rate on the finished product.  This result cannot be obtained with the other methods, under which the lower rate (or exemption) applies only to value added at the particular stage. The subtraction or addition method may facilitate favoring certain activities--say, agriculture--as compared to certain products but is not necessary for this purpose.

An argument can be made for the subtraction or addition methods, on the grounds that the information required is already available in the firms' accounts for income tax and other purposes, whereas the tax cumulated on purchases is not. This argument is of very limited merit, however, especially for the typical small firms in a developing economy, where the accounting systems are rudimentary and inventory records are particularly poor. The ascertainment of tax on purchases is far simpler. Furthermore, the data for the addition method are available only on an annual basis. The addition or subtraction method may be required if the tax is used by states in a federal system (as was the case in Michigan), because interjurisdictional sales complicate the operation of the tax credit system.

On the whole, certainly in developing economies and probably in any country, the tax credit method is to be preferred, particularly because of its contribution to control of the tax.

## Separate Quotation of Tax at the Retail Level

The tax credit method necessitates separation of the tax element from the price on all transactions among business firms. But should the separate quotation rule be required on the sale to the final consumer? There are three principal arguments in favor of this. First, a seller will frequently not know whether a purchaser is buying for business or consumption use. If he itemizes separately on all invoices, the need for this delineation is avoided. Second, as a matter of principle, it may be argued that optimal determination of the level of governmental activity is facilitated by knowledge on the part of consumers of the amount of tax they are paying. Finally, retailers may prefer separate quotation because they do not then need to readjust prices to compensate for the tax, and the likelihood of a full shift of the tax is increased. (Concealment of the tax at the retail level complicates the task of the retailer in calculating his tax liability since he must factor out the amount of the tax due from his gross receipts. For example, with a 10 percent tax, he would divide total tax receipts by 11 and then apply the tax rate to determine his own tax liability. A seemingly simple task proves to be difficult for many retailers. If a simplified rate is provided for retailers that can be applied to the entire gross receipts, then the rate to be used by manufacturers and wholesalers ceases to be an even figure.)

Despite these merits, most European countries prohibit separate quotation of the tax on the sale to the final consumer--following the tradition in those countries of concealing taxes.  About the only argument that may be advanced for such a policy in a developing country is that of minimizing popular resistance to a tax the government regards as essential for aiding economic development.  Others, who stress that the tax may not fully shift forward, argue that the separate quotation of the tax is misleading, in suggesting that the tax is actually shifting forward when in practice it may not be.

## Tax-Inclusive Versus Tax-Exclusive Prices

The tax rate may apply to the figure of sales exclusive of tax, or inclusive of tax.  For example, with a 20 percent tax rate, the tax on an item selling for $100 net of tax will be $20 (before deducting tax paid on purchases) with the tax-exclusive method, $25 with the tax-inclusive method (since the tax element is itself subject to tax).  France used the latter method for a long time but has recently moved to the tax-exclusive method in conformity with the EEC directive.

The tax-exclusive method has the great advantage of simplicity and greater ease in forward shifting of the exact amount of the tax.  The effective tax rate is clearly revealed. The inclusive method is confusing and has no possible merit, except to yield more revenue at a given nominal tax rate.

Bracket Systems.  If VAT is carried through the retail level and separate quotation of tax on the retail side is either required or authorized, it is desirable to prescribe brackets for collection, as is done in the states of the United States with the retail sales taxes.  Thus for example, the schedule may provide, with a 10 percent tax, that a retailer will collect no tax on sales under 5 cents, 1 cent on sales from 5 to 14 cents, 2 cents on sales 15 to 24 cents, and so on.  The use of brackets facilitates shifting of the tax by the retailer.  With appropriately designed brackets, the retailers will collect from their customers almost exactly the amount of tax due the government, particularly if the tax rate is relatively high (for example, 10 percent).  Some jurisdictions attempt to require any vendor collecting more than the sum determined by applying the tax rate to the figure of taxable sales to remit this excess collection to the government.  Any attempt to do so is not worth the trouble.

## Coverage of Firms

A major issue in establishing a VAT structure is the extent of forward and backward coverage--the coverage of retail traders at one extreme, and of farmers, fishermen, and the like at the other. Any VAT would apply to manufacturing and similar processing; the debatable areas center around the forward and backward limits. A sharp distinction must be made at this point between exemption of a seller and zero rating. If a seller is exempt from tax, he is not required to register and pay tax. However, tax will have been collected on his purchases, and he is not entitled to claim a refund of these taxes. By contrast, if particular sellers are subject to a zero rate, the seller must be registered; he then owes no tax on his sales but is entitled to a refund of all taxes paid on his purchases. The choice between the two depends on the government's objectives in the particular instance: Whether the objective is to free the firm from responsibility for registering and paying tax, but to keep some tax on the final purchaser, or to free the consumer of all burden on his purchases.

### Extension of the Tax to Wholesalers

Restriction of the scope of VAT to the manufacturing level, as in Africa, seriously limits the potential gains from use of the tax, since it will suffer from the same defects as the manufacturers sales tax. Producers are encouraged to leave distribution functions to independent firms; burdens on consumers will be uneven; pyramiding is more likely to occur through the application of conventional markups to a cost inclusive of tax; also revenue will be less at a given rate. Bringing wholesalers within the scope of the tax will lessen the seriousness of these defects, as the impact of the tax will be brought closer to the final consumer. The problem of freeing from tax those goods that are first sold to a wholesaler and then exported will be avoided.

### Extension of the Tax to Retail Traders

Currently, following the EEC directive, all the Common Market countries extend their taxes through the retail level (although, as subsequently noted, all provide for some exemptions of small firms, many of which are retailers). The same policy is followed in three Latin American countries now using the tax. In the African countries using the VAT, however, retailers are specifically exempted from tax (as was the practice in France prior to 1968).

Extension of the tax to cover retailing is obviously desirable, if it is feasible. First, the revenue yield at a

given tax rate will be greater. Secondly, all incentive to push
distribution functions forward past the point of impact of the
tax will be eliminated. Thirdly, the need for special adjustments to deal with forward-integrated manufacturers or backward-
integrated retailers will be avoided. Fourthly, equality of
treatment of imported and domestic goods will be easier to
attain. In general, the potential advantage of VAT can be
attained fully only if the tax is extended through the retail
level.

The great obstacle to doing so is, of course, the small-
scale nature of most retailing in developing countries. Many
retail shops are small establishments, the proprietor having
a limited education and keeping inadequate, or no, records.
To collect a retail sales tax from these firms is virtually
impossible, and VAT is even more complicated. However, the
situation does not require exempting retail trade, per se, but
merely providing special treatment for small firms, as
discussed below.

In many developing countries, there are four types of
retail activity. First, there is the large department store,
often foreign or government-owned, plus modern specialized
stores and service establishments: hotels, larger restaurants,
motor vehicle and appliance dealers, record shops, clothing
stores, variety stores, and so on. These are largely confined
to the metropolitan areas. But they are of substantial
importance in virtually all developing countries--certainly in
those that would seriously consider VAT. Second, there is
the typical smaller town general or specialty store and the
smaller stores in the large cities. In much of Africa, these
have traditionally been operated by persons of Asian or
Middle Eastern origin but are gradually passing into African
hands. In parts of Southeast Asia, they have typically been
operated by Chinese. Third, there are sellers in market
stalls, highly important in some countries, and lastly the
itinerant sellers, on the streets, roads, and sidewalks, and
the operators of wayside stands.

The first category can be reached by a VAT without
serious difficulty--particularly the large foreign or
government-owned stores and hotels. The second category can
likewise be reached, although the enforcement problems are
greater. The third and fourth categories must obviously be
excluded. But this exclusion is much less serious than might
at first appear. Many of these are sellers of unprocessed
foods--exempt in virtually all countries. Many of the stall
sellers and peddlers (other than of food) buy from firms that
can be subjected to control--and buy at prices comparable to
those charged by the larger retail stores on sales to
individual customers. As long as the small venders are buying
from controllable suppliers, only the venders' margins escape tax.

Accordingly, there is a strong case for extending the tax through the retail level per se and dealing with small retailers in the same fashion as with other small firms.  As time passes, more and more retailing will come under the scope of the tax, and, meanwhile, the fact that the retail margin of small vendors is escaping tax is not likely to have serious distorting effects by checking the growth of larger-scale retailing.

## Backward Coverage:  Farmers and Other Primary Producers

A major issue is that of the inclusion of farmers within the scope of the tax.  In the developing countries, there can be no question about the typical semisubsistence farmer who clearly cannot be brought within the tax's scope.  Some European countries using the value-added tax do not exempt farmers per se, but in fact most farmers are excluded via the general treatment of small firms.  The same policy is followed in Brazil, although in some of the states of that country farmers are not required to register, tax being collected instead from the firms that purchase farm produce from them. Ecuador in effect excludes farmers from the tax by exempting the first sale of unprocessed agricultural products.  The other developing countries using the tax specifically exclude sales by farmers.  In practice, little revenue would be gained by bringing even large commercial farmers within the scope of the tax, unless they were also processors or merchants.  The products, unless otherwise exempted, are fully taxed at later stages in production and distribution, and no revenue is gained by taxing the farmer.  Much of the farm output is exported in many of the least developed countries, and any tax collected would ultimately be refunded.

Exemption of farmers from liability to register as venders and to pay tax, however, creates one problem:  how to prevent multiple taxation of farm products when the farmers buy taxable items.  The larger farms will purchase seed, fertilizer, feed for livestock, farm equipment, and supplies.  These will be subject to tax.  But since the firms are not registered venders and do not file tax returns, they do not receive a credit or refund for these tax elements.  Therefore, the goods they produce and sell contain a tax element in their prices, but subsequent processors and distributors receive no credit for this against their tax liability.  Thus, in some degree, the tax has entered twice into the prices of the finished product.  The Netherlands attempts to meet this problem by allowing subsequent handlers of farm products an arbitrary credit for tax presumed to have been borne by the farmer.  The same procedure is followed in Ireland; firms purchasing from unregistered farmers or fishermen are allowed to deduct an amount equal to 1 percent of the purchase price as representing

the tax element in the price.  This creates an added
complication and is somewhat arbitrary.  Moreover, it does not
reduce the inhibiting effect on farmers' purchases of
fertilizer, tractors, veterinary services, and so on, as does
the alternative of zero rating sales made to unregistered
farmers.  While the zero-rating approach is the most
satisfactory, it does complicate the application of the tax
somewhat, since the sellers of these products must distinguish
between sales to farmers, which are zero-rated, and sales of
the same items to other purchasers, to which the tax applies.
In the African countries, Uruguay and in most states of the
United States (under retail sales taxes), feed, seed, and
fertilizer are specifically exempted.  Exemption does not
exclude the items completely from tax under a VAT and
seriously complicates the tasks of the venders, as noted.

For developing economies generally, it would appear
futile to attempt to include farmers--but larger farmers could
be allowed to register voluntarily and obtain refund of tax
paid on their purchases, if multiple taxation of farm products
be a significant problem.  Otherwise, the tax element in
prices arising from taxable purchases by a farmer is not
likely to be large enough to warrant adjustments.  The problem
is much more serious in highly developed countries.

Small Firms Generally

In any developing country, there are inevitably substantial
numbers of firms that will be subject to the registration
requirement--particularly if the tax extends through the retail
level, but even if it does not--but that lack the record
systems and educational levels to enable them to apply the
tax correctly.  These include numerous artisan craftsmen as
well as small retailers.  This problem arises with any form
of sales tax.  The states of the United States, and the
Canadian provinces, which use retail sales taxes, are among
the few jurisdictions in the world that do not provide some
exclusion for small firms.  (But even they do to a limited
extent, in exempting door-to-door sales of various items by
children.)  It is difficult to summarize the actual treatment
provided in various countries.  All European VAT and certainly
most of the others provide for the exemption of small firms,
and several countries provide for a forfait system, or
negotiated determination of tax liability for certain small
firms, or a gross receipts tax in lieu of VAT.

Outright Exemption. The following table indicates typical
provisions for outright exemptions of small firms.

| Country | Exemption | Exemption in U.S. Dollars |
|---|---|---|
| Belgium* | B fr 1,500,000 turnover | 41,250 |
| Denmark | Kr 5,000 sales | 890 |
| France | F 1,200 tax liability | 284 tax |
| Germany, Federal Republic of | DM 12,000 turnover | 4,992 |
| Ireland | L 1,800 turnover | 4,374 |
| Netherlands | Dfl 1,300 tax liability | 520 tax |
| Norway | N kr 6,000 turnover | 1,098 |
| Sweden | Dr 10,000 turnover | 2,400 |
| United Kingdom | £5,000 turnover | 12,150 |
| Ecuador | Capital under 50,000 sucres | 2,000 capital |

Similar exemptions are provided in the Malagasy Republic.

When these small firms are exempt, tax still applies to
sales to them, including sales of supplies and equipment as
well as materials and articles for resale, but they receive
no credit for this tax. The aim is to collect as much tax as
possible on the transactions. The result is that only their
margins--and, in fact, only a portion of the margins because
of the tax on supplies and equipment purchases--escape tax.
This provides some artificial advantage to these smaller firms--
a consideration that suggests that the exemption figure should
be set as low as is regarded as feasible.

Only Belgium attempts to meet this problem by making sales
to small exempt firms subject to a higher rate of tax than the
regular rate.

The Forfait Basis. Several countries use a forfait--or
arbitrary agreed-upon assessment--approach to the taxation of
smaller firms, either in lieu of an outright exemption or for
firms somewhat larger than those given outright exemption.

Under the forfait system, the tax liability is determined
by an inspector, often on the basis of such records as the firm

---

*Purchases subject to a higher than normal rate.

has, and on the basis of external criteria of probable sales
volume, as indicated by the size of the establishment, the
number of employees, evidence of the owners' wealth, and so on.
The figures are typically set for a year at a time.

In Belgium, the smallest firms (turnover B fr 1,500,000)
are exempt and their purchases are taxed at a higher rate.
Somewhat larger firms (turnover B fr 1,500,000 to B fr 5 million)
are subject to forfait determination of total turnover.  The
tax rate is applied to this, and the firms are then allowed to
deduct tax paid on purchases from this figure.

In France, the forfait method of calculation is used for
firms with tax liability between F 1,200 and F 12,100 (a
substantial number of firms).

In Italy, the system is used for firms larger than those
exempt, up to ones with turnover of 80 million lire.

In Brazil, under the state levies, there is no exemption
of small firms per se, but there is extensive use of the
forfait system.

Forfait procedures are applied to firms with annual gross
receipts under CFA 30 million (about $173,000) in the Ivory
Coast; under CFA 20 million ($115,000) in Senegal; under
MF 5 million (about $29,000) in the Malagasy Republic.  Similar
policies are followed in the North African countries.

In Senegal, 352 out of 1,345 taxpaying firms are subject
to forfait assessment; in Sao Paulo in Brazil, 174,000 of
382,000 firms are subject to forfait.

Alternative Tax.  The Federal Republic of Germany provides for
a levy of 4 percent of gross receipts in lieu of VAT, for
firms with turnover under DM 60,000.  This approach is based
on the reasoning that a gross receipts (turnover) tax is
easier for small firms to calculate than a VAT.

Evaluation and Recommendations.  In the least developed
countries, and probably in most developing countries, some
exemption of small firms is almost essential.  The smallest
firms clearly cannot be taxed effectively, and it is far
better to exempt them and tax sales to them, even though the
consequence is some loss in revenue and some--though probably
minor--discrimination in favor of small establishments.  Some
problems of implementation of the rule are inevitable--
particularly in ascertaining those firms eligible for exemption.
Doing so necessitates checking the tax liability of firms
apparently only slightly smaller than the exemption figure.
For simplicity, exemption should be stated in terms of sales
volume, not tax liability.

The forfait system as a substitute for exemption, or for treatment of firms somewhat larger than those exempt, has objectionable features.  The use of a forfait system may involve somewhat less of a discrimination in favor of small firms than an outright exemption, but some rather uneven discrimination in one direction or the other is bound to remain.  A forfait system may facilitate the transition between firms just below the size liable for the regular tax and those just above this limit, without undue loss of revenue.  On balance, however, the tax assessment is certain to be somewhat arbitrary and may come to be more or less nominal.  The system, which involves negotiation between a tax inspector and the vender, is particularly susceptible to bribery.  The forfait system also gives rise to questions about the shifting of tax; it is not at all clear what sum the vender will attempt to shift or will be able to shift.  Uniformity of VAT on all consumer expenditures is therefore lost to some degree.  Little would seem to be gained in most cases from the use of this system in preference to outright exemption.

The Federal Republic of Germany's system of using a turnover tax in lieu of VAT on intermediate-size firms is also open to question, since this approach means that the advantages of VAT are partially lost, and it is also likely to be discriminatory among the various firms.  Shifting may be difficult as well.

One basic problem is inevitable with exemption or the use of an alternative tax on small firms--and to some degree with the forfait system:  When other firms buy from exempt and unregistered firms, no VAT appears on the invoice, and therefore there is nothing they can deduct against their own tax liability, even though the purchase price includes some VAT elements.  The result is to discourage purchasing by business firms from small nonregistered venders.  This is identical to the problem noted above with respect to farmers.  One partial solution is to allow any small firm that wishes to register and become a taxpayer to do so, provided its record system is adequate.  Thus, small venders wishing to make sales to registered firms could register and avoid this form of discrimination.  This problem is most likely to be serious in some segments of the construction industry.

If small firms are to be exempted, the dividing line must be set on the basis of the nature of the production and distribution system in the country concerned and the extent of education and record-keeping at various levels of volume among business firms.  As noted, the figures in Europe differ widely.  Denmark and Norway use very low figures, Belgium and the United Kingdom high figures.  In India, with retail and turnover taxes, the exemption figures are all less than $4,800 and some are not much greater than $1,200.  In Honduras, the relatively high figure of $30,000 is used (under a retail tax). The optimal figure is likely to be somewhere between $6,000 and $12,000 annual receipts.  There is some merit in incorporating other elements into the determination, such as number of employees, that may be easier to ascertain and will avoid a dividing line based on sales alone.  Any exemption encourages the splitting of one firm into several.

## Exemption of Certain Institutions

Questions also arise about the tax treatment of various governmental units and charitable, religious, educational, and other institutions.  This is a major question in many developing countries, in which government-owned enterprises are much more important in manufacturing, wholesale, and retail distribution and provision of services than they are in many Western countries.

The answer is obvious, so far as activities that result in the sale of services or goods to the public is concerned. Clearly, under the philosophy of the tax as a levy on consumers, governmental activities should be taxed in the same fashion as private enterprise.  To do otherwise is to impair the government's revenue for provision of general governmental services, to free many consumers from the intended burden, and to favor purchases from governmental enterprises compared to those from private.

As far as basic governmental activities are concerned, however, as well as those of semigovernmental institutions that do not sell services or goods but provide them in effect free of charge to society (defense, police and fire protection, education, public health, and so on), the issue is more complicated.  Clearly, the tax cannot be applied in its usual form since there is no selling price.  There are several alternatives.

First, the tax can be applied to the goods purchased by governments, in the same fashion as purchases by private firms, but a refund or "credit" of tax can be allowed to the governmental agency.  Secondly, the tax may be applied as in the first instance, without refund.  Alternatively, sales to governmental units may be zero rated and credit allowed to the supplying firms for tax paid on goods entering into the cost of products sold to the government.  Again, sales to government may be exempted, without credit for the supplying firms on their purchases.  Lastly, tax may be applied not only to purchases by governments but to a calculated figure of value added by the government as well (the sum of factor input prices).

The last-mentioned would come closest to placing government on the same basis as private firms, and discourage governmental agencies from producing goods with their own labor instead of buying them, as would be encouraged by the second alternative. But this approach would involve very substantial effort for very little gain (for the level of government levying the tax, there would be no net revenue gain on its own purchases) and would increase the financial problems of the local units of government. On the whole, it is not recommended. Both the third and fourth approaches, involving exemption of sales to government, are inadvisable under VAT, particularly in a developing country, because of the complications created for the firms selling to government. Successful operation of a VAT, more than most sales taxes, requires uniformity of application. Exemption of particular sales seriously impedes operations. The fourth alternative would be almost unworkable, because suppliers of governmental units would have to segregate purchases between those involved in sales to government and others. This is virtually hopeless from a compliance stand-point and is unnecessary. The complications from exempting government purchases completely are far more serious than the implications of some tax burden on governmental purchases.

The first and second approaches in no way complicate the operation of the tax per se. There is, however, no great need to allow refunds, as in the first approach, so far as the national government is concerned. The only possible merit is to avoid encouraging governmental units to produce goods with their own labor instead of buying them or contracting for their production. But this danger can be avoided by appropriate budgetary measures. A government may wish to allow local governmental units to apply for refunds in order to avoid complicating their financial problems.

Somewhat similar reasoning applies to various charitable, educational, and religious organizations not producing a service or good for sale. Taxing them on a calculated figure of value added is scarcely worth the effort and may be regarded as undesirable for reasons of general social policy. On the other hand, exemption of sales to them is seriously objection-able from the standpoint of operation of the tax. It is recommended, therefore, that sales to them be taxable; if the government wishes to make concessions to them for reasons of social policy, they should be authorized to apply for a refund of tax paid on major types of purchases, as evidenced by their purchase invoices. In effect, they would be registered as taxpayers, subjected to a zero rate, and thus entitled to refund on tax paid on their purchases.

Imports

The tax applies to importation as well as domestic sales.
Tax paid at importation, of course, constitutes a credit
against tax on subsequent sales by the importer.  In most
developing countries, a high percentage of the tax--well over
half--will be collected at importation.

To minimize the liquidity problems of manufacturers, some
countries permit registered manufacturers to import free of
tax, accounting for tax on their sales.  This policy, however,
may be dangerous for developing countries because the way is
paved for evasion of tax.  There may be merit in allowing
manufacturers of zero-rated products (as, for example, goods
to be exported) to import materials tax-free in order to
minimize refunds, but even in this instance close control is
needed.

## Tax Treatment of Producers' Goods

A question of key importance in VAT structure is that
of the extent to which tax on purchases for business use is
deductible.  A basic characteristic of VAT is that deduction
is permitted of tax paid on purchases of goods purchased for
direct resale, and materials and parts physically incorporated
into goods to be sold.  As noted in the first section, VAT
that limits deduction to tax on these items is called the
product form of tax--with a tax base comparable to that of
many state "retail" sales taxes in the United States.  These
state levies tax sales for business use other than sales for
resale and sales of parts and materials becoming physical
ingredients of the finished product.  At the other extreme,
deduction may be allowed for tax paid on virtually all
purchases made for business use.  This is the pattern followed
by VAT in the EEC and Scandinavian countries.  The taxes in
Ecuador, Uruguay, and Brazil also approach this form.  In
Brazil, however, the exclusion of capital equipment takes the
form of outright exemption rather than tax credit--a policy
that is likely to prove to be a mistake because it involves a
departure from the basic tax credit nature of the operation
of the tax.  Exemption is not provided for the trade sector,
only for manufacturing and agriculture.  The African levies
allow deduction of tax on industrial equipment and some other
specified categories of fixed assets.  The third alternative
is to allow credit for tax paid on durable capital goods on
a depreciation basis rather than a current basis, as provided
in the proposed Mexican VAT.  On capital equipment with a
10-year life, for example, tax paid on its purchase would not
be deductible in full in the year in which the equipment was
purchased, but only over a 10-year period.  This is a much
more complex system.

## The Case for Credit for All Business Purchases

The case for allowing credit for all taxes paid on purchases for business use is very strong. First, only by full credit can some multiple or cascade application of tax to the products be avoided. As stressed by Maurice Lauré, the chief sponsor of the original French VAT, the costs of supplies and capital equipment enter into the prices of final products in the same way as the costs of parts and materials, and there is little logic in confining the credit to tax on items actually incorporated into the final product. Failure to allow credit on some items will result in uneven tax burden on the final consumers of various products, since the degree of multiple application of the tax will vary. Forward shifting of the tax is made more uncertain, and the actual tax element in the final prices of various goods cannot be ascertained with any certainty.

Full credit is also necessary if exports are to be freed entirely from tax and imported goods are to be taxed on the same basis as domestic goods. Without the credit, export prices will include some tax elements. The fact that the EEC countries allow full credit is a further reason for other countries to do so, if they wish to protect the foreign trade position of their producers.

Moreover, credit for tax paid on durable capital goods minimizes any adverse effect the tax may have on investment. Failure to allow credit artificially increases the cost of new investment and therefore tends to lessen the total amount, to the detriment of economic development.

Similarly, failure to provide credit makes some production methods more expensive than others and will distort choice of production methods from the optimum, causing a loss of economic efficiency. In general, labor-intensive methods are encouraged.

Failure to provide credit also encourages firms to produce their own capital goods instead of buying them, since by doing so the labor cost will be excluded from the base of the tax.

Lastly, if credit is allowed for tax on all business purchases, there is no need for the firm to separate tax paid into deductible and nondeductible categories, and the serious complications of deducting on a depreciation basis over the life of the equipment are avoided. The firm must, of course, distinguish between purchases for personal and for business uses.

## The Objections to Deductibility of Tax Paid on All Business Purchases

There are, however, some arguments in favor of restricting the deductibility of tax paid, particularly on durable capital equipment:[8]

First, the yield, at a given rate, will obviously be less if deductibility of tax paid on all purchases is allowed.  This is not a controlling consideration, of course, since the revenue loss can be made up by a higher rate.

The argument is also advanced that developing economies tend to use overly capital-intensive methods of production, and that complete deductibility of tax paid on capital equipment aggravates this capital intensity, while nondeductibility will tend to redress the balance.  There are several possible reasons for excessive capital intensity. First, the production techniques available are primarily those developed in capital-surplus, labor-short, highly developed countries, which are not optimal in the environment of a developing economy.  Second, capital goods are artificially cheap in some developing countries because the exchange rate is maintained at excessively high levels.  Third, top management, often from developed countries, tends to favor the most modern, prestigious--and capital-intensive--methods.  The interest rates of international lenders are also often lower than the levels justified by domestic conditions.  Finally, wages, by contrast, are often artificially high, in part because of payroll taxes, in part because of strong unionization in the industrial, mining, and transport sectors, and in part because wage patterns were inherited from colonial days, when many of the workers were expatriates with wage scales related to those of their home countries.  Accordingly, it is argued that nondeductibility of capital equipment tends to redress the balance to some degree.

Another argument is that evasion may be increased by a broad provision making tax on all business purchases deductible.  Articles are used for both business and personal use.  With the smaller businesses typical of developing countries, there is great danger that the tax paid on articles acquired for the personal use of the proprietors will be credited against their tax liability as though the goods were actually used in the business.  Doing so is difficult with materials and parts, with industrial machinery, or railroad locomotives.  It is easy with motor vehicles and a wide variety of supplies used by business.  Retailers are particularly likely to evade in this fashion.

These considerations must be weighed against the
undesirable consequences of not permitting credit for tax paid
on all business purchases.  If primary stress is placed upon
increasing the total volume of investment and pushing export
trade, full credit is warranted.  If there is greater concern
about over-capital-intensive methods, and if evasion of the
type noted in the previous paragraph appears serious, some
restriction on deductibility may be provided.  In some countries,
the primary restriction on investment is the lack of foreign
exchange and the consequent inability to import capital goods;
if this is the primary bottleneck, there is little gain in
economic efficiency or growth from allowing credit for tax
paid on industrial equipment.  It is common to deny credit for
tax on the purchase of automobiles and entertainment, even if
taxes on all other purchases are deductible, because of the
danger of evasion whereby substantial amounts of tax revenue
will be lost.

## The Transition Problem

If VAT of the consumption type is substituted for
another type of sales tax that does not exempt capital goods,
firms will delay capital equipment purchases during the
interval in which the tax is under consideration.  On the
other hand, if no credit is allowed for tax on capital goods,
firms using pre-VAT equipment will appear to their competitors
to have some artificial advantage, since they will have bought
their capital equipment more cheaply.  Some industrial countries,
therefore, have introduced the deductibility of tax on capital
equipment gradually over several years or have levied special
vanishing taxes on such equipment.  If the transition problem
is regarded as serious, this approach can be used.  In any
event, long delay in enacting VAT from the time of the original
proposal is undesirable.


## Exclusion of Certain Commodities from Tax

Distinct from the question of the treatment of purchases
for business use is that of the exemption or zero rating of
particular types of consumption goods and services.

## Need for Avoiding Exclusion

There is strong justification for a basic rule of
minimizing exemptions--of keeping the base of the tax as
broad as possible.  The broader the base, the greater the
revenue that can be raised at any given tax rate.  Moreover,
some exemptions breed the demand for more exemptions.  If a
basic rule of universality can be followed, there is less
danger of constant erosion of the tax base.

If all sales are taxable, correct application of the tax is rendered relatively easy for most venders. Exemptions or zero rating produce several types of difficulty. First there is the matter of interpretation. Questions will arise constantly about the tax status of various items. If children's clothing is exempt, for example, there will be constant controversy over exactly what constitutes children's clothing. Then there is the question of correct application. Particularly at the retail level, but even to some extent at earlier levels, business firms will have difficulty in ensuring that clerks apply the tax properly. If the attempt is made in connection with the tax credit feature, to disallow tax credit on goods purchased for use in producing exempt commodities, then firms are given a very difficult task of segregating items used to produce exempt goods from those used to produce taxable goods. The chances for evasion are greatly increased if some of a firm's sales are nontaxable and some are taxable. Control and audit of the firms are made much more difficult. Inspectors will have to devote substantial time to checking reported figures of exempt sales instead of other aspects of control.

Lastly, any exemption favors those persons having relatively high preference for the exempt commodities. Thus, if all food is exempt, those persons making substantial purchases of exotic luxury foods are favored.

In general, the tax credit feature of a VAT creates a degree of interdependency of tax paid by various segments of the economy not found with typical sales taxes. Accordingly, the tax works most effectively and easily if application of the tax is universal. This universality rule applies to all sales taxes, but with particular force to VAT.

The Case for Some Commodity Exclusions

Despite the strong argument for general universality, a case may be made for zero rating of certain commodities in order to exclude those goods completely from the tax. Zero rating, unlike exemption, eliminates tax on the full value of the goods (no matter at what stages the value was created).

The strongest case can be made for excluding unprocessed food from tax. In the least developed countries, a large portion of the total real income consists of unprocessed foods produced on a subsistence basis and not entering commercial channels at all. Therefore, taxation is impossible. Of the portion sold, much will be handled only by small local sellers--itinerant peddlers, operators of wayside stands, and market stalls. These cannot be reached effectively by any form of sales tax. Many of the purchasers of such food from larger venders who could be reached are in the lowest-income

groups, most of their expenditures being made on these food
items.  Thus, equity as well as administrative considerations
dictate exclusions--even though some purchases of the higher-
income groups will escape.

There may be justification, in particular countries, for
extending the exclusion to a few processed food items in very
widespread use and of such a nature that the government may
wish, as a matter of policy, to encourage their consumption.
Powdered milk is an example.  To exclude all processed food,
however, is unnecessary and undesirable.  In many developing
countries, a substantial portion of processed food is imported.
It is consumed primarily by the middle- and upper-income
classes, and the income elasticity of demand is high; that is,
a 10 percent increase in income will result in a more than
10 percent increase in consumption.  Thus, on the basis of
revenue, restriction of consumption and importation, and
equity grounds, exemption is undesirable.  The EEC countries,
except for the United Kingdom, do not exclude food from tax.
Ecuador, Uruguay, Morocco and Brazil limit their exemptions to
basic foodstuffs, mostly unprocessed.  The three tropical
African countries exempt most foodstuffs.

A strong argument can also be made for excluding basic
medicines and drugs, in view of the importance to the
developing economies of improving public health standards.
The exemption should be so worded, however, as to minimize
problems of interpretation and application of tax by venders.

A similar argument may be advanced for the exclusion of
books and other educational materials, certainly when acquired
by educational institutions, and possibly in all circumstances.

The EEC VAT and those of most other countries have very
few exemptions, and (apart from the United Kingdom) almost no
zero rating, and this policy is strongly recommended.
Commodity exclusions should not be extended beyond the
categories indicated.  A broad-based, relatively low-rate VAT
can be highly productive of revenue.  Any attempt to reduce
the burden on the lower income groups by excluding numerous
items will erode the tax base and greatly impair the
application and enforcement of the tax.

## Used Goods

A special problem is created by used consumer goods.
The sale of goods used in a business can be treated like any
other sale, since only the drop in value in the hands of the
business constitutes an input to its productive process, and
any recovery from its sale constitutes a diminution in the
proportion of the original cost on which tax should be

deductible. Sales of used goods between consumers can be
ignored, since the price can in principle be assumed to be so
adjusted as to share the burden of the tax paid on the original
purchase between the two consumers in proportion to their use.
But if the transaction is made through a dealer in used goods,
the margin of the dealer is a value added that should, in
principle, be taxed. This will ordinarily be done automatically
if the addition or subtraction method is used, but if the tax
credit method is used there will be no invoiced tax to be
offset against the tax on the gross sales. The easiest
procedure is to tax the gross sales, with no credit with
respect to the purchase price from consumers. This will
result in a double tax on the portion of the value of the
consumer good not used up by the original purchaser, tax
being paid in effect by the original purchaser on the full
value, and then again by the second user. This rule will have
the effect of encouraging dealers to sell as agents, not
taking title to the goods, and encouraging consumers to sell
directly rather than through dealers. This may or may not be
a serious problem, depending on the type of item involved.

A more correct and nondiscriminatory procedure, if
administratively feasible, would be to allow dealers who
purchase goods for resale from consumers to take a tax credit,
against the tax on their gross sales, equal to the tax on the
purchase price paid to the original consumers. The difficulty
is that in the nature of things there can be no automatic
checking of the claims for such credits in terms of taxes on
invoices covering the sale of the item from the initial user
to the dealer, and a special method of computing the tax will
have to be set up.

Perhaps, on the whole, a better compromise procedure is
to zero rate or exempt sales of used goods purchased from
consumers with respect to which no tax credit has been claimed.
This has the effect of exempting from tax the dealer's margins,
including whatever value added has been created in the form of
repairs, refinishing, or other enhancement of the product for
purposes of sale. This is somewhat comparable to the
exemption of certain services that occurs in some value-added
taxes as actually applied. Alternatively, firms dealing
exclusively in used consumer goods could be exempted, as such.

## Purchases to Produce Excluded Goods

A major issue is the deductibility of tax on purchases
made to produce excluded goods; in other words, should goods
be excluded by exemption or zero rating? Failure to allow
deduction results in only partial exemption of consumer
expenditures on the product and seriously complicates the
tasks of firms producing both taxable and exempt goods.

Purchases for the two purposes must be segregated and arbitrary allocations made for tax on goods purchased for use in producing both taxable and exempt goods.  On the other hand, registration of firms producing or selling only exempt goods can be avoided.  On the whole, the advantages of allowing full deduction of tax on purchases for production of excluded goods are so great as to warrant this procedure.  That is, goods for which exemption is desired will technically be zero-rated (a zero tax rate applied) rather than exempted.

When a firm carries on both exempt and zero-rated taxable activities (for example, a physician who also operates a drug and medicine shop), it must be required to segregate purchases for the exempt activity (services of the physician) and purchases for the zero-rated taxable activity (sale of medicine), as it is permitted to deduct tax only on purchases for the latter activity.

## The Concept of Sale and the Timing of Tax Liability

Sales should be defined to include not only transfers of goods in exchange for payment in money or other goods but also leases of taxable goods, transfer from stock for personal consumption by the owners of the business, and production, within an exempt (not zero-rated) firm, of taxable goods.

With the exception of the latter, it is not necessary to require the inclusion of the value of goods produced by the firm for its own use, as it is under other forms of sales tax, since the firm would receive credit on such transactions against the tax liability on its sales.

Liability would be determined by the time at which the sales invoice was issued or of the actual physical transfer of the goods, whichever came first, regardless of the time of receipt of payment from the firm's customers.  Liability based on cash flow would lessen the liquidity problems of venders but greatly complicate the application of the tax and delay receipt of revenue by the government.

The taxable amount would be the actual sale price less discounts actually taken.  The revenue department should be given by law the power to adjust, for tax purposes, any sales price figures not reflecting open market conditions, as, for example, sale of goods by a firm to its owners at nominal prices.

For each month (or other tax period), tax liability would be governed by sales made during the month and tax actually paid on purchases during the month.  There is no justification for the time lag of a month for the credit, as in France.

## Taxation of Services

There is no basic argument for confining VAT to commodities, and, in fact, most present-day value-added taxes do extend to some or a wide range of services. This is true of the taxes in the EEC and Uruguay. The taxes in Brazil and Ecuador do not apply to services. In Senegal and the Ivory Coast, service firms may opt for VAT or the separate services tax. Expenditures on services yield personal satisfaction just as expenditures on commodities do, and they tend to have a relatively high income elasticity. Thus, taxation of services-- if it is possible to include all of them--should make the tax less regressive and possibly even progressive.

## Exclusion of Certain Services

In practice, however, many services are regarded as unsuited for taxation for a variety of reasons. Medical, dental, and hospital services are regarded as unsuitable for taxation because of the importance of their use to economic development and the desire to avoid tax penalties for those persons who are obliged to make disproportionate expenditures on these items. Legal services are regarded as necessary for the maintenance of justice. The case for exemption is much weaker than that for the first group noted, particularly because many legal services are mutually canceling efforts of opposing parties and make no net contribution to national product. But it is difficult to distinguish these from legal services necessary for the maintenance of justice. With legal services that are rendered to firms rather than households, exemption instead of zero rating may lead such firms to hire their own lawyers as employees, rather than obtaining the services of independent lawyers on a contract basis.

Passenger transportation, particularly in urban areas, is an activity with a very high value-added relative to gross receipts because of its high labor-intensity, and one that most governments seek to encourage in order to lessen street and road congestion, the former being extremely serious in many cities in developing economies. There are also strong "economies of scale" in the sense of lower average costs or improved service quality, as the intensity of use within a given service area increases, and efficient allocation of resources would be promoted by a relative subsidy to such industries. This argument also applies to utility services such as electric power, telephone, gas, water, mail delivery, and the like.

Services typically rendered by small-scale noncommercial establishments--the itinerant barber in many African cities, domestic labor--are extremely difficult to reach from an enforcement standpoint.  But there is no need to exempt the service per se; the activity can be covered by the basic rule for small firms.  Unlike the sale of goods, however, virtually the entire charge escapes tax because almost all the charge reflects the proprietor's labor.

Education is of great importance for economic development, and exemptions may therefore be justified in this sector.  Foreign travel expenses (except travel tickets purchased in the country) are beyond the reach of the country of residence except through exchange controls techniques.  Brokerage and other agency fees for services are appropriate for inclusion within the tax.

Some services, however, are difficult to tax under a tax credit regime because the payment for the services is not made explicitly but is included with other charges on which no VAT is properly assessable or is reflected in a reduction in a payment of income.  Thus, if a savings bank were to sell its services as an intermediary by making an explicit charge to cover the costs of its services, either to its depositors or to its borrowers, or partially to both, paying out in interest to depositors exactly what it received from borrowers, in the aggregate, it would be possible to charge VAT on such service charges and credit tax shown on the invoices paid by the bank for its supplies.  Such charges, however, are not made explicitly, and there is no ready mechanism by which the corresponding tax can be charged and the charge announced to the customers of the bank, so that they can take credit for the charges where appropriate, against their own gross tax.  In the case of insurance companies, similarly, the cost of the services performed, which would be the proper base for a VAT, is included in the premiums charged, a major portion of which goes for the payment of indemnities to those suffering losses, and this part of the premium, being merely a redistribution, is not properly subjected to VAT.

The problem is not so much that one cannot compute the value added of the bank or insurance company, since one could, in principle, be either the addition or the subtraction method (though either method would be sensitive to amounts set up as increases or decreases to various reserves or other liabilities).  The problem is how to adjust the tax liability of the business customers for their share of the tax on the value of the services provided by these institutions.  The practical difficulties of doing this are, if not insuperable, at least of formidable dimensions, and it is doubtful if such a refinement would be worth the effort.  If, then, no tax credit is to be available to the customers of the bank or insurance company, and the bank is made to pay a full VAT, the result will be a double taxation of the cost of banking

services or, if banks and insurance companies are exempt, a
double taxation of the amount of the taxable inputs used by
them.  On the other hand, individual consumers of these
financial services would be properly taxed if the financial
companies paid full VAT.  Perhaps the ideal solution would be
to have such companies allocate their operations between
services to final consumers and services to business firms,
and require them to pay a tax based on full rates on the
portion of services supplied to individuals, while zero rating
the services supplied to business.

The rationale for such a treatment, however, is moderately
hard to explain to those who would be involved in enacting,
levying, or paying the tax.  The tax paid would be small or
even negative for most financial institutions having
predominantly business customers.  The more likely treatment
appears to be complete exemption, and this appears to be the
general practice at present.  Yet such exemption creates
problems:  since it is not desired to free the banks from tax
on their purchases, they are given incentives to provide
internal services, such as computer operation or printing,
using their own employees instead of acquiring them from
outside firms, and to own rather than to rent their quarters.
One could avoid this bias by allowing such institutions a
refund on taxes paid on their purchases, but this would be
widely misunderstood and resented; moreover, allowing such a
refund would require such institutions to be sharply limited
in the scope of their activity lest they compete unfairly with
other firms.  Indeed, this problem arises even with exemption:
consider the phenomenon of employee cafeterias and the like.
Quite possibly the preferable alternative would be full
taxation on an addition basis:  The resulting double taxation
of financial services would at least not create an incentive
for such institutions to encroach on other fields of activity.

Inclusion of the taxation of services, other than those
specified for exclusion, under VAT is greatly preferable to
the use of a separate tax on these services, uncoordinated with
VAT, as found in Brazil, Ecuador, and other countries.  The
result of the latter practice is likely to be some multiple
taxation, as the services tax applies to purchases by business
firms, but they receive no credit, while VAT applies to
purchases by service firms.  An important characteristic of
VAT is that the most satisfactory operation requires maximum
breadth of coverage within the scope of the tax, and the use
of separate services taxes results in partial loss of the
major advantages of the levy.

## Housing Services and Real Property Contracts

A major problem with VAT is the treatment of housing services, a problem complicated by the fact that some housing facilities are owner-occupied.  There are several options.  First, there is complete exemption of all housing, including the costs of construction.  Second, there may be taxation only of commodities utilized in the construction of housing, as under most state sales taxes in the United States and the tax in Ecuador.  Third, the entire cost of new housing construction may be taxed, with no taxation of contractual or imputed rents.  This is the policy in Uruguay.  Fourth, there may be taxation of rental charges, with credit for tax paid on the construction of the housing; the imputed rent of owner-occupied housing  may be taxed with comparable credit for tax paid on new construction.  Last, there may be taxation of construction cost of owner-occupied housing but not of imputed rent.

The first and second approaches involve unnecessary loss in revenue and erosion of the tax base.  Only if the government strongly desires to encourage housing construction is either of these warranted.  The fourth approach is in many ways the most logical from an economic and equity standpoint but involves serious enforcement problems and is therefore not recommended--certainly not in developing economies.  Primary problems would arise with imputed rents and the collection of tax from large numbers of homeowners.  The fifth approach avoids the imputed rent problem but still suffers from compliance difficulties if there are large numbers of small proprietors of rental housing.  It also favors the owners of existing homes, as compared to persons acquiring new ones.  Thus, the third approach appears to be the most satisfactory, although it, too, favors the owners of existing homes, who bought them prior to tax.  It reduces somewhat the potential tax revenue compared to the fourth and last alternatives, but it avoids the task of collecting rent from many small landlords.

There is little merit in taxing subsequent sales of houses, except for firms buying and selling them as a business activity.  Otherwise, any gain is a capital gain, not reflecting value added.

A related problem is that of rental charges for nonhousing facilities and the costs of their construction.  There is no objection to taxing the rental charges--as is the policy in the African countries, the tax of course being deductible against the firm's tax liability.  But at the same time, not too much is gained by doing so.  An alternative is to tax the construction cost, but this would result in unnecessary loss of revenue on existing buildings.  Thus, taxation of the

construction costs, with provision of credit for this tax
against tax due on the rentals, and of tax paid on the rentals
against tax due on the lessee's own sales, appears to be the
most satisfactory, given the desire to maintain as broad an
overall coverage as possible. Sale of buildings and other
real estate would not be taxed. In practice, however, tax is
applied to the sale of buildings by registered venders in
African countries, with credit for tax paid in construction.
The Latin American countries do not tax the sale or rental
of buildings.

## Rate Differentiation

In developing countries, a higher tax burden on luxury
goods is typically regarded as essential, given the objective
of discouraging luxury consumption and imports, and the
desire to attain greater equity. As explained in the first
section, several of the European taxes employ more than one
rate. Brazil, Bolivia, and Vietnam use single rates,
Uruguay two rates. All African value-added taxes use several
rates (two in the Malagasy Republic, three in most others)
except that of Tunisia.

### Objections to Multiple Rates

The use of several rates materially complicates the
operation of the tax for much the same reason as exemptions.
Firms at all levels in production and distribution must
delineate the commodities in the various rate groups and apply
the tax correctly. (All pre-retail transactions could be taxed
at the top rate. But this rule would also create complications
and result in large refunds for retailers of lower-rate
commodities.) This differentiation must be carried through
the retail level, or the intended objective will not be
attained--but it is very difficult to ensure that retailers
apply more than one tax rate. Consequent complications for
the operation of the tax are so great, in developing countries,
as to lead to the conclusion that a uniform rate should be
utilized, certainly if the tax extends beyond the manufacturing
level.

### Excise Tax Supplements

There are, of course, other ways of introducing
differential rates in commodity taxation. The most satisfactory
method is to use a supplementary excise tax on importation and
domestic production, at the manufacturing level, on those
commodities the government wishes to single out for higher
rates. The excises will, therefore, be kept entirely
distinct from VAT. These commodities must also be subjected to

VAT in order to avoid the complications of additional
exemptions at the wholesale and retail level, but no credit is
given against VAT liability for the excise payments.   The
objections to the manufacturers' form of sales tax apply in
part to these excises.   But the administrative advantages of
this approach compared to differential rates in VAT are so
great as to dictate its choice.

## Import and Export Transactions

VAT is universally established on a destination basis,
imports being subject to tax at the time of importation (but
not necessarily at the same rate; some of the taxes in
Africa apply higher rates to imports)--and on subsequent
sales--and exports being free of tax, with full refund of all
taxes paid on previous transactions in the good in question.
At given exchange rates, this is the most satisfactory approach
whereby to protect the country's position in world markets and
ensure that within the country imports are not favored over
domestic goods.   The alternative method, of applying the tax
to exports but not to imports, could be followed, with
appropriate changes in the exchange rate, but countries are
reluctant to attempt this approach.

The destination basis, however, does not function smoothly
in a Common Market area once fiscal frontiers are abandoned.
It is difficult for the country of destination to enforce
payment of the tax, if the sale is made to an individual, just
as it is difficult for the states to do so in the United States
in the case of retail sales taxes.   The origin basis is much
simpler, since the country can enforce jurisdiction over
firms located within its jurisdiction.   Under this form, there
would be no export rebates on sale for delivery within the
Common Market countries; instead, each country would give
credit for tax imposed in the country of origin.   Such a system
is much simpler and has been accepted by the EEC countries as
the ultimate objective.   But its initial adoption requires that
the VAT rate should be more or less uniform among the countries;
otherwise, until such time as exchange rates or relative price
levels are adjusted, manufacturers in the low-tax countries
will have an advantage over those in the high-tax countries,
which are unable to protect their firms by tariff barriers
within the Common Market area.

A special problem is presented by purchases by tourists
of commodities they take home with them.   Administratively, it
is far easier to tax these (items purchased for shipment out
of the country by the vender are, of course, exempt as
exports).   But, to many developing countries, the tourist
trade is highly important, and governments are eager to

encourage tourism and domestic purchases by tourists.  One
possible procedure is to define as an export transaction any
sale in which the purchased item is delivered aboard the
aircraft at the time of the person's departure--but this is a
nuisance to the vender and favors shops located in airports.
Allowing the sale to be made tax free as an export on the basis
of a signed statement by the customer, held in the vender's
file, is the method most convenient for tourist and vender, but
obviously is open to abuse.  Abuse could perhaps be guarded
against by requiring the vender to provide a voucher to the
purchaser to be surrendered at the departure point along with
the exhibit of the tax-free item itself, compliance by the
purchaser being enforced by a notation made by the vender in
a space provided on the tourists' exit slips.  Compliance by
the vender could be enforced requiring him to record the
serial number of the exit slip to be exhibited, if called for,
in order to obtain the credit.  If the corresponding exit slip
does not bear the appropriate endorsement, fraud is indicated.
If the government decides to use such a system as a concession
to tourists, the exemption should be restricted to larger
purchases.

## Summary

The most important requirements for successful operation
of a value-added tax are universality and simplicity.  Because
of the tax credit feature, the tax works best, and its
advantages are most fully attained, only if it applies uniformly
to all forms of economic activity.  Inevitably, administrative
and equity considerations dictate some departures from this
rule, but success of the tax requires that these exceptions be
minimized.  More specifically, the following recommendations
about tax structure are offered:

1.    The tax credit method of calculating tax liability is
far superior to the other forms, particularly from an
enforcement standpoint.

2.    For simplicity of understanding, the tax rate should
be quoted on a tax-exclusive basis, the tax element itself not
being subject to tax.

3.    The tax should be extended through the retail sector
to attain the full advantages of this form of levy, with small
retailers receiving the same treatment as other small firms.
When VAT is first introduced, coverage of only the manufacturing
and wholesale sectors may be desirable as a first step, to be
extended ultimately to the retail sector.

4.   It is not feasible in a developing economy to apply the tax to farmers generally (although farmers should have the privilege of registering as taxpayers if they wish).  Some multiple taxation results but is not likely to be serious; if it proves to be so, zero rating of major farm purchases, such as fertilizer, may be necessary.

5.   Small firms must of necessity be exempted from the tax, with tax applying to their purchases rather than their sales.  The dividing line must be selected in terms of the circumstances of the country.

The forfait system of determining the tax liability of small firms and the use of an alternative gross receipts tax are subject to serious objections, but may be necessary to avoid undue discrimination or impairment of revenue.

6.   Governmental units selling services or goods for prices should be subjected to tax in the same fashion as private firms, since the tax is intended to be a levy on the consumer.  It is not feasible, or necessarily desirable, to apply the tax to value added by governments on their basic governmental activities, but there is also no need to exempt them on their purchases.  Exemption inevitably complicates the operation of the tax.  If desired, local governments may be authorized to apply for refund of tax paid on their purchases.

Similar rules should be applied to charitable, educational, and similar semigovernmental institutions.

7.   The case for allowing credit for all tax paid on purchases for business use is less strong in the developing countries than in the highly developed countries, because of the tendency toward excessive capital-intensity in production. But, all things considered, there is a case for doing so, particularly in view of the importance of stimulating investment and avoiding any tax penalty on export products.

8.   It is extremely important that exclusions of commodities from tax should be held to a minimum:  unprocessed food (most of which cannot be reached by the tax anyway) and possibly a very few processed food items, basic medicines and drugs, and books.  If complete freeing from tax is desired (as for powdered milk, for example), zero rating is required, rather than exemption, so that producers can obtain credit for tax paid on goods purchased for use in the production of the commodity.  Zero rating greatly simplifies the tasks of the firms.

9.   In general, the tax should apply to all services as well as commodities, with several exceptions:  (a) medical,

dental, and hospital services; (b) possibly legal services;
(c) public passenger transport; and (d) education.

In addition, banks, insurance companies, and other
financial institutions may need special treatment, since their
customers will in general have no basis for computing a tax
credit.

10.  Housing services create a major issue.  The most
feasible rule is to tax the full contract price of new housing
construction, but not to tax housing rents, either contractual
or implicit.

11.  Sale of real estate should not be subjected to tax;
this is not a consumption expenditure in the usual sense and
new construction is reached by the tax.

12.  Second-hand goods sold by venders should be taxed,
with a credit for taxes paid on purchases from registered
sellers as evidenced by invoices, but credit, if at all, only
for the tax on the price paid to the previous individual user.

13.  Simplicity and effective operation require the use
of a single rate for VAT.  The higher burden desired on certain
luxury goods, such as motor vehicles, can be obtained by
separate excise taxes at the import and manufacturing level.
It is extremely important that excise-taxed goods should not
be exempted from VAT.

14.  VAT should be applied to imports; exports should be
subjected to a zero rate, with full refund of tax previously
paid.  Within a common market area, however, use of the origin
basis, with credit given by one country for the tax paid in
another, greatly simplifies enforcement.


IMPLEMENTATION OF VAT

This section is concerned with the details of the
implementation of VAT once the decision has been made to
introduce the tax.  The law must be drafted and information
disseminated, an administrative organization must be established
and personnel hired, and firms must be registered.  Decisions
must be made about computerization and a system of returns and
payment established.

Law and Regulations

## The Law

The actual drafting of the legislation must be placed in the hands of a lawyer familiar with the tax jurisprudence of the country. Substantial benefit can be gained, however, from analysis of VAT legislation of other countries using similar levies. The draft should be reviewed by the persons in charge of revenue administration and by Finance and Planning Ministry economists, to be sure that the structure is such as to permit effective administration, on the one hand, and to be consistent with development planning and equity considerations on the other.

It may be helpful to have one or more consultants from outside the country who are familiar with the tax elsewhere to assist in the drafting at least part of the time, but it is important that primary responsibility should rest with persons of the country and not from outside.

## Regulations

Once the law is enacted, it is possible to draft regulations defining various aspects of the tax and setting out the provisions of the act in greater detail.

## Rules and Instructions

It is also necessary to prepare detailed rules and instructions affecting various types of businesses, in order to clarify the law and regulations. A series of circulars explaining the tax as it affects various lines of business--importing, manufacturing, handicraft production, wholesale distribution, retailing, service industries, restaurants, farm marketing organizations, and so on--can be of great assistance to firms and improve the overall operation of the tax.

There is also great merit in preparing a general information booklet explaining carefully the nature and operation of the tax in nontechnical terms. This is important for VAT, which appears to be more complicated than it really is.

## Publicity

Particularly in a developing country, it is of the utmost importance to publicize the introduction of VAT as widely as possible. This can be done by newspaper and trade journal advertisements, and by radio and TV announcements, as

well as through the delivery of information to business firms.
Regional meetings, at which VAT personnel explain the operation
of the tax to merchants and other interested parties, are
desirable.  Simple understandable answers to questions from
traders and others about the tax must be provided.

Similar policies must be followed on a continuing basis,
so that changes will be widely publicized, and firms will have
ready access to information and obtain immediate answers to
questions.  New firms must be given pertinent information
about the tax, particularly the general information pamphlets
and circulars relating to the type of business.

## Lead Time

If a country is changing to VAT from another form of sales
tax, four months' preparatory time from the date of passage of
the legislation should be adequate to implement the new law.
If no sales tax has been in use, six months is a minimum time.

## Administrative Organization

If VAT is being substituted for another form of sales
tax, the same administrative organization and personnel can be
utilized, although the change may offer an opportune time to
reorganize the administrative structure and bring in new,
highly qualified personnel.  If there has been no sales tax,
an entirely new organization is required.  A suggested
organizational structure appears in Figure 2.1.

## Location of the VAT Division

The exact location of a VAT administration will be
influenced by the overall structure of the revenue department
or departments.  There is strong justification, however, for
concentrating responsibility for VAT in a single unit.  It is
a levy that differs substantially from customs duties and
excises, on the one hand, and income taxes, on the other, as
far as control and inspection are concerned.  To divide
responsibility for the tax among various functional units
(enforcement, inspection or audit, legal, and so on) that
also handle other taxes, as has occurred with sales taxes in
some countries, is likely to impair effective operation.
Centralization of responsibility for operation of the tax is a
necessity.

There are three possible structural arrangements:

1.   A VAT Administration, separate from Customs, on the
one hand and Income Tax, on the other, with coordinate status.

FIGURE 2.1

Suggested Organizational Structure for VAT Administration

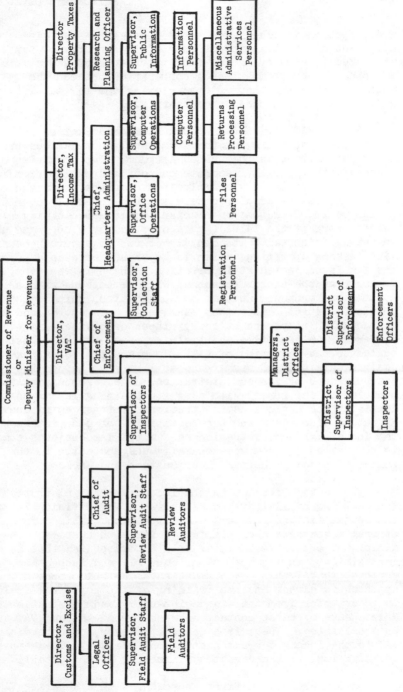

This approach is likely to be the most effective, given the different characteristics of each of these forms of tax and is warranted in view of the revenue importance of VAT. This approach, however, may lessen cooperation between the VAT administration and that of other levies and may multiply administrative overhead unnecessarily.

2.   A VAT Division in the Customs and Excise Administration, following the Commonwealth of Nations tradition based on practice in the United Kingdom. The countries of the Commonwealth typically separate customs and excise from income tax administration very sharply into separate departments. The sales tax, value-added or otherwise, has generally been placed in the realm of customs and excise. This approach may be satisfactory if the sales tax is operated by a separate unit in the division, with its own director. It assures cooperation with customs operation, which is important because a portion of the tax is collected at importation. There is, however, great danger that the senior personnel will be persons with a customs background. Customs administration, which emphasizes physical control rather than examination of records and direct contact with taxpayers at their places of business, is very different, in tradition and training, from the kind best suited to the operation of VAT. To place the sales tax against this type of background is likely to lessen the effectiveness of its administration, unless responsibility is centered in one person with adequate training in tax as distinct from customs administration. This organizational structure also minimizes the possibility of cooperation with the income tax administration on audit. The business community in the United Kingdom was generally unsympathetic to the policy of placing the tax under Customs and Excise.

3.   A VAT Division in the Income Tax Administration. The third possibility is to establish a VAT division in the income tax (inland revenue) administration. This offers several advantages over placing of VAT with customs. The senior personnel are familiar with a form of tax that is much more similar, in its operation, control, and inspection aspects, to VAT than customs duties. The philosophy of approach is closer and the training of the personnel is likely to be superior from the standpoint of VAT administration. Maintenance of close contact between income tax and VAT audit is facilitated. There is a danger, however, of subordinating VAT to the income tax administration--certainly if a separate VAT division, with a competent director, is not established.

On the whole, the first approach, with a separate VAT administration coordinated with customs-excise and income taxes, is likely to give the most satisfactory results. But close cooperation both with customs, for the collection of VAT on imports, and with income tax, for the exchange of audit information, is essential.

## Regionalization

In large countries, there is great merit in decentralizing administration to some extent. This is particularly important in developing countries, where roads are poor and passenger transport either very poor or very expensive (air). District offices should be established in major centers, and enforcement and inspection personnel assigned to these centers. The district offices should be headed by personnel with training in both inspection and control work. These offices should be accessible to the public as sources of information.

Regionalization always poses some problems of attaining uniformity in policy throughout the country and may result in favoritism. Accordingly, headquarters personnel must check the inspection and enforcement activities in each district, and regular reports must be required. Headquarters review of all audits is necessary for uniformity of policy.

In summary, regionalization offers significant advantages: travel time and cost are materially reduced; personnel are able to live at home most of the time; and inspectors are familiar with local activities and can more easily spot firms that have failed to register, gone out of business, and so on.

### Personnel

Personnel can be grouped into two general types: headquarters and field.

## Headquarters Personnel

Headquarters personnel should consist of the following:

1.     The director of the VAT Division and an assistant if necessary.

2.     The heads of the enforcement and audit units and the supervisor of headquarters operation. The audit unit would have jurisdiction over all auditors and inspectors.

3.     Senior review auditors.

4.     Senior enforcement and collection personnel, to deal with hard-core delinquents.

5.   A legal officer, to handle rulings and questions of interpretation.

6.   Personnel providing information to firms.

7.   Computer personnel, either a small number to work with the personnel of a central computer agency, or, if the unit has its own computer, personnel to program and operate the system, including keypunch operations.

8.   Filing clerks and stenographic personnel.

Obviously, in a small country, some of these posts may be combined, and the subordinate personnel may be very limited. There may, for example, be only one senior auditor, who is director of the audit work and does all the reviewing of audits.

## Field Personnel

These are persons carrying on actual enforcement and audit and inspection work. Although some may work out of the head-quarters office, they are distinct from headquarters personnel per se.

It is recommended for VAT in a typical developing economy that there should be three types of field personnel in addition to the district supervisors and clerical personnel:

1.   Auditors. These persons would be trained in true audit work, with training and experience comparable to personnel of public accounting firms. They would be assigned to the audit of manufacturing and wholesale establishments, larger retailers, and other large firms, such as hotels, electric power agencies, large transport firms, and so on.

2.   Inspectors. These persons would have a basic knowledge of bookkeeping systems and accounting, business practices, and some training in auditing the accounts of smaller venders--craft producers, typical retail traders, service establishments, and so on. They would not have training in high-level auditing. Given the great scarcity of persons with such training and the large number of relatively small firms under VAT of such a nature that auditing is relatively elementary, it is preferable to set up this separate category of inspectors--whereas it is not advisable to do so with the typical manufacturers' sales tax or retail tax in a highly developed country. The inspectors and auditors would both be assigned to the audit and inspection unit, under the Director of Audit and Inspection.

3.    Enforcement personnel.  These persons would not be
trained in accounting or auditing per se; their primary task
would be to ensure that all firms were registered for tax and
to obtain returns and payment from firms failing to file as
required by law.  This type of work requires less training
than that needed by auditors and inspectors, and somewhat
different characteristics--the ability to bring delinquents
into line, rather than to determine if correct amounts of tax
are paid.  In remote areas, persons would do both inspection
and control work, with training in both fields.

## Sources and Qualifications of Personnel

Senior personnel for the new tax may be obtained from the
income tax administration, from other government agencies, or
from private firms.  In countries extremely short of persons
with accounting and administrative training, key personnel
must be obtained from abroad on contract.  It is obviously
desirable to move away from the use of expatriate personnel as
soon as possible, but some initial use may be unavoidable at
first.  If expatriate personnel are employed, it is essential
that they should be persons with training in sales tax
administration, preferably in VAT administration, and that a
portion of their time should be allocated to instructing their
successors.

Sources of field personnel vary with the type of work:

1.    Auditors.  The audit staff may be borrowed in part
from the income tax administration and in part hired away from
private firms.  Again, some countries may find it necessary to
use expatriate personnel for several years, until a sufficient
number of auditors are trained.  As a continuing process, the
audit staff should be recruited from university graduates in
accounting; but in many countries no such degrees are offered,
and it is necessary to recruit persons who have received
their training through some form of apprenticeship with
accounting firms or in accounting departments of industrial
firms.  Once an audit program is well under way, some
recruiting of new personnel through in-service training of
inspectors will become possible.

2.    Inspectors.  The inspectors require some knowledge
of accounting but at a much more elementary level.  An ideal
source consists of graduates of commercial colleges, where
available.  These schools give a one- or two-year course for
secondary school graduates, stressing bookkeeping, business
management, and related topics.  Alternatively, older persons
with substantial business experience and some knowledge of
bookkeeping can be employed.

3.  Enforcement personnel.  The enforcement personnel can be recruited from among secondary school graduates and persons with business experience.

## Training

When VAT is introduced, no one within the country is likely to have had contact with such a tax previously.  If VAT is replacing another form of sales tax, the task is simpler than if no sales tax has been used.  In the replacement situation, it is recommended that key personnel--the director of the Sales Tax Division and the heads of audit and enforcement work--be sent to a country using VAT to study the operation of the tax.  The country selected should be one with somewhat similar characteristics and a reputation for effective administration.  Several weeks constitute a minimum period. Upon their return, these persons should train other personnel. The change in the form of tax may also provide an occasion for sending senior sales tax personnel for outside training, such as that provided in the International Monetary Fund courses, the Harvard Law School International Tax Program, the Tax Institute at the University of Southern California, the National School of Taxes in France, and so on.

If the country has not had any form of sales tax, the procedures are of necessity somewhat different.  In this instance, it is even more essential for key personnel to spend some time in a country with VAT to study methods and procedures, and for some of the personnel to be sent through an IMF or similar course.  With this knowledge, the senior personnel will then conduct training courses for audit, inspection, and enforcement personnel.  The audit instruction would be the most lengthy and detailed, since even the most qualified auditors will know nothing about VAT auditing per se.  Again, it may be possible to borrow an auditor from a country with experience with the tax to operate the training courses.  Once the operation of the tax is under way, all new personnel who are hired must likewise be given training.  In a large country, with several new auditors being hired at intervals, it is possible to provide the training through formal courses. Otherwise, after a few days' general instruction, in-service training involving work in the field with trained personnel is the primary approach to instruction.

It is also important to provide some system of continuing education in accounting and auditing, through correspondence or extension courses, to enable enforcement personnel to gain the training necessary for inspection work and for inspectors to move up to the rank of auditors.  This may be arranged through cooperative arrangements with colleges and universities or developed independently.

## Numbers of Personnel

The size of the staff must, of course, be related to the number of firms, the complexity of their operations, and their geographical distribution.

1.   Auditors.  Based on experience elsewhere, there should be roughly one auditor per 100 registrants of the type for which audit personnel is required, as a minimum, and perhaps one to 50--the exact number depending upon the complexity of the audits.

2.   Inspectors.  One inspector per 300 registrants is a reasonable figure.

3.   Enforcement personnel.  One per 500 registrants is suggested.

In summary, a country with 1,000 larger firms subject to audit and 10,000 others would need roughly 10 auditors, 30 inspectors, and 22 enforcement officers.  These are, of course, rough estimates based on experience elsewhere.  Excessively small numbers result in false economy.  While this is commonly expressed by stating that the revenue loss will far exceed the cost of additional staff; the revenue loss per se is a mere transfer, and the more important consideration, in terms of the economy as a whole, is the loss of morale and the distortion of economic activity that result from evasion efforts and the uneven impact of the tax.

## Assignment

The relatively small audit staff, in the typical developing country, can be used most effectively if it is assigned either to headquarters or to two or three major industrial and commercial areas.  Thus, for example, in a country with the geographical pattern of Kenya, the auditors would be assigned to the two principal cities (Nairobi and Mombasa in this instance).  A country having a high concentration of industry and larger-scale trade in one city (for example, Sierra Leone) would assign all audit personnel to headquarters.

The inspection staff would be assigned to the district offices and possibly to specific segments of the district area, particularly when towns are far apart.  Each inspector, therefore, would have responsibility for a particular group of registrants.  Alternatively, in the larger cities, inspectors would simply be assigned to the entire city as a group, and assigned to specific tasks by the district director of audit and inspection.

Enforcement personnel in virtually all cases would be assigned to specific territories, including portions of a city, since it is important that they should be highly familiar with the firms in the particular area.  But since excessive familiarity may lead to the development of favoritism or even corruption, it may be advantageous to relocate the personnel at intervals of several years.

## Personnel Policies

It is obvious that salaries competitive with private business and other government agencies must be paid to obtain competent personnel and to lessen the danger of bribery. Hiring rules that will ensure that only qualified persons are employed are necessary, as well as the provision of protection against discharge without cause.

## Registration of Venders

The first step in the actual operation of a VAT is the registration of firms subject to the tax and the development of a master roll of taxpayers.

## Notification of Prospective Registrants

The first action is to notify firms of their responsibility to register.  If the VAT replaces an existing sales tax, particularly a cascade tax, the basic list of registered firms is presumably already available; firms registered under the turnover tax need merely to be notified to reregister under the VAT.  But if there is no satisfactory turnover tax list, if another form of sales tax is in use in which registration is limited, or if there is no sales tax, other means must be used to ascertain which firms are to be notified.  These include the use of lists of taxpayers under the corporate income tax, although this will cover only a small portion of VAT registrants, holders of municipal licenses, and so on. A number of the firms can be found in telephone directories. A list is made up from these sources of likely registrants, and these firms are notified, either by mail or by hand delivery of the information.

In addition, it is almost essential, in a developing country, to make a door-to-door check.  The newly hired staff of inspectors and enforcement officers can be used for this purpose.

## Registration Form

A registration form is necessary. Figure 2.2 shows a form used by Kansas for retail sales tax; the form for VAT is very similar, except that it is desirable to request the firm to indicate its major suppliers--the names of firms from which it makes purchases in large quantities. These forms can be sent out with the notices for prospective registration and delivered to traders and artisan craftsmen by the inspectors. In fact, for many smaller firms, it will be desirable for the inspector or enforcement officer to assist the proprietor in filling out the form, or actually to fill it out.

## Review

Either after the form is returned, or at the time it is prepared with the assistance of an inspector, a decision must be made as to whether the firm is liable for registration. Given the universality of coverage of the tax, the only decision, as a rule, is whether the firm's receipts exceed the designated figure for exemption. The vender will be asked to make an estimate, and the inspector will decide upon its reasonableness on the basis of such records as the firm has, the number of employees, the size of the inventory, data from income tax returns, if any, and so on. All decisions by inspectors will be reviewed by senior personnel.

At the same time that the inspector makes this review, he should explain carefully the responsibilities of the firm, if registered, with regard to the tax--separate quotation or not, listing on invoices, record systems, time for filing returns, deduction of tax paid on purchases, penalties for errors, and so on. At the time of review also, a decision must be made about the need for a security bond, if such a system, noted in the next section, is employed.

## Coding by Type of Business

It is essential that each firm should be coded by type of business--for example, manufacturer of clothing, retailer of food products, restaurant, and so on. A classification of firms suitable for the purpose--preferably the standard one for census and other purposes--should be employed. The initial suggestion should be made by the vender, approved by the inspector, and finally sanctioned by registration personnel at headquarters. Coding is important as a basis for supplying relevant information to the firm, for various aspects of control, for the selection of firms for inspection and audit, and for audit procedures.

Each firm must also be coded by geographical area of location.

FIGURE 2.2

Sales Tax Application:
STATE OF KANSAS

APPLICATION FOR CERTIFICATE OF REGISTRATION

As Required By Section 8 of the Kansas
Retailers' Sales Tax Act of 1937

(Do not fill in this space)

S. T. D.—1
Rev. 4-69

Send this application to:

DEPARTMENT OF REVENUE

DIRECTOR OF REVENUE
SALES TAX DIVISION
TOPEKA, KANSAS 66612

1. Name under which business will be conducted and as

   you desire it to appear on Certificate of Registration

2. Full name of owner
   (Name of Owner if Different from Name on Above Line)    Residence Address

3. Names and addresses of all partners,

   or principal officers

   and title, if a corporation

4. Indicate in the proper space    Individual ☐    Copartnership    Corporation ☐    Association
   type of ownership:                               or Company ☐                    or Club ☐        Other _____ ☐ (Specify Type)

4a. If Incorporated, Give the State of Incorporation

5. Location of business _____
                        (Street and Number)        (City or Town)        (County)

6. Type of business _____
                     (Specify major category of sales made, i. e., food, hardware, clothing, drugs, etc.)

7. Forms for returns to be mailed to _____
                                      (Street No.)        (City or Town)        (State)        (Zip Code)

134

8. Date started making retail sales at this address in Kansas _____

9. *Returns will be computed on a Cash Basis ☐          Accrual Basis ☐

10. Have you, or any member of firm, previously held a Kansas Certificate of Registration? Individual ☐  Copartnership or Company ☐  Corporation ☐

11. If so, show Certificate of Registration number, or name under which same was issued _____

12. Do you owe any sales tax? _____

13. If you are buying the business, give name of party from whom it    Seller's Sales Tax

    is being purchased _____          Certificate of Registration No. _____

14. Has the seller furnished you with evidence that the Kansas Retail Sales Tax has been paid up to the time of your purchase? _____

15. If not, why? _____

16. How many places of business do you operate within the State of Kansas? _____

17. Give registration numbers, if not reporting on a Consolidated return _____

18. If you operate at more than one place of business, do you prefer to file a ⎱ Consolidated Tax Return ☐
                                                                                ⎰ Tax Return for Each Location ☐

    FILL IN THE QUESTIONS ON THE REVERSE SIDE AND SIGN IN THE SPACE PROVIDED

| R. A. C. O. | Co. No. | C/R No. | I. | C. | K. | A. | No. L. | City | Bonded | S. | Q. | Col. 13 Code | Date | Former No. Code |
|---|---|---|---|---|---|---|---|---|---|---|---|---|---|---|
| Tax Exam. | Auditor | Group | Type | Minor | | | | | | | | | | Audit |

PAID Thru _____

* Cash Basis means reporting sales tax on actual total cash receipts.
Accrual Basis means reporting sales tax on total gross sales whether sales for cash or on credit.

(continued)

135

# FIGURE 2.2 Continued

19. Where are consolidated records kept? _____

    If you operate more than one place of business, separate and complete application must be made for each location (for which a Certificate of Registration will be issued).

20. Do you own Stock in trade? _____ Value of Stock in trade _____

21. Do you own all of the Equipment and Fixtures? _____ Value of Equipment and Fixtures _____

22. Are Equipment and Fixtures free of Encumbrances? _____

    If not, what is your Equity $ _____

23. Has Kansas Sales or Compensating Use Tax been paid on Equipment and Fixtures used in this business? _____

    (The Director of Revenue may examine any books or records of persons who purchase tangible personal property subject to this tax on all property used, stored, or consumed in Kansas.)

Section 79-3612 Kansas Retailers' Sales Tax Act creates a lien upon the property for unpaid taxes upon the sale of a business. "The purchaser shall be personally liable for the payment of any unpaid taxes of the seller, to the extent of the value of the property received by the purchaser, and if a receipt is not furnished by such seller within twenty (20) days from date of sale of such business, the purchaser shall remit the amount of such unpaid taxes to the Director of Revenue on or before the last day of the month succeeding that in which he acquired such business or property."

**Under the provisions of Section 8 of the Kansas Retailers' Sales Tax Act of 1937, the above named hereby makes application for a Certificate of Registration. Said Certificate of Registration issued to Applicant in response to this application will be accepted with the condition and agreement that Applicant will pay any and all Taxes due under said Kansas Retailers' Sales Tax Act of 1937 to the State of Kansas.**

**This application shall be signed by the owner if a natural person; by all partners if a partnership; by an executive officer or some person specifically authorized to sign the application as a corporation. On applications of corporations it is required that written evidence of authority to sign the application be furnished.**

X _____

X _____

X _____

136

Witness _____

X _____
     (Field Representative)

X _____   SIGNATURE(S) AND SOCIAL SECURITY NUMBER(S)
     (Date)

A "Retailer" is defined in the Kansas Retailers' Sales Tax Act as, "a person regularly engaged in the business of selling tangible personal property at retail or furnishing electrical energy, gas, water, service or entertainment, known to the trade and public as such, and selling only to the user or consumer and not for resale."

Persons regularly serving meals to the public must register as retailers under the provisions of this Act.

Remarks and recommendations _____

_____

_____

_____

_____

32-8372     1741-N

137

## Account Number

It is imperative with VAT to assign each vender an account number. These may be assigned simply on a sequential numerical basis, or they may include business and location code numbers. It would be desirable, if possible, to use the same account number as is employed for payroll, income, and other tax purposes, but a VAT in a developing country involves many small traders not subject to other taxes, so complete identity of account numbers for all taxes is difficult. But the principle should be followed as far as possible. A multiple-unit firm-- such as an oil company operating a number of service stations-- may be given a single registration number, with subnumbers identifying each branch, or alternatively, each branch may be given a number but the firm allowed to consolidate the figures for the various branches on a single return.

## Registration Certificate

Because of the small-scale nature of many of the traders, it is desirable to issue registration certificates and require them to be posted in the firm's place of business, so that inspectors and customers can quickly check to see if the vender is registered. A certificate of exemption should be provided for those firms exempted because of small volume.

## Master File

A master file of registrants must be prepared at head-quarters. The exact form of the file will depend on the extent to which computers are used. Without computers, the file will consist simply of a series of ledger cards, kept in sequence of the account numbers, plus index cards as noted below. With a card computer system, the master file will be a set of master IBM-type punched cards, one for each registrant. These can be printed out onto visible cards or normal computer printouts for convenience in use. With the most modern computers, the master file consists of a magnetic tape with an entry for each firm or an entry in some form of memory call. The data on this file can likewise be printed out as desired. A card index file, the information typed when the ledger card is prepared in noncomputerized systems or printed from the master cards or tape, in account number sequence, is also prepared, together with a separate card index file in alphabetical order. Each index card shows the account number as well as the name, address, and business coding of the vender.

As new registrants are added, new entries are made, and new index cards are prepared; as firms go out of business, the entry is removed from the master file and the cards pulled

from the index files and kept in a separate accounts-closed
file.  Most jurisdictions find it difficult to keep their
files free of firms no longer operating; a systematic
procedure is necessary to ensure that as firms quit business,
as discovered by notification, by visits from inspectors or
enforcement personnel, or by continued failure to file returns,
the entry in the master file is canceled.

With regional organization, it is imperative for each
district office to be given a list of registrants in its area.
This can be accomplished by producing duplicates of the
numerical and alphabetical file cards and sending them to the
district office, or sending a computer printout of registrants
at intervals.  The geographical coding of each firm facilitates
this process.  Similarly, the addition of new registrants and
the cancellation of old ones require notification of the
district offices.

If each enforcement officer is assigned to firms in a
specific area, he too requires either an index card for each
firm or a computer printout, reissued at frequent intervals,
of the firms for which he is responsible.

## File Folders

In addition to the master file entry and index cards, a
manila folder should be established for each registrant and
arranged in account number sequence, to hold the registration
application and other documents and correspondence (but not
the periodic tax returns).

## Continuing Check on Registration

A primary responsibility of both the inspectors and the
enforcement personnel is to watch for potential new registrants.
As new places of business are established, or as an unregistered
firm obviously expands the scope of its operations, the
enforcement officer and the inspector in the area should visit
the place of business to check upon registration and provide
information.

## Tax Returns

VAT, like any sales tax, requires the use of tax return
forms.  A number of issues must be resolved relating to them:
the type of form, the information required, the filing interval,
and the system of processing.

## The Form

A government has the choice of two general forms, the
traditional paper return and the IBM card-type or postcard
return.  The paper form provides space for more information,
whereas the card form is easier to handle and to store and
can be punched for filing in sequence of account number.  The
paper returns are much more laborious to store and file.  The
general experience with cards has been quite satisfactory in
the jurisdictions using it.  As suggested below, an annual
return in addition to the regular returns has great merit;
this can be a paper return to allow more space, while the
periodic returns are cards.

## Information Required

Several items of information are imperative, in addition
to the firm's name and account number:

1.    Total sales, including transfers from inventory to
personal use of the owners.

2.    Zero-rated sales, such as sales for export.

3.    Sales exempt, but without credit for tax paid on
purchases, if the law provides for such exemptions.

4.    Taxable sales.

5.    The gross tax--the figure obtained by applying the
tax rate to the taxable sales figure.

6.    The sum of taxes paid on purchases during the period
as cumulated from purchase invoices.  If the law provides for
exemptions as well as **zero-rated** firms or commodities, this
category must be broken down into two parts:

(a) Tax paid on purchases related to exempt sales on
    which no credit is allowed for tax paid on purchases.

(b) Tax paid on all other purchases.

7.    The tax due:  (5) - (6), or (5) - (6b)

Thus, the return might appear as follows:

1. Total sales, including transfers from
   inventory to personal use of the owners of          _____

   ─────────────────────────────────────────

2. Exempt sales                                         _____

3. **Zero-rated sales**                                 _____

4. Taxable sales $(1 - \sqrt{2} + 3\sqrt{})$            _____

5. Taxable sales times tax rate (gross tax)             _____

6. Tax paid on purchases, not including tax of
   _____ paid on purchases related to
   exempt commodities.                                  _____

7. Tax due (5 - 6)                                       _____

As long as there is only one tax rate, no other data would
be required. When there is more than one tax rate, separate
lines must be provided for sales and tax at each tax rate, as
shown in Figure 2.3, the VAT return form used in Ireland.

If there are several forms of exemptions or transactions
subject to zero rate, it may be desirable to request the firm
to break down the total by type of exemption, as is common
with retail sales taxes (see Figure 2.4, which reproduces the
United Kingdom VAT return form).

It is highly important that the return should be kept as
simple as possible and that no unnecessary information should
be required. The Danish tax return form (Figure 2.5) is a
particularly good example.

Another major question is whether to require the firm to
show on the return the amounts of tax paid to various
suppliers (in excess of a specific figure) by name of
supplier. The number typically would not be large, although
this rule might necessitate paper rather than card return
forms. This is useful information for the auditors, but it
would appear to be most useful on an annual basis. There is
little gained by requiring this information monthly, since it
cannot be used effectively except for annual periods.

Annual Return

There is great merit in requiring firms to file an annual
summary return showing the total of the monthly returns and
itemizing purchases from particular suppliers in excess of a
specified figure--perhaps the equivalent of $100. Some
additional work is required of the firms, but the gains from

FIGURE 2.3

VAT Return Form:  Ireland

Office of the Revenue Commissioners, Teach Earlsfort, Hatch Street, Dublin 2.

Date as Postmark.

*Below is a copy of the form on which to make your return for value-added tax for the taxable period just ended. This return, which is due between the 10th and the 19th instant, should be sent together with a remittance in settlement of the tax payable, so as to reach me not later than the 19th instant.*

*When completing this form, please read Appendix A of the Guide to the Value-added Tax.*

**S. P. BEDFORD**
**Collector-General**

FOR TAXABLE PERIOD

REGISTERED NO.

THIS FORM BECOMES A
**RECEIPT**
WHEN ENDORSED BY THE
RECEIPTING MACHINE IN THE
OFFICE OF THE COLLECTOR-
GENERAL.

**Received from the above named the sum mentioned below in respect of value- added tax.**

# VALUE-ADDED TAX  Return for the taxable period

## VAT 3

FOR OFFICIAL USE

REGISTERED NO.

## DELIVERIES OF GOODS AND RENDERING OF SERVICES

Show consideration rounded down to the nearest £ exclusive of VAT.

| | 6.75% | 19.5% | Zero% | Exempt |
|---|---|---|---|---|
| (A) DELIVERIES OF TRADING STOCKS | | | | |
| (i) Deliveries to other persons | A1 | B1 | D1 | |
| (ii) Self-deliveries | A2 | B2 | D2 | |
| (B) RENDERING OF SERVICES AND DELIVERIES OF GOODS OTHER THAN TRADING STOCKS. | A3 | B3 | D3 | E3 |
| | TOTAL (A1,A2,A3) | TOTAL (B1,B2,B3) | | |

@ 6.75%  =

@ 19.5%  =

| | TAX £ p | p |
|---|---|---|
| Z1 | | |
| Z2 | | |
| T1 | | |
| T2 | | |
| T3 | | |
| T4 | | |

GROSS VAT PAYABLE (Z1+Z2) →

GR0SS VAT DEDUCTIBLE (FROM OVERLEAF) →

⊗

**NET VAT NOW DUE** (EXCESS OF T1 OVER T2)

Or **NET VAT REPAYABLE** (EXCESS OF T2 OVER T1)

DECLARATION
I/We declare that according to the best of my/our knowledge and belief, this is a true and correct statement of the value-added tax for the period specified.

.............................. Signed

Date

FIGURE 2.3 Continued

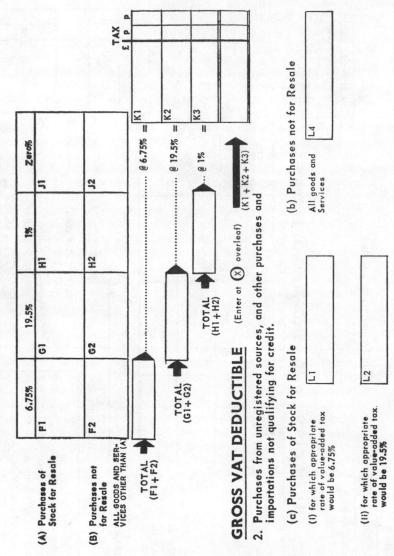

# EX

# PURCHASES AND IMPORTATIONS

**1. Goods and Services charged with tax and qualifying for credit.**

SHOW CONSIDERATION ROUNDED UP TO NEAREST £ EXCLUSIVE OF VAT.

| | 6.75% | 19.5% | 1% | Zero% |
|---|---|---|---|---|
| **(A) Purchases of Stock for Resale** | F1 | G1 | H1 | J1 |
| **(B) Purchases not for Resale**<br>ALL GOODS AND SER-VICES OTHER THAN (A) | F2 | G2 | H2 | J2 |
| | **TOTAL (F1 + F2)** | **TOTAL (G1 + G2)** | **TOTAL (H1 + H2)** | |

.......... @ 6.75% = K1

.......... @ 19.5% = K2

.......... @ 1% = K3

(Enter at (X) overleaf) (K1 + K2 + K3)

| | TAX |
|---|---|
| | £ p p |
| K1 = | |
| K2 = | |
| K3 = | |

# GROSS VAT DEDUCTIBLE

**2. Purchases from unregistered sources, and other purchases and importations not qualifying for credit.**

**(a) Purchases of Stock for Resale**

(i) for which appropriate rate of value-added tax would be 6.75%

L1

(ii) for which appropriate rate of value-added tax would be 19.5%

L2

**(b) Purchases not for Resale**

All goods and Services

L4

144

an audit standpoint are substantial.  Much of the cumulation
is required for income taxes anyway.

## Return Intervals

In view of the large number of relatively small firms,
there is merit in requiring payment of tax at relatively
frequent intervals, to avoid the accumulation of liabilities
that the firm cannot meet.  One month, as used in Ecuador,
some of the EEC countries, and the African countries (see
Figure 2.6, the VAT return form used in Senegal), may be
regarded as a suitable interval.  Brazil requires an even
shorter interval for certain types of firms--10 to 15 days--
but this would appear to be unnecessarily short and, given the
exemption of very small firms in most countries, is probably
not necessary.  Monthly returns and payments also provide an
even flow of money to the government and smooth out the work
load, as compared to quarterly or longer intervals.  (Periods
of less than one month may be desirable for exporters and
others who receive large refunds.)

One slight modification that lessens the amount of paper
work is to allow firms to file returns on a quarterly basis
but to pay installments on an estimated basis, with a very
simple return, during the other two months of the quarter.
This minimizes accumulated tax liability and smooths the
flow of revenue, but reduces paperwork to some extent.

Problems always arise with firms that operate on a
seasonal basis, for a few months of the year, since it is
difficult to get them to file returns during the period when
they are not operating.  Some identification of such firms and
the period of typical operations is necessary, or they will
appear on delinquency lists.  Some jurisdictions find it more
satisfactory to have them file a single return for the entire
period of operation, if this is short.

## Computer Systems

Further discussion of the operation of the tax requires
a digression on the alternative record keeping and computer
systems.

## Purely Manual Operation

A country with a small number of registered firms may
not find the use of computers worthwhile.  A ledger card
(preferable to a page in a ledger volume) serves as the basis
for recording the filing of returns and the amounts paid.
These may be recorded by hand, or more commonly by a simple

FIGURE 2.4

## VAT Return Form: United Kingdom

H. M. Customs
and Excise

### Return of Value Added Tax
For the period
01 08 75 to 31 10 75
These dates must not be altered without the
agreement of Customs and Excise

A Wholesaler Ltd
22 North Road
LONDON
N12 4NA

**For Official Use**

# SAMPLE

| Registration No. | Period No. |
|---|---|
| 912 3456 78 | 31 |

Please quote this Registration No. and Period
No. in all correspondence about this return.

*The registered person named here must complete
and return the form to the Controller, VAT Central
Unit, H.M. Customs and Excise, Alexander House,
21, Victoria Avenue, SOUTHEND-ON-SEA X,*

*not later than* 30 November 1975

*Tax payable must be paid by the same date, by
remittance enclosed with this form or by National
or Bank Giro.*

*A pre-paid addressed envelope is enclosed.*

RATE A IS THE HIGHER RATE
IGNORE RATE B BOX

**Before completing any item on this form please open out the form and read the corresponding note.**

A return which is incomplete or qualified in any way (e.g. marked "Provisional") does not satisfy the legal
requirements. Failure to make a return or to pay the full amount of tax payable by the due date is an offence.

**PART A. Account of tax payable or repayable**
*This part must be completed by all registered persons. Please complete all boxes, writing "NONE"
where there is no amount to be entered.*

|  |  |  |  | £ | p |
|---|---|---|---|---|---|
| **TAX DUE** for this period | On **OUTPUTS** (sales, etc.) | at the standard rate | s | 2595 | 80 |
|  |  | at rate a | a | 632 | 20 |
|  |  | at rate b | b |  |  |
|  | **TOTAL OUTPUT TAX** (Total of amounts at standard rate, rate a and rate b) |  | 1 | 3228 | 00 |
|  | Tax due on imported goods and goods from bonded warehouse |  | 2 | 183 | 30 |
|  | Underdeclarations and/or underpayments of tax in previous periods, notified in writing by Customs and Excise |  | 3 | NONE |  |
|  | Other underdeclarations made on previous returns |  | 4 | 213 | 70 |
|  | **TOTAL TAX DUE** (Total of amounts in boxes 1, 2, 3 and 4) |  | 5 | 3625 | 00 |
| **TAX DEDUCTIBLE** for this period *Partly exempt persons should also see box 24* | On **INPUTS** (purchases, etc.) |  | 6 | 2536 | 30 |
|  | Overdeclarations and/or overpayments of tax in previous periods, notified in writing by Customs and Excise |  | 7 | NONE |  |
|  | Other overdeclarations made on previous returns |  | 8 | 271 | 60 |
|  | **TOTAL TAX DEDUCTIBLE** (Total of amounts in boxes 6, 7 and 8) |  | 9 | 2807 | 90 |
| **NET TAX** | payable or repayable for this period. | (Difference between boxes 5 and 9) | 10 | 817 | 10 |

If the amount in box 5 is greater than the amount in box 9, then the tax in
box 10 is payable to Customs and Excise. In this case please tick box P        P ✓

If the amount in box 5 is less than the amount in box 9 then the tax in
box 10 is repayable by Customs and Excise. In this case please tick box R        R

| METHOD OF PAYMENT to Customs and Excise *Please tick the appropriate box* | National Giro | Bank Giro ✓ | Remittance enclosed | In your own interests you should not send notes or coin through the post. | PLEASE TURN OVER |
|---|---|---|---|---|---|

**FOR OFFICIAL USE**

Fold | Here (left margin)

Fold | Here (right margin)

VAT 100                    F.3790 (Oct. 1974)

## PART B.  Value of outputs and inputs (excluding any Value Added Tax)

This part must be completed by all registered persons. Please complete all the boxes, writing **"NONE"** where there is no amount to be entered. Pence should be disregarded.

Pounds only

| | | | |
|---|---|---|---|
| **OUTPUTS** (sales, etc.): (All values shown should exclude Value Added Tax) | Value of outputs chargeable at the standard rate, rate a and rate b | 11 | 35654 00 |
| | Exports | 12 | 1582 00 |
| | Zero-rated taxable outputs (other than exports in box 12) | 13 | 703 00 |
| SAMPLE | Total taxable outputs (total of amounts in boxes 11, 12 and 13) | 14 | 37939 00 |
| | Exempt outputs (if you insert an amount here, see Part D) | 15 | NONE 00 |
| | Total outputs (total of amounts in boxes 14 and 15) | 16 | 37939 00 |
| **INPUTS** (purchases, etc.): | Value (excluding Value Added Tax) of total taxable inputs, including zero-rated inputs | 17 | 29648 |

## PART C.  Retailers' special schemes

This part must be completed by any person who has used any of the special schemes for retailers – see Notice No. 727.

Show the scheme(s) you have used by ticking the box(es) below the appropriate letter(s)

| Scheme | A | B | C | D | E | F | G | H | J | K | L | M |
|---|---|---|---|---|---|---|---|---|---|---|---|---|
| 18 | | | | | | | | | | | | |

## PART D.  Partly exempt persons: calculation of deductible input tax

Except as explained in the notes, this part must be completed by all taxable persons with exempt outputs. It should **NOT** be completed by any other registered persons.

| | | £ | p |
|---|---|---|---|
| Enter 1, 2 or 3 in this box to show which method you have used | 19 | | |
| Amount of any input tax wholly attributable to taxable supplies | 20 | | |
| Amount of input tax partly attributable to taxable supplies | 21 | | |
| Percentage used to attribute input tax $\left(\dfrac{\text{box 14} \times 100}{\text{box 16}}\right)$ | 22 | | |
| That part of the amount in box 21 which is deductible for the period $\left(\dfrac{\text{box 21} \times \text{box 22}}{100}\right)$ | | | |
| Total deductible input tax for the period (total of amounts in boxes 20 and 23). (Enter this total also in box 6 overleaf) | 24 | | |

## PART E.  Declaration by the signatory

This part must be completed by or on behalf of all registered persons.

I............... ALAN   NORMAN   OTHER ...............

(full name of signatory in BLOCK CAPITALS)

declare that

(i)   the information given in this return is true and complete in respect of all business or businesses carried on by the registered person (except in so far as he is separately registered if so required) and, **except as notified, none of the changes listed in Notice No. 700 (Section 11, last paragraph) has occurred during the period covered by the return,**

(ii)   the amounts shown as deductible input tax in this return relate to tax which may be deducted by virtue of section 3 of the Finance Act 1972 and Regulations made under that section, and I claim deduction of input tax accordingly,

(iii)   where I have used any of the retailers' special schemes I have complied with Notice No. 727.

Signed ............... A.N. Other ...............

(*Proprietor, partner, director, secretary, responsible officer, duly authorised person)

Date ............... 25/11/75 ...............

*Delete as necessary

**BEFORE RETURNING THIS FORM PLEASE DETACH THE NOTES**

147

# FIGURE 2.4 Continued

**PART. B. Value of Outputs and Inputs (Excluding any Value Added Tax)**

The information in this Part is required for statistical and control purposes and is particularly important in the case of partly exempt persons. Enter **POUNDS ONLY.** Ignore any pence.

The values entered should be net amounts after deducting any credits allowed to your customers or received from your suppliers, **but without any deduction for cash discounts given or taken.** If it is your practice to record in your accounts the net values of your inputs and outputs after deduction of cash discounts, these values should be adjusted to gross figures by adding to them a reasonable estimate of the discounts.
Retailers using any of the special schemes to calculate output tax (see Notice No. 707) should follow the instructions for retailers given below; they should also include in the amounts entered in boxes 11, 12 and 13 the value of any supplies for which they are using the normal method.

Item 11. Enter the value (excluding VAT) of all supplies BY you which are chargeable with tax, including any taxable self-supplies, goods applied to personal use and gifts and loans of goods.

Note for retailers: For outputs covered by a special scheme, multiply the special scheme output tax by 100, divide by the standard rate of tax and enter the result.

Item 12. Enter the value of all your zero-rated exports, including:-

(a) any goods exported under retail export schemes (see Notice No. 704);

(b) any tax-free sales of motor vehicles to tourists etc. (see Notice No. 705); and

(c) any supplies of zero-rated services under the Finance Act 1972 Schedule 4, Group 9, or Group 10, item 5 (see Notice No. 701).

Item 13. Enter the value of all other zero-rated supplies BY you.

Note for retailers: For outputs covered by a special scheme, deduct the special scheme ouput tax and the amounts shown in items 11 and 12 from the total gross takings for the period and enter the result.

Item 15. Enter the value of all exempt supplies BY you, but exclude:-

(a) capital sums receivable for the grant, assignment or surrender of an interest in land or buildings that you have occupied in the course of your business; and

(b) the value of securities or secondary securities within the definition in section 42 of the Exchange Control Act 1947 which are issued, transferred or received, or dealt with in the course of your business, unless you are wholly or mainly in business to negotiate or undertake transactions in securities or to make arrangements for such transactions.

The following do not count as exempt supplies and their value should not be included here:-

(i) zero-rated supplies (enter in box 12 or 13 as appropriate);

(ii) disposals of motor cars on which you did not have to account for output tax (see Cars in Section IV of the VAT General guide); and

(iii) any transactions that are not classed as a supply for VAT purposes, unless Customs and Excise have directed that partly exempt persons are to include them (see Notice No. 706).

Item 17. Enter the total value (excluding any VAT) of the standard-rated and zero-rated inputs recorded in your accounts for this period. Include the value of any such inputs for which there is no tax invoice (for example because the supplier is not a registered taxable person) and of any goods which you imported or removed from a bonded warehouse, but exclude:-

(a) non-deductible inputs; and

(b) any transactions that are not classed as a supply for VAT purposes.

**PART C. Retailers' Special Schemes**

Please read Notice No. 707 before making any entry in box 18.

Item 18. Enter the scheme number(s) of the scheme(s) you have used to calculate output tax. It is not necessary to indicate that a modified scheme has been used. For example scheme 1 modified should be entered as scheme 1.

**PART D. Calculation of Deductible Input Tax**

Write amounts like this: £ 4236 : 30  or, if there are no pence, like this £3182 : 00

Please read Notice No. 706

If the value of your exempt outputs (box 15) is less than **either** £100 a month on average **or** 5 per cent of your total outputs (box 16):-

(a) you need not complete this part if you are using Method 1 ;

(b) if you are using Method 2 or any other approved method under which some of your input tax is fully deductible, you must complete boxes 19 and 20, but need not make any entries in boxes 21 to 24.

In either case, you should enter your deductible input tax for this period in box 6.

Item 19. If you are using Method 1 or 2 to calculate your deductible input tax, enter the method number.

If you are using any other method approved by Customs and Excise, enter the figure "3".

Item 20. If you are using Method 1 write "None" in this box.

If you are using Method 2, enter all input tax for the period on supplies of goods TO you for resale as taxable supplies in the same state.

If you are using any other approved method, enter all the input tax which is fully deductible by that method.

Item 21. If you are using Method 1, enter all input tax on supplies TO you for the period **except non-deductible input tax (see Notice No. 701).**

If you are using Method 2, enter all input tax on supplies TO you for the period (except non-deductible input tax) **less the amount already entered in box 20.**

If you are using any other approved method, enter the amount of input tax which has to be apportioned between taxable and exempt supplies by that method.

Item 22. Express the percentage as a whole number; ignore any fraction.

Item 23. Enter the result of the calculation.

**PART E. Declaration by the signatory**

The return must be signed by the proprietor of the business (if an individual), by a partner in the case of a partnership, by a director or the secretary in the case of an incorporated company, or by a person authorised in writing by one of them. For Government Departments, local authorities or corporations the return should be signed by a responsible officer who is authorised to sign on behalf of the Department, authority, corporation etc.

There are heavy penalties for furnishing a return which is false in any material particular.

## HOW TO FILL UP THIS FORM

Please read these notes carefully before starting to complete the form, and refer to them for guidance as you come to each box.

Please refer also, where necessary, to the VAT General guide (which gives an illustration of a completed return form) and to other relevant Customs and Excise Notices.

All registered persons must complete Parts A, B and E of the form.

A retailer must also complete Part C, if he is using a retailer's special scheme for the calculation of output tax (see Notice No. 707). A registered person with exempt outputs (a partly exempt trader) must complete Part D, except as explained in the notes on that Part.

Any alteration should be made by deleting the incorrect entry and inserting the correct figure(s) above it (but within the box). The alteration should be initialled alongside the box by the person who signs the return. It should look like this:-

Please complete ALL the boxes in Parts A and B, **writing "None" in any box where there is no amount to be entered.**

Any correspondence regarding VAT returns and payment or re-payment should always quote your VAT registration number and tax period concerned.

### PART A. Account of Tax Payable or Repayable

Write amounts like this: £4236│30  or, if there are no pence, like this £3182│00

Item 1. Enter the OUTPUT TAX chargeable on all supplies of goods and services BY you, including any taxable self-supplies, goods which you have applied to personal use, and gifts and loans of goods. Enter the net amount after deducting any tax credits allowed to your customers.

Item 2. Enter any tax not already paid, if you imported goods or removed them from a bonded warehouse in the period (see Notice No. 702).

Item 3. **Do not enter any amount here unless it is an under-declaration or under-payment of tax notified to you by Customs and Excise.**
The note on item 4 tells you how to deal with other adjustments of this kind. "Under-declaration" means that a previous return showed too little tax payable to Customs and Excise or too much repayable to you. "Under-payment" means that an amount you declared on a previous return has not been paid in full.

Item 4. Enter any other amount of tax which you under-declared or over-claimed on a previous return. But do not use this box for errors which have been adjusted in another way, e.g. by sending a supplementary tax invoice or a debit note to a customer and recording the extra tax in your accounts as output tax due for this period.

Item 6. Enter the DEDUCTIBLE INPUT TAX on supplies of goods and services TO you and on any goods which you imported or removed from a bonded warehouse. Enter the net amount after deducting any tax credits received from your suppliers.

Do **not** include non-deductible input tax on motor cars and business entertaining expenses (see Notice No. 701) or tax on goods or services that were not for the purpose of your business. If you are a builder see Notice No. 708 about non-deductible input tax.

**If you are partly exempt and have to apportion your input tax for this period the amount to be entered here is the same as the amount in box 24**, so you should read the notes on Part D before making any entry here.

Item 7. Do not enter any amount here unless it is an over-declaration or over-payment notified to you by Customs and Excise. The note on item 8 tells you how to deal with other adjustments of this kind. "Over-declaration" means that a previous return showed too much tax payable to Customs and Excise or too little repayable to you. "Over-payment" means that the amount you paid for a previous period was more than the amount you declared.

Item 8. Enter any other amount of tax which you over-declared or under-claimed on a previous return. But do not use this box for errors which have been adjusted in another way, e.g. by passing a credit note to a customer and deducting the tax credit in your accounts from the output tax due for this period. And do not use it for correcting an over-charge of tax to a customer (see ADJUSTMENT OF ERRORS in Section X of the General guide).

Item 10. Enter the difference between box 5 and box 9, as well as ticking the appropriate box alongside box 10.

You can pay either by cheque or by credit transfer. Please show the method you choose by ticking the appropriate box. Cheques should be made payable to H.M. Customs and Excise and crossed. Credit transfers may be made either through a bank or through National Giro.

In your own interests, you should not send notes or coin through the post.

VAT 100 (Notes)                    Sec. F 3790 (April 1973)

FIGURE 2.5

VAT Return Form:  Denmark
(Front and Back Sides, facsimile)

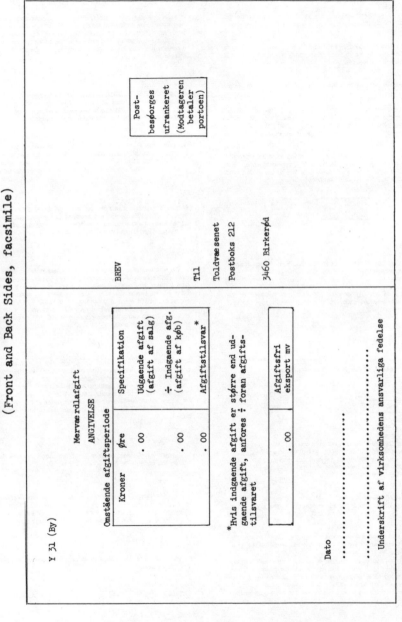

Toldvæsenet

**Merværdiafgift**

Afgiftsperiode

Forfaldsdag

Sidste rettidige Indbetalingsdag

Angivelsen må kun benyttes vedrørende ovenstående afgiftsperiode.

Angivelsen skal i udfyldt og underskrevet stand indsendes sidste rettidige indbetalingsdag, også selv om der ikke skal betales afgift.

Såfremt den 20. i betalingsmåneden er en lør-dag, søndag eller helligdag, anses den nærmest følgende hverdag for sidste rettidige angivelses- og indbetalingsdag.

Angivelsen kan indsendes portofrit.

POSTKVITTERING

til postgirokonto nr 636

Toldvæsenet, Postboks 212

3460 Birkerød

er indbetalt af nedennævnte ADRESSAT

kr 0 0 øre

Eftersendes ikke ved vedvarende adresseforandring men bedes returneret med oplys-ning om den nye adresse

Udfyldes af postvæsenet

........................
Postvæsenets stempel og underskrift

(Poslvaesenets erstainingsplift opherer, nar kravet ikke er anmeldt for postvæsenet inden 1 ar efter indbetalingen).

151

FIGURE 2.6

VAT Return Form: Senegal

RÉPUBLIQUE DU SÉNÉGAL

MINISTERE DES FINANCES
DIRECTION DES IMPOTS
ET DES DOMAINES

RECETTES DES TAXES INDIRECTES
Bloc Fiscal - DAKAR

BOITE POSTALE 1561 DAKAR
COMPTE CHÈQUE POSTAL 370

TÉLÉPHONES : 210-25 - 222-50

TAXE SUR LE CHIFFRE D'AFFAIRES

N° de DECLARATION

N° de COMPTE

DECLARATION
DES AFFAIRES IMPOSABLES

RÉALISÉES AU COURS DU MOIS DE

Nom ou Raison Sociale

Adresse

Profession :

| | | | TAUX | BASE IMPOSABLE | IMPOT |
|---|---|---|---|---|---|
| 101 | Montant des AFFAIRES RÉALISÉES y compris les affaires non imposables | | | | |
| 101 | Montant des affaires à l'exportation | | | | |
| 101 | Montant des AFFAIRES EXONÉRÉES autres que les exportations | | | | |
| | NATURE DES AFFAIRES IMPOSABLES | | | | |
| 111 | PRESTATIONS DE SERVICES | | | | |
| 112 | TRAVAUX IMMOBILIERS | | | | |
| 113 | VENTES A CONSOMMER SUR PLACE | Taux normal | | | |
| | | Taux réduit | | | |
| 114 | REVENTES EN L'ETAT | Taux normal | | | |
| | | Taux réduit | | | |
| 115 | VENTES, LIVRAISONS ET TRAVAUX A FAÇON portant sut des produits fabriqués. | Taux normal | | | |
| | | Taux réduit | | | |
| 190 | TOTAL DE L'IMPOT EXIGIBLE | | | | |
| 190 | TAXE A DÉDUIRE (Indiquer nature et détail au verso) | | | | |
| 190 | NET A PAYER | | | | |
| 190 | ou CRÉDIT A REPORTER | | | | |

Mode de paiement utilisé :   BANQUE   C. C. P.   ESPÈCES      DATE

IMP. GUTENBERG DAKAR

## COMPTABILITÉ (Partie détachable)

ARRÊTÉ A LA SOMME DE (en toutes lettres) ........................................

.................................................................................

A ....................... le ....................... Signature : .......................

### T. C. A.

Mois de .......................

Nom ou Raison Sociale .......................

Adresse .......................

Profession .......................

MODE DE PAIEMENT    BANQUE : **3** ; C. C. P. : **2** ; ESPÈCES : **1** ; NON PAYEMENT : **0**

ESPÈCES - QUITTANCE    N° .......................

CHÈQUE BANCAIRE    N° ....................... Sur .......................

C. C. P.    N° ....................... Compte N° .......................

Les chèques bancaires doivent être barrés et libellés à l'ordre du RECEVEUR DES TAXES INDIRECTES

Les chèques postaux doivent être libellés à l'ordre du RECEVEUR DES TAXES INDIRECTES - C.C.P. 370 - CENTRE DE DAKAR

NUMÉRO DÉCLARATION

NUMÉRO DE COMPTE

PAIEMENT

Montant

Date

N° Bordereau

N° Quittance

Signature du Caissier

153

bookkeeping machine, which any jurisdiction, no matter how small, can use economically.  The ledger cards serve as the record of payments and the basis for identifying nonfilers.

## Card Computer Systems

The earlier forms of computer, such as IBM 1401, involve simply the use of punch cards.  The information on the tax return is punched onto a card by a card-punch operator.  The card serves as the basic record of filing and of payments and the basis for totaling payments and identifying nonfilers. This is a relatively inexpensive system and is still optimal for small jurisdictions.  It is, however, slow compared to modern computers and cannot provide information of the types forthcoming from the latter.

## Magnetic Tape Operation

The next step in computer systems is the use of a magnetic tape, with a master tape listing the registered firms.  A returns tape is prepared each month from the data contained on the tax returns.  The information may be entered from punch cards or from paper or magnetic tape encoders, which are much quieter.  Processing is much faster with this type of operation.

## Memory Cells and Direct Access

The most modern computers provide for entry of the relevant data into memory cells, either from punch cards or tape, or directly via the keyboards of the video cathode tube units. The memory can be read for the necessary information, and information on any account can be obtained instantly, either on a video screen or printed paper copy, simply by entering the account number on the keyboard.  This is of great advantage in checking quickly on particular accounts.  But the system is too expensive and demanding of trained personnel for most developing countries to use.

Regardless of their exact form, computers perform several functions:  (1) providing the master file of registrants, with necessary information; providing the basic data record--of payments, delinquency, and so on; identifying nonfilers in each return period; balancing accounts; cross-checking taxes reported as paid by certain firms against the tax return data of others; selecting accounts for audit; and preparing statistics for internal control purposes and for economic planning and other units of government.

Evaluation of Computer Systems

Accuracy is greater with a properly functioning computer system than with manual operators.  Much more information can be generated, and the process of operation is much faster (for example, identification of nonfilers).  The cost may well be less.  There are, however, problems.  Many developing countries lack personnel trained in computer operation and maintenance, and in computer programing.  It may be necessary to send persons abroad for this training, and they may be lost immediately to private industry on their return.  Long delays may be encountered when the system is not functioning properly.  The costs of the computer system may not be warranted, in the light of the small number of accounts and the cheapness of labor.  The feasibility of use of computers is much greater if the same computer can be used for other taxes and other governmental programs, such as payrolls and the issuance of motor vehicle licenses, both activities that lend themselves very well to computer operation.  If a computer is shared over too many activities, however, the VAT unit may have difficulty in having its work scheduled when required.  A less sophisticated and much less expensive system used solely for VAT and related taxes may be far superior to shared use of the most modern direct-access memory cell system.

The actual decision about the choice of computer must be made on the basis of careful analysis of the relative costs of various alternative systems, given the task to be performed, and the relative advantages of the various systems.  It is important to take advantage of potential gains from computers-- and the VAT is a form of tax that lends itself particularly well to computerization.  But it is highly important to avoid selecting expensive, sophisticated equipment far beyond either the needs of the revenue administration or its capacity to keep it in satisfactory operation.  A computer system that does not function properly is far worse than a manual system, since ferreting out the difficulty and correcting errors is very difficult.

The Processing of Returns

Regardless of the system employed, there are certain common elements in the handling of VAT returns:

## Distribution of Return Forms

The ideal system is to address the return forms from the computer or from addressograph plates[*] each month and distribute these each month to each registered firm, either by mail if the mail system permits, or by hand delivery from the district offices. There are several advantages to this approach. First, the returns have the account number, name, and address of the firm printed on them when they come back in, and thus there is much less danger of misrecording the information onto the wrong account. Second, distribution reminds the firms that the time has arrived to file and pay. Third, the month is indicated on the return, which facilitates more accurate recording. When the return forms are IBM cards, they are prepunched with the account number for subsequent sorting.

If the distribution of returns to each firm monthly is not feasible, blank return forms should be made widely available--sent by mail on request and supplied in local revenue offices and post offices.

The firm should be given two copies of the return form each month and should be required to keep the duplicate in its own file. There is no justification for requiring the firm to file a number of copies, as for income tax in many countries. There is likewise no need to require the notarization of returns, since misreporting is a criminal offense whether the document is notarized or not.

## Place of Filing

The task of filing should be made as simple as possible. Filing by mail should always be authorized, the firm being allowed to mail both the return form and the payment to the revenue office (preferably but not necessarily headquarters).[**] Requiring payment to be made in person is archaic and nonsensical. But the firm should also be given the option of filing and paying at a local revenue office or, if possible, at

---

[*]Without a computer, the relatively inexpensive addressograph offers the best way to address return forms. With computer systems, the return forms may be addressed from master cards, or tape, or the addressograph may still be used if there is a shortage of computer time.

[**]Drastic improvements in the postal system are required for effective operation of the tax in some countries.

a post office or bank.  It is entirely feasible to allow post
offices to receive both the payment and the return form.  It
is also feasible for the government to negotiate agreements
with the banks, whereby the banks will receive both payment
and return, crediting the money to the government account and
forwarding the return to the VAT division.  The requirement
in some countries that payment should be made to a bank or
other office and the return and the receipt then filed at a
different place, all in person, is highly objectionable and
complete unnecessary.

## Date of Filing

Firms must be given a reasonable length of time to
ascertain their tax liability and file their returns after the
end of the period.  Experience elsewhere suggests that three
weeks after the end of the month is a reasonable interval.  In
Africa, the 25th of the following month is the deadline.  Too
short a period results in excessive numbers of nonfilers, while
too long a period delays receipt of the money by the government
and increases the danger of accumulating liability that the
firm cannot meet.

The legislation should permit the sales tax division to
grant extensions for filing.  Hardship cases, such as the
illness of the proprietor or his bookkeeper, arise and make
filing and paying on time impossible.  Firms in very remote
areas may find it impossible to get a return in on schedule.
Large multiple-unit firms with centralized bookkeeping may be
unable to assemble the information in time.  However, the
extension privilege can be abused and should be extended with
care.

## Initial Processing

There are several steps:

1.  Validation.  Returns and payments coming in by mail
are typically validated by placing a number on the check or
other form of payment and on the tax return.  When payments
are made in person and a receipt issued, the number of the
receipt is placed on the return form.  At this point, the
money is separated from the returns, a bank deposit slip
prepared, and the money placed in the bank for deposit, while
the returns go forward for processing.

2.  Batching.  The returns are placed in batches of 50
to 100 and kept in these during subsequent processing.  Each
batch is numbered.

3.  Arithmetical check.  A manual check with the use of a calculator is made of the returns to ascertain that the arithmetic is correct.  (This can be done by computer at a later stage, with modern computer systems.)

4.  Posting.  The data from the returns are then posted to the firm's account.  This may be done by entry onto a ledger card by hand or by bookkeeping machine, or with computers, punched onto a returns card for the vender or entered, either through the cards or by encoder or video cathode tube unit, onto the master tape or memory cell.  Some jurisdictions prefer to enter the data onto a ledger card as well as into the computer, to guard against errors.  Others print the information out from the computer, either onto visible ledger cards or printout sheets, so that it will be readily available.  This is not necessary with the direct access systems, which provide instant information on any account.

5.  Balancing of accounts.  Internal control requires balancing of totals reported on the returns and entered into the venders' files against the total amounts of money deposited. This is usually done by batch and the batch figures are then summed.

Storage of Returns

Various systems are used for storage of returns.  If the return forms are of the IBM card type, with prepunching, the returns are sorted mechanically and merged with the previous returns for the taxpayer account, so that the returns for a two- or three-year period are readily available for each account.

With paper returns, mechanical sorting is not possible. One system involves the setting up of return folders for each account, and the filing, manually, of the returns into these folders each month.  This ensures that all of the returns for each account for several years are readily available for the auditors and for checking.  But this is a laborious task if the number of returns is great, and the danger of misfiling is high.  A misfiled return is very difficult to find.

Another alternative is to leave the returns in the batches in which they are initially placed, with the number of the batch entered onto the ledger card or into the computer file at the time of entry of filing and payment.  In the event of a need to check the return itself, it can be found via the batch number.  This approach is more laborious when it is necessary to find a return but saves a great deal of filing time and lessens the danger of misfiling.  If the returns are used subsequently by auditors as a routine matter, this system is less satisfactory; if they are not used by auditors, there is little objection to batch storage, since for other purposes a check back to the return is seldom necessary.

After two or three years, the returns are typically sent into dead storage, where they can be found if necessary in the event of legal action. Some jurisdictions microfilm the returns after three years or so and then destroy them. A few jurisdictions microfilm all returns as they are received and use the microfilm rather than the original return when checking is necessary. But many employees find microfilm much less satisfactory to work with than the returns themselves.

## Office Audit

It may be considered desirable to check each return for probable accuracy, as a basis for obtaining additional information from the taxpayer about certain items, and as a basis for selecting accounts for audit. The office auditors, usually senior clerical personnel, look for items that appear to be greatly out of line with typical figures--excess of tax paid on purchases over gross tax on sales, for example. If annual summary returns are used, as suggested, there is much less need to check the monthly returns in this fashion; the annual returns are greatly superior for the purpose because month-to-month fluctuations in sales and in ratios of purchases to sales are evened out.

## Refunds

Taxpayers will frequently have a net credit for the period rather than owe tax payment. This will occur when many of the firm's sales (for example, exports) are zero-rated or when it has made substantial purchases of capital equipment during the period, with the tax on such purchases being deductible. There is merit in avoiding the payment of small refunds when possible, by requiring the firm to carry forward the credit against its tax liability in succeeding periods. But this is feasible only if the credits are nonrecurrent, and it is not desirable for large amounts. Thus, an exporter may have a net credit over an extended period. Accordingly, provision must be made for payment by the government, perhaps when there is a net credit at the end of a three-month period, or when the amount exceeds a certain figure. Firms should also be allowed to credit VAT refunds against their income tax liability.

## Taxpayer Records and Invoices

Effective operation of a VAT requires that the venders
subject to the tax maintain adequate record systems.  Since
record systems differ widely among various types of businesses,
it is undesirable to prescribe one exact form.  The law,
however, should require that the vender keep an adequate set
of records and keep copies of all purchase and sales invoices,
with provision for denying credit for tax paid on purchases
unless the firm can produce the invoices showing these amounts.
It is not desirable to require that invoices be issued,
particularly on smaller transactions.  It is desirable,
however, to require that invoices be issued on all sales to
other registered firms, and on all sales in excess of a certain
monetary sum.

There would be merit in providing for a standard invoice
form for these transactions.  The forms would be supplied by
the government free of charge to the taxpayer, each with the
taxpayer's registration number included on it in magnetic ink
or some similar form.  This would provide a basis for ultimate
computer matching of a given taxpayer's sales records with the
tax credit invoices used by the firms buying from him.  This
approach may not be feasible in the earlier years of the tax,
but ultimately a system of this sort would greatly facilitate
its operation.


## ENFORCEMENT:  INSPECTION AND AUDIT

The successful operation of VAT, like any form of sales
tax, requires two major elements:  (1) enforcement of the tax,
in the sense of ensuring that all firms file returns and pay
tax to the government at the specified times, and (2) inspection
and audit--the checking of firms' records and accounts to
ensure that the correct amounts of tax have been reported.


## Enforcement Procedures

Enforcement requires an accurate up-to-date master file
of registered firms--with all firms registered that are
required to do so; a system for ascertaining failure to file
and pay; techniques for ensuring that the delinquents--as the
nonfilers are called--do file and pay; and methods of dealing
with hard-core delinquents who fail to pay despite notices and
visits.

## The Master File

The steps to build up the master file were noted in the preceding section. It is extremely important that constant checks be made to ensure that all firms are registered. This is a minor problem in highly developed countries but a major one in many developing countries. This type of check is made by the enforcement officers, who are assigned particular territories, and to some extent by the inspectors.

## Identification of Nonfilers

The system used to identify those firms that have not filed in each time period depends on the types of computer installation, if any. These include the following:

1. Manual systems. With noncomputerized operations, the check is made manually. Several systems are workable. A simple one involves the transfer of the ledger cards from one file to another, as they are taken out of the file for recording of filing and payment. At the end of the period, the cards remaining in the original file show the nonfilers. After delinquency has been noted and a list prepared, the index cards are put back into the file for use during the succeeding period. Alternatively, the ledger cards are checked visually at the end of the period to identify those on which there are no entries for the month. Or a notation is made on an index card that the return has been filed, and those with no notation at the end of the period are listed as nonfilers.

2. Card systems. With the simple type of card computer operation, a returns card is punched for each firm as its return is processed during the period. At the end of the period, the returns cards are run through the collator against the master cards. The collator throws out the master cards for which there is no return card, and these master cards are then run through the printer to print the delinquency notices and prepare the list of delinquents.

3. Tape and memory cell systems. With the most modern sophisticated computers, there are several procedures, determined by the exact form of computer installation. With a magnetic tape system, a returns tape is prepared from the returns as they are processed. This is then run against the master tape on which all registered firms are listed to produce a delinquency tape, which in turn is used to print the delinquency notices and prepare the list of delinquents.

With the memory systems, the entries for the period are made in the memory cell for each firm, and at the end of the

period the cells are read to identify those for which no entry
has been made.

## Timing

The tax returns and payments are due on a certain date, as
noted.  Usually a few days of grace are given.  The optimal
cutoff date for identifying nonfilers is from two to three
weeks after the filing date; those filing between the end of
the period of grace, say three days after the due date, and
the cutoff date are assessed penalties.  Those not filing by
the cutoff date are listed as delinquents (nonfilers).  To cutoff too soon after the due date results in substantial
unnecessary effort, since experience shows that many of those
not filing by the due date will do so within two weeks anyway,
and action to notify them during the two-week period is
wasteful.  On the other hand, to allow notification to go much
beyond two or three weeks increases the danger of the loss of
revenue, since many of the nonfilers are firms with little
capital.

## Firms Not Paying

The primary problem is with firms that fail both to file
and to pay.  Occasionally, however, a firm will file a return
but not pay--usually because it is out of funds.  These firms
are listed separately, assessed the tax (with penalties), and
the amounts are listed in accounts receivable.  Otherwise,
these delinquents are treated in much the same fashion as firms
that fail to file.

## Automatic Penalties

Firms not filing and paying by the due date are subject to
automatic penalty and interest charges.  These are assessed at
the time of the check for delinquents and are applied to the
firms that have paid between the end of the grace period and
the cutoff date as well as those that have not yet filed.
These penalties and interest charges are applied automatically
without court action; they are not criminal penalties but
simply charges for failure to file and pay on time.  The amount
of the penalty is a percentage of the amount due, perhaps 10
percent, rising to 25 percent after three months, with a
minimum expressed in monetary units in order to discourage
firms that have little or no tax liability from failing to
file.  In addition, interest is assessed, often at 1 percent
a month for the entire period of delinquency.

These automatic penalty and interest charges are highly
effective in encouraging firms to file and pay on time and can
be applied simply and quickly.

## Initial Action

The initial step, in the parts of the country where firms can be reached easily by mail or by hand delivery, is the sending of a delinquency notice--a statement that no return has been received--with a demand that the return be filed and payment made immediately. One copy of this notice is kept in headquarters and two duplicates are sent to the district office, which in turn forwards one to the enforcement officer in the subdistrict to alert him. Experience shows that such a letter will clear many delinquents, often as many as half, without further action.

Where the sending of a notice is not feasible, the initial action is the same as the second action in instances in which the first action consists of notification, as explained below.

## Second Action

Initially where notification cannot be sent directly to the firm, and as a second action when it is, an enforcement officer visits the firm at its place of business. As a second action, this is undertaken about two weeks after the initial notice has been sent. Alternatively, a second notice may be sent to the firm before a visit is paid. At the end of the two-week period, with the delinquency file cleared of those who have filed and paid, a second listing of delinquents is prepared. The district offices are given this list, with a copy to each enforcement officer containing the names of the nonfilers in his subdistrict. His task is to visit each nonfiler and attempt to obtain the return and the payment. Or he may accompany the proprietor to the local revenue office, bank, or post office and ensure that he does file and make payment. If he does not succeed, he informs his superior to that effect, indicating the apparent reason for the failure to file and pay, and the superior determines the next action to take. In many instances, the enforcement officer will find that the firm has gone out of business or has closed up for a period of time, and he will so notify his superior. The district office, of course, keeps a list of the delinquents, and the enforcement officer will be required to report on each vendor on his list after a certain number of days-- perhaps 14 or 21.

## Additional Action

Before adopting final collection techniques, the director of enforcement in the district office may decide upon additional action. He may himself visit the proprietor and perhaps seek to work out a system of delayed payment if the owner is desperately short of cash but has some prospects. Ultimately,

the district enforcement officer will notify the enforcement
unit at headquarters of his inability to obtain either a
return or payment, and further action will be decided upon in
headquarters.

## Legal Action to Collect

As the first step toward legal measures to enforce
collection, headquarters personnel will make a formal assessment
of the tax apparently due.  This is built up from past sales
and tax figures and is often set deliberately high.  The amount
is entered into accounts receivable.  The taxpaying firm is
then notified of this assessment, and given a certain period,
perhaps two weeks, in which to pay, and warned of the action
that will be taken if it does not file.

There are several alternative policies that may then be
followed to enforce payment, some jurisdictions stressing one,
some another.  No one is necessarily "best."  The optimal
method in a particular situation depends upon the circumstances,
the legal environment, the attitude of the courts, and other
factors:

1.  Warrants.  The revenue department prepares a warrant,
often called a distress or distraint warrant, authorizing
either revenue department personnel or a law enforcement
officer to seize the property of the taxpayer in order to
obtain payment of the amount due.  The net effect, in many
instances, is to put the firm out of business.  This is an
action that local law enforcement officers and even revenue
personnel may be reluctant to take, but it may be necessary as
a final resort.  Threat of it and the preparation of the
warrant, without actual execution, often brings payment.
Granting revenue department personnel the right to execute
warrants avoids problems of noncooperation by local law
enforcement officers.

2.  Court order.  The revenue department may obtain an
order from the appropriate court requiring the firm to make
payment or to cease operations, and authorizing the seizure
of its property.  This action is in some respects easier to
enforce than a warrant, since failure to obey the order
constitutes contempt of court, but it requires more time and
the cooperation of the courts, which may have a long backlog
of business and may not be too cooperative in dealing with
tax violations.

3.  Revocation of certificate.  An alternative used
effectively by some states in the United States with their
retail sales taxes is to threaten initially to revoke the

firm's certificate, and ultimately to revoke it if the firm does not then file and pay.  The threat is often enough; if the firm does not pay and continues to operate, it is subject to criminal penalties for operating without a certificate.  Power to revoke the certificate should be given to the revenue department by the tax legislation.

4.  Immediate criminal prosecution.  An alternative used by a small number of jurisdictions is to undertake immediate criminal prosecution for failure to file and pay.  To be successful, however, this approach requires the cooperation of the courts, which may not be forthcoming.  It is not uncommon for judges to regard the collection of delinquent taxes as being outside their appropriate sphere of action.  It is often easier to obtain conviction on failure to file than it is on failure to pay, as the former does not directly involve the collection of money.

Quite distinct from action to prosecute for failure to file and pay is prosecution for fraud--for deliberate misrepresentation of sales and of taxes paid on purchases. Usually prosecution for fraud is undertaken only in extreme instances because of the difficulty of proving intent to defraud.  But occasional use is helpful as a means of warning firms to be more careful.

5.  Liens.  A technique to enforce payment that is sometimes used alone but more often in conjunction with other techniques is the filing of a lien against the property of the firm.  The firm is then severely restricted in its ability to sell or mortgage the property or to borrow, and the interests of the government are protected more effectively in the event of bankruptcy.

6.  Attachment of bank accounts.  The blocking of the firm's bank account, as practiced in Senegal, is a technique that has been found to be effective with those firms that have such accounts.  It discourages the use of bank accounts, however--a serious consequence in a developing economy.

It is highly important that VAT legislation give the revenue department adequate powers to deal with delinquents-- particularly of the hard-core type:  automatic penalties; the power to revoke certificates of registration; the power to execute warrants and to seize property without reliance on local law enforcement officials; and adequate criminal penalties for fraud.

## Summary of the Time Cycle

The exact optimal timing for the various steps in the handling of delinquents varies with the circumstances--the size of the country, speed of communications and transportation, and so on. But the following may be suggested as a rough guide for a developing country. The particular month of January is taken as an example.

## Time Cycle for Enforcement

| Return period | Month of January |
|---|---|
| Due date | February 21 |
| Cutoff date for identifying delinquents | March 7 |
| Notices sent or delivered to nonfilers | March 14 |
| Notice to enforcement officers to visit firms | March 28 |
| Deadline for enforcement officers to report action | April 15 |
| Initiation of legal action | May 1 |

There is merit in operating portions of the cycle more rapidly if possible, but, in most cases, much greater speed is not feasible.

## Causes of Nonfiling

An analysis of filing practices suggests several major causes of failure to file and pay: (1) oversight--failure to realize the deadline has been reached; (2) carelessness--not bothering to file; (3) illness or other casualty in smaller firms; (4) shortage of funds--either no money to pay, or the desire to use the tax money as working capital; and (5) deliberate attempt to defraud--the proprietor has vanished with the assets.

Primarily, nonfilers are smaller firms, but a number of larger ones, particularly those running short of working capital, are not infrequently delinquent.

## Delinquency Experience

With sales taxes generally, initial delinquency--failure to file by the due date--runs from 5 to 25 percent, and even higher in some jurisdictions. In the states of the United States, with their retail sales taxes, the average figure is 8 percent. In Chile, with the turnover tax, the figure averaged around 25 percent. Even the Canadian manufacturers' sales tax shows a surprisingly high 18 percent at the cutoff

date, although the figure falls to 5 percent a week later.
Most jurisdictions should be able to hold the figure under 10
percent if they develop adequate and timely procedures, and
if the penalty provisions of the law are adequate.  The high
rate in some countries reflects a failure to take adequate
action.

## Security Bond Requirements

A technique that helps to lessen loss of revenue through
failure to pay requires some form of security bond from
registered firms.  The bond may take a variety of forms:
surety bond, cash, certificates of deposit (in banks),
securities, and so on.  While a bond may be required of all
firms, this is rare and unnecessary.  More commonly, a bond
is required of new firms, particularly those with limited
assets, and of firms with chronic delinquency records.  The
amount of the bond required is related to the estimated
monthly tax payment--perhaps twice the amount.  When bonding
is required of new firms, the firms are frequently freed from
the requirement after several years of good experience.

Bonding offers substantial protection to the government
against losses through the failure of business firms, although
some firms may have difficulty in raising the necessary amounts.

## Audit Programs

The key to the successful operation of VAT, like any sales
tax, is careful inspection and auditing--examination of the
records of firms, their suppliers, and their customers, to
determine if the correct amounts of tax have been reported.
Self-assessment is imperative with VAT, but this self-assessment
must be subjected to careful review in order to ascertain
errors and misinterpretations as well as to prevent outright
evasion.

## Separate Versus Integrated Audit

A major issue is to decide whether the audit program for
the VAT should be integrated with that for the income tax or
whether it should be operated separately.  Both approaches
are used.

Integrated audit offers certain advantages:

1.  The nuisance and expense caused to firms by visits of
auditors are minimized, since during the period the firm will
have to deal with only one auditor or audit team rather than two.

2.  The expense of auditing should be lessened somewhat, since the total time involved in travel, making appointments, getting access to books, and learning the firm's bookkeeping procedures will be minimized.

3.  Some of the information needed to audit one tax is also needed for the other, and cross-checking between the tax returns for the two taxes is facilitated.  Errors discovered in common figures--for example, gross sales--can be corrected for both taxes at the same time.

The advantages, however, are not fully on the side of integration.  There are several disadvantages:

1.  The criteria for selecting accounts for audit is not the same for the two taxes.  The firms that require the most frequent checking for VAT may not be the same as those that require it for income tax purposes.

2.  The emphasis in audit is substantially different. VAT auditing, while sharing the interest of the income tax in gross sales, is primarily concerned with the reported figures of tax paid on purchases of exempt sales.  By contrast, income tax auditing stresses depreciation, inventory, and the deductibility of various expense items.  Thus, the time saving through integrated audit is less than it might first appear to be.

Because of the differences, substantial difference in training is required; a person can become an expert income tax or VAT auditor much more quickly than he can become an expert in both.  Experience suggests, also, that individual auditors tend to become more interested in one tax or the other and consequently to stress it in their auditing work.  There is a common tendency for personnel to become specialized in one tax, and actual integration in practice is often much less than it would appear to be.

3.  There is some tendency for one tax or the other to become dominant in auditing work.  For example, for a long period in Chile, the income tax dominated auditing even though the sales tax was by far the more important tax from a revenue standpoint.

On the whole, it is not obvious that integration of the auditing of the two major forms of tax is desirable.  Close cooperation and exchange of information is imperative, but separate auditing staffs may result in more effective operation of VAT.

## Allocation of Firms Between Auditors and Inspectors

As indicated in the previous section, in developing countries, in contrast to highly industrialized countries, it is desirable to have two separate but closely coordinated staffs to examine taxpayers' records. The audit staff per se, with highly trained personnel, would examine the accounts of the larger business firms, in the same fashion as in the highly developed countries. The inspectors, with substantially less training, would conduct the examinations of the smaller firms. Both would be under the jurisdiction of the Director of Inspection and Audit.

The allocation of firms to the two staffs would be based primarily on the volume of business and the complexity of operations. The exact dividing line would depend upon the nature of the economy and the relative availability of trained auditors. But in general, the audit staff would be assigned the firms typically subject to a manufacturers' sales tax, plus wholesale firms, importers and exporters, and the larger retailers--the department stores, multiple-unit stores, motor vehicle dealers, and any others with sales volume in excess of the designated figure. Auditors would also control governmental agencies subject to tax, public utilities, larger transport firms, larger hotels and restaurants, professional men if subject to tax, and so on.

The inspectors, therefore, would have jurisdiction over typical traders (those large enough to be subject to tax), craft producers, and most service establishments subject to tax. The number of firms in this second group would almost certainly be greater than in the former. In Ghana, for example, there are less than 1,000 manufacturers subject to the present manufacturers' sales tax; the number of larger establishments would probably not exceed 2,000 under VAT, while there would be several times as many traders, even if the very small ones were exempted.

## Frequency of Audit and Inspection

It is difficult to define exactly the optimal timing of audits. To audit every firm every year is not economical nor possible in most countries because of shortage of personnel. The following standards are suggested.

Those firms subject to auditing, as distinguished from inspection, should be subjected to a thorough audit no less frequently than every third year, with some firms being audited at one- or two-year intervals, as determined by experience. In any country, a substantial portion of the revenue will be obtained from these firms. While they are, on the average, less inclined than smaller firms to evade tax deliberately, and their records are better, the chances of unintentional error are greater and the amounts of money involved are very much larger.

The smaller firms subject to inspection should receive, at the minimum, a brief check from an inspector every two years, with more careful examination of those firms about which the inspector has doubts. The brief inspections would involve little more than a look at the record system, a check on a few invoices as a test, and consideration of the reasonableness of the figures shown on the return in the light of the size of the establishment, inventory, number of employees, and so on. Each of these venders should have a careful examination at least once every five years. While more frequent coverage would be desirable, it is not likely to be attainable. The states of the United States do not have so complete a coverage; on the average, no more than 3 percent of the venders are audited annually. It is widely recognized, however, that this coverage is inadequate, and the environment in the developing economies is substantially different.

## Selection of Firms for Audit Priority

Since inspecting or auditing each firm every year is obviously an impossibility, some system of priorities must be established. There are several types of approach, which countries have developed on the basis of experience.

1. Firms may be classified by type of business and size. Experience in various countries suggests that firms in certain industries are more prone to error than those in others, depending in large measure on the complexity of the tax as applied in various fields. There are, inevitably, in some industries, questions about the deductibility of taxes paid on certain purchases. If, for example, tax on the purchase of motor vehicles is not deductible, questions will arise about the exact definition of motor vehicles. If some food is exempt, application of the tax to firms handling food products will be much more complex.

Giving priority to the larger firms is prompted primarily by revenue considerations. There is no particular evidence that large firms are more inclined to make errors than small firms; if anything, the opposite may be true. But the amount of tax revenue involved is much greater, and therefore the tax recovery per audit hour is larger.

As an illustration of this system, Canada, with its manufacturers' sales tax, classifies all registered firms, on the basis of type and volume, into two-, three-, and four-year groups, all firms in each group being audited at the frequency interval indicated. The state of California with its retail sales tax has a very elaborate "cell" system. The potentiality of error in various industries, with firms of various size, is determined by experience, and all firms are classified into cells on the basis of this probability. The top-priority firms will be audited annually; the low-priority cells very rarely. But such a sophisticated system is not feasible or necessary for most developing countries, certainly in the early years of the tax.

2. Deviation from norms. The procedure here involves the development of norms or standards and the selection of those firms that show substantial deviation from the norms. One of the most useful norms with VAT is the ratio of tax deducted as having been paid to suppliers to gross tax liability. Firms can be required to identify in their annual returns the tax paid on purchases of materials and goods for resale, the tax paid on durable capital equipment, and the tax paid on other items. The first item, typically by far the largest, should be relatively uniform, as a percentage of gross tax, among firms in particular lines of business.

Firms that deviate from these norms can be ascertained initially by office audit--that is, by checking the returns, preferably on an annual basis. Ultimately the computer system can be used to ascertain all firms deviating from the established norms by more than a certain percentage.

Other norms may also be established: the ratio of export sales to total sales, the ratio of other exempt sales to total sales, or gross sales for particular types of businesses in cities of various sizes.

3. Other techniques include audit of all new firms and follow-up of leads. There is great merit in auditing all firms as soon as possible after the initiation of the tax, even though these audits must be cursory. The primary purpose is to ensure that firms are applying and recording the tax correctly and using the appropriate procedures in determining tax liability. After the tax has been in operation for a time, however, each new firm starting business should be audited within six months after the date of starting, for the same reason. For these early audits, there is merit in a policy of not assessing penalties and interest but merely warning the firm to correct its methods; subsequent repetition of the errors then brings penalties.

One audit often leads to another, particularly with VAT. Check on the tax reported as paid by a firm will frequently reveal errors in the application of the tax by the firm's suppliers and lead to an audit of the supplier and of other customers of this particular supplier.

Income tax audit will also suggest the need for a VAT audit as well (and vice versa); hence, a systematic exchange of information between the VAT division and the income tax division is imperative.

Likewise, a firm found to be making frequent errors, particularly on borderline questions where the firm has given itself the benefit of the doubt consistently, is a prime candidate for a repeat audit at a relatively early date.

4. The geographical approach. At the inspection level, the remoteness of many towns in developing countries suggests that some use must be made of the geographical approach; an inspector travels through an area with three somewhat isolated towns, each having only three or four registered firms and inspects all these firms. Given the desirability of reasonably frequent checking of all traders, this approach is less wasteful than it is in a highly developed country, where it leads to a high percentage of unproductive audits.

## Regional Versus Centralized Selection

With the usual regionalization, it must be decided where selection is most appropriately made--at headquarters or at the regional offices. With auditing as such, there is little question: If all the auditors are attached to headquarters, obviously the selection must be made at headquarters. If they are assigned to two or three regional offices, the selection may be made at either location, although there is still some merit in centralization. At the inspection level, the situation is different. While headquarters will provide the guides and establish priorities, and ultimately, with computer assistance in selection, furnish information about deviation from norms, the actual selection should be made in the district office. The decision will be made by the supervising auditor, often in cooperation with the inspectors since they are in much closer contact with the venders and with local conditions. Standard policy is not to allow an inspector to make his own selections, although he is encouraged to recommend priorities to the supervisor. There is danger if the inspector has the ability to go ahead on his own that he will give priority to the easy accounts to audit, those located in seaside resorts, or those with other characteristics not relevant for optimal selection.

## Audit Manuals and Forms

Preparation of an audit manual, with instructions and guides to the auditors, is highly desirable, especially when the tax first goes into operation and the auditors are not experienced. The manual should contain information on various aspects of the tax and detailed explanations of auditing procedures. Separate manuals are desirable for auditors and inspectors, given the differences in the complexity of their work and the types of firms with which they deal. Forms to be filled in should be included as well as samples of audit reports. Not only do the manuals aid the auditor and improve the quality of the audit, but they also increase uniformity of policy throughout the country.

A country introducing a new VAT may be able to develop its first audit manual by making use of ones developed in other countries using the tax, as well as of manuals from countries with single-stage forms of tax.

The audit report forms require a detailed reporting of the procedures followed, the records checked, the errors discovered, and the apparent reasons for the errors. Substantial detail is requested in order to facilitate the review of the audit findings by senior auditing personnel. Other information, such as the time spent on the audit, the nature of the firm's records systems, the persons in the firm contacted, and so on, are required as a routine matter.

The reports for the inspectors are basically similar but much simpler and less formal.

Policies differ with respect to the information provided to the auditor or inspector when he is starting an audit. The usual procedure is either to provide him with copies of the returns from the firm or to have him examine the returns and make his own notes. Either approach is satisfactory for the audits per se, but not for inspections. The inspector works from the district office while the returns are in headquarters, and it is not usually worthwhile to produce duplicates for the district offices, although this can be done if necessary. With modern computers, each district office can be provided with a monthly printout of the data on the returns, or, much more simply, of the annual returns, which serve as the basis for most audit work anyway. Or, the computer can produce a separate printout for each account, showing the information on the returns for the period the audit will cover. But in developing countries few computer systems have reached this level; the overall printout is the best that can be expected. An alternative as far as inspections are concerned is to give the inspector nothing except the list of firms to be inspected,

requiring him to check the duplicate copies of the returns that
the firm is required to keep.  Unfortunately, if these are not
available, the inspector must contact headquarters for further
information.

Virtually never is an auditor or inspector given the
actual returns to take with him, because of the danger of loss.

Auditing Procedures

VAT audit involves several major steps, some of which
differ substantially from those for other forms of sales tax.

Verification of Reported Gross Sales

Underreporting of gross sales will of course reduce the
firm's tax liability, as well as, if the same figures are
used, its income tax liability.  There are several approaches
to checking this.

1.    Examination of basic records, including the sales
journal and the general ledger.

2.    Reconciliation of sales invoices with entries into
the sales journal and the general ledger, to ensure that all
invoices are being entered correctly.  Otherwise, the gross
sales figure that serves as the basis for calculation of the
tax will be in error.  Unfortunately, there is always a
danger that sales will be made without invoices, as is common
with retailers, that invoices may understate the actual sales
figure, and that invoices will be destroyed.  Many of the
smaller traders will not have duplicates of sales invoices,
or they may have issued none.  More modern stores may have
only cash register tapes.

3.    Comparison of gross sales as shown on VAT returns
with those shown on income tax returns.

4.    Casn analysis of deposits and payments from bank
accounts, if these are used.  This approach is of little use
with small traders but will provide some rough verification
of the sales of large firms.

5.    Check on inventory.  The inventory on hand gives
some indication of likely sales figures.

6.    Comparison of reported figures of sales with those
of purchases of goods for resale and of materials.  A key
element in the VAT audit of traders is the reconciliation of

reported figures of sales with figures calculated by applying
a markup to purchases of goods for resale as shown in the
purchase journal. Either a customary markup figure or the
firm's actual markup is used, the latter ascertained by a
review of the purchase prices and selling prices of a sample
of commodities. This figure is then applied to the total of
purchases and the result compared with the figure of reported
sales. Any significant discrepancy must be justified by the
trader, as, for example, by showing a comparable change in
inventory.

One device that may be used with certain types of service
establishments such as hotels is to require them to issue
invoices to all customers from a specified form of invoice
book with numbered invoices. These are then checked against
the reported total receipts. This system is not foolproof and
is not workable with many service establishments, but it may
assist in certain fields. Another device is to require
receipts to be issued on numbered forms, these forms then
being in effect lottery tickets entitling purchasers to a
chance for a prize, so as to motivate them to insist on
delivery of a receipt.

Especially with service firms, but in some instances with
others, there may be no way to build a figure of total sales
except by somewhat arbitrary measures: the size of the
inventory, the number of employees, floor space, and so on.
The revenue department should be given adequate legal powers
to make assessments on these criteria when a firm does not
keep accurate records as required by law. Sometimes it is
worthwhile to station an inspector or enforcement man in the
place of business for several days, to make an actual record
of sales or to observe the operation on a number of sample
occasions as a basis on which to build up figures for a
longer period.

On purchases other than materials and goods for resale,
there is very little incentive to conceal the amounts and
the firm will wish to deduct tax paid on these purchases. If
the firm bought an item tax-free, it will have no tax to
deduct and will pay more tax itself. A problem arises only if
the tax on some items is nondeductible; the firm will then
have an incentive to try to buy these items tax-free if it can
and then not to report use of them or pay tax on them. This
is a serious problem with single-stage taxes; it should not
be of any great consequence with a well-designed VAT without
exemptions, since there is no way the firm can buy tax free.

## Analysis of the Handling of the Tax

Since the firm is required to collect the tax from the customer and quote it separately on the invoice, at least on sales to registered firms, sample check of invoices is necessary to ensure that the tax is being calculated and shown correctly.

The tax-credit form of VAT computation gives rise to a special form of evasion. A firm overstates the tax on the invoice, but not its gross sales. The purchaser pays at least part of the excess tax willingly because he can deduct all of it from his tax liability, while the supplier calculates his tax on his total sales figures, thus pocketing the rest of the excess tax he has collected. A check on invoices is necessary to detect this practice.

Some firms will establish a tax account (a practice required in the United Kingdom), credit the tax collected from customers to this account, and debit the account with tax payments made to the government. A useful check is to see, on a test basis, whether tax as shown on invoices is being properly credited to the tax account, and whether the total shown as credit to the tax account during the period is equal to the figure of the tax rate times taxable sales--that is, gross sales less exempt sales, as noted below. If it is not, the source of the discrepancy should be found.

## Reported Figures of Tax-Paid Purchases

Two types of verification are required for the figure reported as tax paid to suppliers. First, the figure itself may be overreported; firms may report that they have paid more than they actually have. A basic rule is imperative: They can deduct only amounts that they can prove by showing the suppliers' sales invoices with the amount of tax itemized. A firm that has lost some of its purchase records can presumably obtain a duplicate from the supplier. But a further check is necessary; these figures must be checked against the data on the tax returns of the suppliers, to ensure that the amounts have actually been paid. Otherwise, as noted above, connivance between the firm and its supplier could result in fictitious invoices, reporting tax that was never actually paid to the government. Thus, on each audit, the auditor or inspector must obtain or prepare a statement of the tax reported as paid by the firm to its various suppliers, listed by name and account number of the supplier. This information will be supplied through headquarters to the person auditing the records of the supplier. This cross-checking cannot be done perfectly, but it can be done to a sufficient degree to catch large-scale evasion and discourage firms from attempting the practice. Ultimately computers can do much of the cross-checking.

Second, a check must be made to ensure that there is no deduction of tax on purchases made for the personal use of the owner of the business, unless, of course, the use by the owner has been reported as a sale in the records of the firm and tax has been applied to it as to any other sale. This is essentially the same problem as that of deducting personal expenses as business expenses under the income tax.

There is a great temptation, with the typical smaller proprietorship or partnership business, to deduct tax that has been paid on purchases for personal use--television sets, furniture, and other items. The basic trouble is that no sharp distinction is made by the establishment between the business per se, and the financial affairs of the family operating the business. It is not easy to catch all such errors (not all of which are deliberate). The inspector can pick up some items from purchase invoices: a shoe store deducting tax paid on a television set, for example, or on restaurant meals. Such deductions could be legitimate (the TV set might have been purchased solely to entertain customers, the meal have been a special luncheon for employees). But at least they suggest the need for inquiry. At the same time, the auditor or inspector can inquire into transfers from inventory to personal use, which are inevitable in almost all small businesses and even in larger ones, to be sure that these are reported in gross sales and tax applied to the sale. There is no foolproof check, however. Problems also arise, as with the income tax, as to whether an item is a legitimate business purchase or not. Was the airline trip necessary to visit customers or suppliers or was it a pleasure journey? It is probably desirable to ban by law deduction of tax purchases from certain types of establishments--places of entertainment, for example.

## Zero-Rated and Exempt Sales

As noted, export sales are universally not subject to tax, or, in other words, are zero-rated. Thus, tax paid on purchases of goods that are exported and other tax items entering into their costs are deductible. The firm must therefore provide verification that transactions reported as export sales were actually exports. This can be evidenced by invoices and bills of lading, postal receipts, and so on. If tourist purchases delivered, say, aboard planes are exempt, there must be some system for verifying reported sales of this type.

Hopefully, zero rating in VAT will be confined to exports and to an absolute minimum of exempt commodities, but others may in practice be provided. So far as commodities are concerned, firms must have evidence of the portion of total sales consisting of exempt or zero-rated goods. There are several approaches for an auditor or inspector:

1.     Relation to typical pattern. If only unprocessed foods are exempt, the ratio of exempt to taxable sales is likely to be reasonably uniform for urban grocery stores per se. Any deviation from this standard suggests detailed investigation.

2.     Spot check of sales invoices and cash register tapes, if any. The exempt commodities must be identified in some fashion on the sales record. Unfortunately, many of the retail firms of this type will have very inadequate records.

3.     Purchase invoices. Primary control must depend upon purchase invoices. If half of a firm's purchases consist of unprocessed food, and markups are the same on food and other goods, half of the sales should consist of taxable goods. If purchase invoices on unprocessed food are inadequate, as they will be if the purchases are primarily made directly from farmers, then reliance will be placed on the purchase invoices for the taxable goods, which are more likely to be available and correct (with a check on the firm's suppliers if necessary).

4.     In-store check. Again, at times, it may be necessary to station an enforcement officer in the store for several days, to keep a record of the no-tax and taxable sales, and then to expand the ratio thus ascertained to the entire tax period. The law should sanction assessments made on this basis.

Exemptions to certain classes of buyers should be held to an absolute minimum. But if some are provided (to churches and diplomats, and sales to farmers of feed, seed, and fertilizer), the control methods must be much the same as those used for exports. The seller must be able to document the exempt nature of the transaction through sales invoices, which can be checked with the purchaser if necessary. Checking with most farmers is, unfortunately, impossible.

## Rate Differentials

As noted earlier, it is highly desirable to use only one rate in VAT. If, however, two or more rates are employed, a major new task is created for the auditors:  to ascertain the accuracy of the reported sales by rate class. Numerous errors of misinterpretation and of simple erroneous application of tax are almost certain to occur. The auditor or inspector will rely on much the same tests as those for taxable versus exempt sales: checking, on a sample basis, of sales invoices, and checking against purchase invoices. Again, if half of the firm's purchases consist of commodities subject to a 5 percent rate and half to a 10 percent rate, the same ratio should be found with sales, if the same markups are used with the two. The tendency for the trader to rely on the classification of the commodities used by his supplier suggests the need for a careful check on wholesale suppliers and on manufacturers. When an inspection or audit suggests that a particular supplier is misapplying the classification, an immediate audit of the supplier is in order.

## Forfait Systems

If a forfait approach is used, the inspector responsible for the initial assessment will follow much the same procedures as in actual inspection. He will ask the vender for an estimate of his probable sales or, as in the African countries, require the trader to keep a detailed record for a few days and expand this to an annual basis. The inspector will then check this figure against the purchase records. Where these are inadequate, the inspector will seek to gain more information from the firm's suppliers. When this proves impossible or when there is doubt about its accuracy, the inspector must resort to somewhat arbitrary measures based upon numbers of employees, floor space, and so on. The VAT division should prepare guidelines for the inspectors to follow in building up the tax liability figure, and all assessments made by inspectors must be subject to careful review by senior personnel, if for no other reason than to lessen the danger of bribery.

If a forfait system is to be used, it is highly desirable to have the forfait assessment relate to the sales figure alone and to allow credit only for tax actually proven to be paid, rather than having the forfait assessment made for tax due. This procedure forces the firm to keep records of purchases or lose its tax credit, and these purchase records are of great assistance to the inspector in arriving at a reasonable figure of probable sales. It requires little effort for the trader to keep his purchase invoices showing the tax paid on his purchases.

## Audit Periods and Test Periods

An audit will usually be made for the entire period since the last audit, subject to the constraint of the statute of limitations.  In the audit itself, the use of test periods is imperative from the standpoint of the time both of the auditor or inspector and the firm.  In some instances, the auditor or inspector will make a brief test-period check to see whether the circumstances warrant a more careful audit.  If an audit is decided upon, the auditor will usually seek to obtain the consent of the firm to use two or three months, or even a shorter period, as the basis for the entire audit findings. The results of the test period will be extended to the entire period covered by the audit.  With a VAT, this approach is primarily usable for verifying figures of sales and of relative sales of taxable and exempt commodities.  It is less suitable for verifying tax reported as paid to suppliers.  It may be used for the latter when the purchases and the tax paid on purchases are more or less uniform through the year. If they are not, figures for the entire year must be used. The annual basis may also be necessary for obtaining data for checking on the tax reported as paid by suppliers.

## An Ultimate Goal:  Cross-Check by Computer

As noted earlier, one of the great merits of VAT is the possibility it offers for checking the tax reported as paid by one firm to its suppliers against the tax reported as due and payable by the suppliers.  Auditors can check these figures.  The use of a standard invoice form would aid in cross-checking.  But there is also the ultimate possibility of a complete check by computer.  Firms will be required, on annual returns, to report the tax paid to various suppliers, identified by name and account number, during the year.  These figures will be entered into the computer, which will sum them for each supplying firm and compare the sum with tax reported as paid by the supplying firm.  This total, of course, does not include data of sales to persons other than registered firms and thus is of little value with traders and service establishments, but it is of great value in checking on the accuracy of the reported sales figures of manufacturers and wholesalers, and of the deductions for tax claimed as paid by all registered firms, including traders.

Another potential form of automated check is that of tracing subsequent sales of imported goods.  If smuggling is prevented and valuation figures at import are reasonably accurate, a country in which most manufactured goods are still imported has an accurate check of goods entering the domestic distribution channels.  The importers can be required to report sales (in excess of some relatively small figure) to specific purchasers; these figures can then be cumulated for each wholesale distributor buying from importers and compared after proper markup adjustments with the sales reported by these firms.  This procedure is undoubtedly beyond the computer capacity of many developing economies, at least initially.  But it does offer great potential over a longer period of time.

## Steps in the Audit

The overall field audit process involves several steps:

1.    Assignment.  The firm is selected for audit by the audit supervisor, and the audit is assigned to a particular person (or perhaps team in some instances).

2.    Arrangement for audit.  The auditor will contact the firm and arrange for a time and for provision of records and working space.

3.    Actual conduct of the audit.

4.    Completion.  The auditor will explain his findings to the appropriate official of the firm or the proprietor, call attention to defects in the record and control system, and indicate errors and the audit assessment.  He will also explain his methods.  He will then seek to get the official or proprietor to approve the findings.  Normally the auditor does not actually collect money due, although with examinations by inspectors of smaller traders it may be desirable for the inspector to require the proprietor to go to the nearest office and pay the additional tax at once.  It is highly important for the auditor to report a net overpayment, if there is one, as well as an underpayment.  The excess, once the audit is reviewed, will be refunded or credited against the next period's tax liability.

5.    Report.  The auditor will file his report and working papers with the supervising auditor.  The supervisor or senior review auditor will then review the audit in detail. This may be done at headquarters or in the regional offices. The reports by inspectors will be reviewed by the supervising auditor in the district office and then forwarded to head-quarters for further review in the interests of uniformity.

6.    Assessment.  Following review, the senior auditor will make the formal assessment of the amount due, or the certification for credit if the audit has revealed overpayment. The taxpaying firm is then notified, by mail or delivered notice.  With inspections, the inspector will visit the place of business with the formal assessment and ask for payment to be made within the specified time.  Upon assessment, the interest charge for late payment will be applied as a routine matter.  Whether penalties (comparable to those for late filing) should be applied should be left to the discretion of

the supervising auditor.  Commonly, no penalty is applied when
the errors were clearly unintended, especially on the first
offense.  On the other hand, when there is evidence of
deliberate attempt to defraud, the auditor may recommend that
the person should be prosecuted for fraud.  The final decision
is made by the director of the VAT Division.  In many countries
it is difficult to obtain a conviction for fraud because of
the need to prove intent to defraud.  But an occasional
prosecution is useful as a warning to firms.

7.    Appeal.  There is obviously a need to provide a
channel for review of the audit findings.  Commonly, the first
appeal is a highly informal one, the taxpayer visiting the
supervisor of audit in the district office in respect to
inspection examinations, and the supervising auditor or
director of audit at headquarters on audits per se.  Beyond
this, there is merit in establishing some form of VAT appeals
board, set up solely for this purpose and consisting of
persons not directly affiliated with the government who are
experts in the field.  Final appeal is to the courts, but in
most countries the number of cases reaching the courts is very
limited.

## Control over Auditors and Inspectors

Auditors report directly to the chief auditor at headquarters or in the regional office, inspectors to a supervising
auditor in the district offices.  Apart from the control
exercised over them through review of their reports, other
supervisory techniques may be employed.  For example, they may
be limited as to the amount of time they may spend on any one
audit, without specific approval.  They may be expected to make
a certain number of audits or inspections per year.  As long as
such a rule is used with care, it is not unreasonable, but,
particularly with auditors, consideration must be given to the
complexity of the audit.  Inspections lend themselves more
readily to control over the time spent.  While certain standards
should be set up as to revenue productivity per audit, too much
stress must not be placed upon revenue per se, since the
primary purpose of audit is to attain more correct reporting
of tax; the assessments are merely steps toward that objective.
Excessive stress on the money produced, with prizes for the
maximum recovery, lead the auditors and inspectors to press
the taxpayers unreasonably hard in borderline cases and to
ignore all aspects of audit other than those most productive
of additional money.

One of the most serious problems in some countries is the
strong tie that may arise between inspector and proprietor
from the extended family system.  The inspector's dominant

loyalty is to his family members and to report a family member for underreporting tax is contrary to strong traditional moral standards. The problem arises even with senior revenue officials. A partial answer is to try to assign inspectors to areas where they do not have family ties.

## Responsibilities of Firms

The introduction of a VAT creates a number of tasks for the firms subject to the registration requirement:

1.  To obtain necessary information about the tax.

2.  To ascertain whether the firm is subject to the registration requirement or not, and to register if required.

3.  To establish a system for control and operation of the tax, including the creation of a tax account to which the amounts collected as tax are credited.

4.  To instruct billing clerks and sales persons about the tax and liability for the tax.

5.  To ensure that the tax is added to the invoice on each sale, with separate quotation of tax as required.

6.  At the end of each tax period, to total taxable and exempt sales and the tax collected.

7.  To total purchases by major category and tax paid on these purchases.

8.  To prepare the VAT return, filing the return and making payment.

9.  To record the tax paid to each supplier (in excess of the minimum established by law) and report this information to the government on each annual return.

10.  To file annual returns as required.

11.  To keep the relevant records and make them available to inspectors or auditors. Records must be retained for the period specified by law.

12.  To obtain and preserve evidence, such as bills of lading, of sales for export, and other exempt sales.

NOTES

1.   The experience is reviewed in the book by R. D. Ebel, The Michigan Business Activities Tax (East Lansing:  Michigan State University, 1972).

2.   This conclusion is strongly opposed by Norman Ture, who rejects the assumption of differential incidence and concludes that factor prices will fall.  See his "Economics of the Value Added Tax" in Value Added Tax:  Two Views (Washington: American Enterprise Institute, 1972), pp. 69-95.

3.   See ibid.

4.   A recent discussion of the expenditure tax is to be found in the paper by R. E. Slitor, "Administrative Aspects of Expenditures Taxation," in R. A. Musgrave, ed., Broad Based Taxes:  New Options and Sources (Baltimore:  Johns Hopkins Press, 1973).  The most outspoken proponents of this form of tax include Nicholas Kaldor; note his book, An Expenditure Tax (London:  Allen and Unwin, 1955); and Irving Fisher and Herbert W. Fisher, Constructive Income Taxation:  A Proposal for Reform (New York:  Harper and Brothers, 1942).  In principle, advocacy of this tax goes back to John Stuart Mill's Principles of Political Economy (1848).

5.   R. J. Chelliah, "Trends in Taxation in Developing Countries," International Monetary Fund (IMF) Staff Papers 18 (July 1971): 254-331.

6.   J. F. Due, Indirect Taxation in Developing Economies (Baltimore:  Johns Hopkins Press, 1970), chap. 2.

7.   The tax credit system is also opposed by those who insist upon regarding VAT as resting upon factor incomes rather than in relation to consumer spending.  But this is a small minority.  Note Ture, in Value Added Tax:  Two Views, op. cit.

8.   See M. Gillis, ed., Fiscal Reform for Colombia (Cambridge:  Harvard Law School, 1971), pp. 593-647.

## SELECTED BIBLIOGRAPHY

The volume of literature on value-added taxation is now tremendous. Only major references are listed below, with emphasis on those most relevant for developing countries.

Asociacion Latin Americano de Libre Comercio (ALALC). Impuestos de Tipo Valor Agregado: Anteproyecto de Modelo Mexico, D.F., 1972.

Bird, R. M. "A Value-Added Tax for Singapore: Comment." Malayan Economic Review 12 (April 1967): 39-41.

Cnossen, S. "Sales and Excise Tax Systems of the World." Mimeo. Washington, D.C.: International Monetary Fund, 1974.

Edwards, C.T. "A Value Added Tax?" Malayan Economic Review 13 (October 1968): 22-49.

Guerard, Michele. "The Brazilian State Value Added Tax." International Monetary Fund Staff Papers 30 (March 1973): 118-69.

Hill, John H. "Sales Taxation in Francophone Africa." Ph.D. dissertation, University of Illinois, 1973.

International Monetary Fund. "Bibliography on Value Added Tax." Mimeo. Washington, D.C.: IMF, 1972.

Lent, G.E., Casanegra, M., and Guerard, M. "The Value Added Tax in Developing Countries." International Monetary Fund Staff Papers 30 (July 1973): 318-78.

McKinnon, R.I. "Export Expansion through Tax Policy: The Case for a Value-Added Tax for Singapore." Malayan Economic Review 11 (October 1966): 1-27.

McLure, C. E., and Ture, N. B. Value Added Tax: Two Views. Washington, D.C.: American Enterprise Institute, 1972.

Spain. Instituto de Estudios Fiscales, Ministerio de Hacienda. El Impuesto sobre el valor anadido. Madrid, 1971.

Sullivan, Clara. The Tax on Value Added. New York: Columbia University Press, 1965.

Tait, A. Value Added Tax. London: McGraw-Hill, 1972.

Tax Institute of America.  A Value Added Tax.  Papers presented
     at the symposium conducted by the Tax Institute of America,
     1972, published in Tax Policy 39 (October-December 1972).

Wheatcroft, G. S. A.  Value Added Tax in the Enlarged Common
     Market.  London:  Associated Business Programs, Ltd.,
     1973.

# 3

## TAXATION IN THE
## MANAGEMENT OF
## PRIMARY COMMODITY
## MARKETS
### Albert G. Hart

Since the sensational rise in 1973-75 of the price of petroleum under management by the Organization of Petroleum Exporting Countries (OPEC), there has been lively political and journalistic discussion of the possibility that developing countries that export primary commodities other than oil might score substantial economic gains by organizing to manage markets for their export commodities. Most of this discussion seems to rest on the assumption that primary commodity prices can be set by fiat; though, of course, those who are trying to devise practical ways and means for raising prices are aware that to do so requires obviating excess supply. This chapter explores the possibilities of the systematic use of tax policy to cope with the excess supply problem, and simultaneously to avoid the perverse distributional consequences and the dissipation of potential development capital that will be brought about within developing countries if commodity-agreement techniques are applied without appropriate tax policies.

Unless explicitly stated to the contrary, the analysis in this chapter accepts for purposes of argument a somewhat doubtful assumption, which permeates much of the literature on commodity agreements--namely, that the market for whatever commodity is in question is one in which demand is inelastic with respect to price, so that if exporters raise their price and accept whatever reduction in export quantum may result, they will find their export proceeds increased. In view of the ability of the industrial countries to economize on the use of the commodities that may be involved, and to generate competing production of many of them, this may be a misleading assumption. Towards the end of the chapter, consideration will be given to the corrections of the argument that would be in order if this assumption proved false, and to the possibilities of feeling out the situation rather than merely gambling on the validity of this assumption.

COMMODITY AGREEMENTS IN THE ABSENCE OF TAX ELEMENTS

The image of a commodity agreement that seems to be in
the minds of most participants in political and journalistic
discussions is extremely simple.  They seem to assume only
that (1) a "fair" price for the commodity will be worked out
by some sort of negotiation and that (2) participating
governments will administer imports and exports in such a way
that no international trade in the commodity in question will
take place below the agreed price.  The participating
governments may be only those of countries that export the
commodity, or they may also include governments of importing
countries.

## Problem of Excess Supply

It will be evident instantly to anyone who has either
business experience or some grasp of technical economics that
an agreement framed along the above lines will soon run into
problems of excess supply.  Setting a price higher than the
"market-clearing price" that would exist in the absence of
the agreement will create incentives for users to cut down
their absorption of the commodity.  At the same time, it will
create incentives for producing enterprises (both in the
exporting countries, which we may think of as largely but
perhaps not exclusively developing nations, and within the
importing countries, unless climate and the like forbid) to
expand their capacity for production, and to use existing
capacity more fully.  With output larger than at the market-
clearing price and consumption smaller, there will be a
tendency for production to outrun consumption, and for
unconsumed stocks to pile up.

(Economists, of course, can always think up exceptions to
any proposition.  In this instance, it is plain that commodity
agreements are apt to include clauses that call for developing
new uses for the commodity and alternative lines of production
for the producing enterprises--and for drawing the attention
of the firms and governments involved to whatever opportunities
may be uncovered on either side.  There is no way to prove
a priori that this kind of research-development-and-promotion
effort may not take hold strongly enough on the market to
absorb the excess supply.  But it would be hard to compile an
impressive list of concrete successes along this line.
Successful promotions do not go well with a high-price policy.)

Experience with markets tells us that in the presence of
excess supply, prices tend to soften.  If total sales are not
large enough to satisfy all the producing enterprises that
want to sell, some or all of these enterprises will be

frustrated.  If the aggregate shortfall of demand is small
(which it may be if demand is highly inelastic and the price
rise is moderate) and if the shortfall spreads itself out
fairly evenly over the producing enterprises, would-be sellers
may be happy to accept the higher price on an output that is
only slightly reduced, and the tension of excess supply may be
so slight that the price will rule at the agreed level.  But
if the aggregate shortfall of demand is even a small number
of percentage points, it is likely that the distribution of
the shortfall will be uneven; and of course a small percentage
of the world total will be large enough relative to the output
of any particular producing enterprise to make the shortfalls
very painful to some individual producers.*  Producing
enterprises that feel they are not getting a fair share of the
market at the agreed price will feel justified in shading the
price to attract buyers--and may even be unable to survive
unless they do so.

## Buffer Stocks

Two methods for dealing with the threat of excess supply
are commonly considered in framing commodity agreements.  One
is to arrange for a buffer stock, the other to agree upon an
allocation of sales among exporting countries.  A buffer stock
arrangement requires finding or setting up some body to
function as residual buyer--acquiring and holding off the
market any goods offered for sale that do not find other buyers
at the agreed price.  A sales allocation arrangement throws
responsibility back upon individual governments of exporting
countries (or upon associations of producing enterprises).
This responsibility must then be executed either by setting
up buffer stocks or "surplus disposal" schemes within
countries or by allocating national quotas to specific
enterprises.

Buffer stocks (whether international or national) must be
financed, for it is in the nature of their operations to buy
more than they sell whenever the agreed price generates excess
supply.  In addition, they will have to face costs of operation
(including storage costs and interest on any financing they

-----

*When all suppliers offer the same price, buyers will
ordinarily turn to suppliers toward whom they feel "loyalty,"
and from whom they can expect reciprocal favors if the market
becomes tight.  Such claims to "loyalty" are unlikely to be
evenly distributed.  A consideration much in point in the
present context is the likelihood that specific industrial
countries will commonly focus their "loyalty" on their ex-
colonies, and especially on enterprises in those countries in
which residents of the metropolitan country retain an interest.

obtain by borrowing).  If they are financed by levies on the
commodity in question, we enter the realm of taxation, which
will be considered in the next phase of the argument.  If they
are otherwise financed, they will absorb general tax revenues
or borrowing power for which, particularly in a developing
country, there may be urgent alternative uses.  Purchases for
"surplus disposal" (whether by physical destruction, by down-
graded use such as the transformation of cocoa into margarine,
or by subsidized sale to users not on the regular market) also
present financing problems.  Allocation of national export
quotas to producing enterprises may obviate financing problems
but will entail difficulties in structuring and administering
the quotas--unless the enterprises involved are in the public
sector.  Furthermore, if quota allocations rest on productive
capacity (generally the most straightforward basis that
presents itself), producing enterprises are given incentives
to create additional capacity, which as long as the quota
system lasts will be underutilized and thus high cost.

## Role of Importing Countries

While it is not impossible to manage a primary product
market through a commodity agreement subscribed to only by
exporting countries, prospects that an agreement will prove
viable rise sharply if importing countries are also parties to
the agreement.  To begin with, the financial strength of
importing, mostly industrial countries, offers a safeguard
against inadequate financing of buffer stocks.  Secondly,
verification that transactions actually conform to the terms of
the agreement is much more administratively feasible if
officials of the importing country share the responsibility
for such verification.  Thirdly, if importing countries can be
persuaded to spread their purchases over different sources in
an agreed pattern, the danger that some exporting countries
and some producing enterprises may carry much more than their
share of the burden of the probable sales shortfall is much
abated.  Fourthly, participation by importing countries may
include commitments to check rather than stimulate production
of the commodity in question within their own borders.
Lastly, if governments of the importing countries attest to
the fairness of the agreement, there is less prospect of a
buildup of resentments and of devices for bypassing the
agreement among the people of the importing countries.

From the standpoint of the importing countries' own
interests, the very existence of an agreement may be mostly
harmful.  If the agreement has the effect desired by the
exporting countries of giving them a larger physical flow of
industrial product imports in exchange for a somewhat
curtailed physical flow of primary product exports, the effect

on the importing countries is plainly to call for the transfer
to overseas suppliers of primary products of part of the real
income that citizens of importing countries would otherwise
have enjoyed.  As may be seen from experience with petroleum in
the last few years, such a transfer can be painful, and the
direct and indirect inflationary effects in the importing
countries are regrettable.  Furthermore, the likelihood that
the agreement will succeed temporarily and collapse after a
few years means a risk that people in the importing countries
will be induced to invest in the production of the commodities
involved--and to be ready with substantial flows of output just
in time to be bankrupted by a sharp postagreement drop in
prices.*  Hence, if refusing to be parties to agreements (or
even negotiations over agreements) will prevent an effective
agreement from being framed, industrial importing countries
have strong incentives to refuse.

The situation is different if governments of industrial
countries believe that, even without their participation, a
strong agreement can be set up by governments of overseas
exporting countries.  "If you can't lick 'em, join 'em!" says
a venerable dictum of practical politics.  If there is going
to be an agreement, there is plenty of room for it to be
better or worse from the standpoint of an importing country.
Industrial country governments will derive strong bargaining
power from the considerations mentioned above and can do a
good deal to mitigate the drawbacks of the agreement for their
citizens.  They can moderate the price to be agreed upon and
set up the structure of the agreement so that it is less likely
to produce a drastic price collapse after a sharp rise, and
thus to tempt enterprises inside the importing countries to
walk into traps.  Moreover, in this era of confrontations
where groups of exporting countries may try to enforce their
demands through embargoes, industrial importing countries that
participate in negotiating and operating commodity agreements

---

*Awareness of this aspect of the commodity agreement
problem is reflected in proposals of the US State Department
for "floor prices" on petroleum.  But to safeguard against
bankruptcy of the new producers within the importing country is
surely a very inadequate response.  The device of the "floor
price" tends to make permanent a rise in primary product
prices, which might otherwise be transitory, to subsidize at
the expense of producers what may be a very inefficient use
of resources, and to create a permanent disability for enterprises that use the material in question in competition with
enterprises in other industrial countries that will be able
to get the material cheaper.

may be taking out valuable insurance against disastrous
interruptions of supply.

It must be kept in mind, also, that industrial countries
do not approach international markets for primary products
purely in terms of national self-interest.  Public opinion in
the industrial importing countries gives a good deal of
credence to the claims of third-world governments that primary
product prices are and have long been "unfair" and that third-
world countries are entitled to much more than they have had in
the way of capital resources for development.  Furthermore, it
is a fact of political experience (visible especially in the
agricultural policy of almost all industrial countries) that
where citizens recognize a claim for giving a larger share of
income and wealth to some disadvantaged group, they are more
willing to make the transfer by the vehicle of a higher price
than by increasing income taxes and giving away the proceeds.

The claim that commodity agreements can benefit the
poorer countries of the world by making them richer and giving
them more resources for development, accordingly, is bound to
carry weight with the governments of the United States and of
other industrial countries.  This claim will make industrial-
country governments more inclined to want agreements to be
successful in maintaining higher relative prices for primary
products and more willing to enter upon negotiations with a
view to participating in the resulting agreements.  Furthermore,
looking at agreements as mechanisms for producing a fairer
distribution of income and wealth and generating capital for
development provides criteria for deciding what constitutes
improvement (from the standpoint of world public interest) in
an agreement under negotiation, and what changes should be
sought in a proposed agreement.

## Distributional and Development Effects within Developing Countries

To reach clarity on the problems of distribution of
income and wealth and capital resources for development, we
must apply much more discrimination than is customary in the
use of such terms as "country" and "producer."  It tends to
be taken for granted that if "Zambia" exports copper, "Burma"
exports rice, the "Dominican Republic" exports sugar, then
those countries as a whole will gain if prices rise for
copper, rice, and sugar.  If asked to explain, the casual
visitor in this domain of policy thinking will naturally
reply that "producers" in these countries stand to gain, that
producers of these key commodities are an important part of
the population, and that benefits to producers will spread to
other groups in the population.  Furthermore, he will tell us
that since "producing countries" for copper and sugar are "poor

countries" by comparison with the "consuming countries," a
rise in these prices will distribute income and wealth more
equally over the world and that the savings of "producers" of
copper in Zambia and of sugar in the Dominican Republic will
furnish development capital for those countries.

It should give us pause to reflect that, not many years
ago, the effect within the Dominican Republic of a rise in the
price of sugar would have been almost exclusively to enrich
further the person then heading the government, who had somehow
managed to become the owner of most of the sugar mills.  This
reflection illuminates a semantic trap.  When we use the word
"producers" in relation to sugar, we think of the people whose
lives go into planting and cutting the cane, fetching it to
the mill, processing it, and providing the management and the
equipment without which the operation would be at best
inefficient.  But when we say that "producers gain" when the
price of sugar rises, the content of the expression is quite
different:  It means that there are gains for the profit
takers along the line.  If the price rise is managed by
curtailing production (as it will be if engineered by a
commodity agreement), the effect will be to reduce employment
in the industry and to curtail the market of people who
provide the sugar industry with supplies.  Gains to others than
the profit takers depend on a "trickle-down process"--on the
extent to which additional profits are captured by taxes or
drawn upon to support otherwise unobtainable wage-rate
increases.

To trace the distributional or developmental effects of
a commodity agreement that raises the price of sugar or copper
or rice or palm oil, we must start with an awareness that the
primary beneficiaries are these profit takers.  This fact
alters the redistribution analysis.  To enrich poor-country
producers of sugar at the expense of consumers of sugar in
rich countries sounds like a Robin Hood gesture.  But although
the rank and file of sugar consumers in the industrial
countries are undoubtedly richer than the rank and file of
citizens in the overseas countries that export sugar, the
profit gains to sugar "producers" must accrue very largely to
elite groups in the overseas countries, who are far richer than
the rank and file sugar consumers.

The argument in favor of levying through higher price
upon the consumers in industrial countries in order to
generate development capital in primary producing countries
is not settled by the foregoing argument.  We could certainly
imagine that the profit takers might use their gains to save
more and pour capital into the industries crucial for development (as seems to have happened to a large extent when the
Industrial Revolution was in process in the countries that

today are industrialized). The mere fact that the profit takers
might also put part of their gains into luxury consumption is
not conclusive. Yet the case for relying on saving by these
profit takers as an engine of development is a weak one. On
the whole, the profit takers in developing countries are known
for their high marginal propensity to consume rather than save
(including heavy consumption of imports), for their tendency
to invest savings abroad rather than in their own countries,
and for their tendency to invest in their own industries
rather than in other lines of activity. Since, under the
conditions that go with a commodity agreement, their investment
in their own industry is apt to generate excess capacity, it
seems likely that the percentage of gains to these profit
takers that will go into developmentally urgent lines of
investment will be very small.

From both the distributional and the developmental standpoint, the only reasonably certain benefits from this process
of enriching the profit takers result from the taxes they pay.
Fortunately, profits of this type tend to arise from transactions of high visibility, and even in countries where income
taxation is very ineffective, a large proportion can often be
registered as taxable income of enterprises or persons. To
the extent that their taxes enable governments to abate
regressive taxes or abate inflation, there are presumably
benefits to the rank and file of the population. To the
extent that their taxes enhance the ability of their governments
to execute "public saving," they constitute a source of
development capital. But the fraction of additional profits
that will be constructively used in this way must be modest.

## THE ROLE OF EXPORT TAXES IN COMMODITY AGREEMENTS

Two important difficulties with commodity agreements have
been stated above: (1) their chronic tendency to generate
excess supply; (2) their tendency to redistribute income in
favor of profit takers, without any assurance that doing so
will generate development capital. The crucial argument of
this chapter is that both these difficulties can be abated by
a single policy measure--the imposition of an export tax on
the commodity. Hence, the likelihood that a commodity agreement will work out constructively as an instrument of development in the overseas countries that export primary products
can be greatly enhanced by making such a tax a central feature
of the agreement.

## The Effect of Export Taxes

Since this inference is not part of the "conventional wisdom" of those interested in commodity agreements, export taxes will be justified in some detail, using a traditional microeconomic "tax incidence model," set forth graphically in Figure 3.1. We suppose that demand for the commodity (pounds per annum exported, as a function of price per pound) is represented by curve $D_aE$ and that supply (pounds per annum made available for export, as a function of price per pound) is represented by curve $S_tES_a$. In the absence of market management, the market will tend toward the equilibrium price $OP_e$, with supply and demand for exports equal at the quantum $OQ_e$. Export proceeds will be measured by the rectangle $OP_eEQ_e$.

We now suppose that a commodity agreement is negotiated, setting the price at $OP_a$. At this price, the buyers for the industrial countries that import the product will take a quantum $OQ_t$, slightly smaller than $OQ_e$. Export proceeds will be measured by the rectangle $OP_aD_aQ_t$. (The figure is drawn to match the assumptions on which the argument for a price-boosting agreement is regularly based, so that the export proceeds are substantially higher at the higher price.)[*] If the price $OP_a$ is made available to all comers by a buffer-stock agency acting as residual buyer, the supply curve tells us that quantity $OQ_a$ will be made available for export, and the buffer stock must acquire $Q_tQ_a$ pounds, corresponding to the excess supply indicated by the length of the line $D_aS_a$, which lies between the points at which the agreed price is found on the

---

[*]Three caveats about Figure 3.1: (1) it does not purport to locate the maximum-profit price for the industry in question but merely supposes that an agreed price has been set. As drawn, it implies that the maximum-profit price for the industry (if operated as a monopoly) would lie considerably higher than $OP_a$. (2) While the supply curve carries implications about the industry's cost structure, no precise measurement of cost (or correspondingly of profit) is specified. Information about fixed costs and cost externalities would be needed for such precision. (3) The chart is static. We may suppose that both the demand curve and the supply curve will tend to be shifted to the right from year to year by growth in both exporting and consuming countries. But speculative behavior and other specifically dynamic elements of the situation are ignored. All this is standard practice in a preliminary general exposition of the sort appropriate to this chapter. No specific advice about a concrete commodity-agreement situation could be offered without going into the considerations that are simplified out of this figure.

FIGURE 3.1

Tax Incidence Model

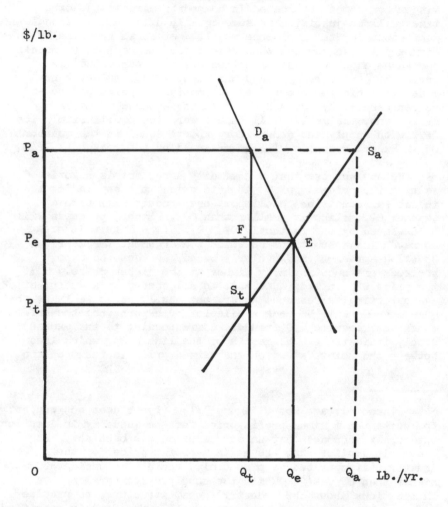

demand curve and supply curve respectively. Total gross
receipts of the producing enterprises (if we simplify by
assuming demand within the exporting countries is negligible)
will be measured by rectangle $OP_aS_aQ_a$, out of which $OP_aD_aQ_t$
will be covered by export proceeds, and $Q_tD_aS_aQ_a$ must be
covered by buffer-stock financing. If the situation
represented by the chart corresponds to a normal year (and not
to a transitory situation where the supply curve has been
pushed to the right of its usual position by a bumper crop,
or the demand curve pulled to the left by an industrial

depression), the position of the buffer-stock agency is untenable: The stock will pile up till it exhausts either its storage capacity or its ability to finance.

Now suppose the agreement includes a provision that all exporting countries will levy a uniform tax (measured like the price in cents per pound) on all exports of the commodity. If this tax is set at the level $P_aP_t = D_aS_t$ and the price is left to market determination, price will turn out to be just what we previously supposed to be the agreed level, namely $OP_a$. At this price, the buyers for export will take $OQ_t$ pounds. As for the suppliers, the price they realize (net of tax) being $OP_t$, the supply curve tells us they will put $OQ_t$ pounds on the market, so that the amount supplied will match the amount demanded and excess supply will be eliminated. It will be observed that the rate of tax that has this effect is greater than the excess of the agreed price $OP_a$ over the original equilibrium price $OP_e$; we get this result because the supply curve incorporates the assumption that the supply function, though relatively inelastic, is not completely inelastic with respect to price.[*]

The upshot is that there exists some rate of tax that will bring the price to $OP_a$ without generating excess supply. If a buffer stock agency is established, it will have to make purchases to hold the price at $OP_a$ in years when transitory factors make supply unusually strong or demand unusually weak, but it will be able to make corresponding sales without pulling price below $OP_a$ in years when transitory factors work in the other direction. Hence, the tax can make it possible to work a buffer stock scheme without danger of overflowing the storage facilities or exhausting a moderate provision for financing. In addition, of course, pooling of part of the tax proceeds can provide a source for buffer stock financing.

If the tax is smaller than we have just supposed, it will not fully eliminate the excess supply. But to abate the problem of excess supply without eliminating it would still make the agreement much more viable. If we imagine a buffer stock arrangement that has a breakdown point (either when physical stock reaches a certain cumulative limit or when

---

[*]It will be noted that along with the simplifications mentioned in the preceding footnote, no distinction is made between short-run and long-run elasticity of supply. If we read the supply curve as corresponding to short-run supply elasticity, we must suppose that the long-run supply curve will be more nearly horizontal and that maintaining the tax at $P_aP_t$ cents per pound over several years will pull output below $OQ_t$ and push price above $OP_a$.

funds expended, net of recoveries from sales in favorable years, reach a certain amount), the presence of a tax will raise the expectation value for the period, which will elapse before the breakdown occurs.

(It should be mentioned that, besides buffer stocks, market management schemes sometimes provide for permanent removal of "surplus" from the market. Thus coffee is sometimes burned; cocoa is sometimes turned into margarine; wheat is sometimes given to people who are supposed to be so poor that they would never use wheat if their only choice was to buy it.

(In the absence of a tax, a surplus-disposal scheme would have to be financed with resources from outside the market. But if a tax is levied, smaller than would be required to eliminate excess supply but still substantial, it becomes possible to finance surplus disposal within the limits of the agreement system. For example, suppose the tax has been set at $P_aP_e$ /equal to the excess of agreement price over the initial equilibrium price/. Demand will then still be for the quantum $OQ_t$, and there will be excess supply of $FE=Q_tQ_e$ pounds. To buy up the excess supply will cost a sum measured by rectangle $Q_tFEQ_e$, while tax proceeds will be measured by rectangle $P_eP_aD_aF$. At the cost of diverting the tax proceeds from use as a source of development capital, it becomes feasible to finance the surplus disposal without going outside the resources of the agreement program itself.

(This is scarcely a program the economist would recommend: to use resources that could be put into development merely to produce additional pounds of resources that will be disposed of rather than used entails a social loss. But the argument confirms the generalization of the text that commodity agreement programs focused on a tax are more viable than otherwise similar programs that lack the tax element.)

The model of Figure 3.1 can be used also to illuminate the problem of income redistribution and provision of capital for development. Suppose that in the absence of a tax the agreement price is established at $OP_a$ and that production for export is limited by the device of setting national quotas that add up to $OQ_t$, and inducing each national government to suballocate its quota among its producing enterprises. Under these conditions, if the quotas are so determined that production is no less efficient than it would be under an unmanaged market in a year when the equilibrium price was $OP_t$ because of a temporary weakness of demand, the agreement will enhance the profits of producing enterprises at least by the amount measured by rectangle $P_eP_aD_aF$. This amount measures a transfer from rank and file consumers in the industrial countries that import the commodity to the profit takers in the developing countries (presumably an elite group).[*] Of this amount transferred, some fraction will be captured by the governments of the exporting countries through their taxes on profits of enterprises and personal incomes.

If we consider the tax alternative, the levy of a tax rate equal to $P_aP_t$ will capture a share of what would otherwise be profits of producing enterprises, which is measured by the area of rectangle $P_tP_aD_aS_t$. All of this, instead of only a fraction of it, goes to the fiscal authority. Part of the proceeds may be used for personal income redistribution by reduction of regressive taxes. Part is available for capital financing of the development process. In view of the inefficiency for both redistribution and development of presenting the whole amount to the profit-taking elite and relying on "trickle-down" processes to spread the benefit, one must put a very low value on the efficiency of governments in developing countries as engines of development in order to avoid the conclusion that, on the redistribution and development side, a commodity agreement focused on export taxes is far superior to mere price boosting.

The upshot of this argument for the policy of industrial country governments that are under pressure to participate in commodity agreements is that the best answer is likely to be "Yes, if...." If the exporting countries in the third world are seriously interested in using commodity agreement mechanisms to relieve poverty and to generate development capital, importing countries in the industrial world may well find on due consideration that they feel an obligation to impose sacrifices on their citizens by accepting higher prices. On the other hand, if the governments in the third world reject the tax element of the program and are interested merely in price boosting, the proposition becomes one of burdening the rank and file in the industrial countries in order to enrich the elite in the third world--a much less meritorious program.

----

[*] Social evaluation of the transfer will plainly depend partly on what kind of people the beneficiaries are. Cocoa growers in Nigeria, though a favored group within the Nigerian income distribution, are less likely to be above the income level of consumers of their product than are coffee planters in Brazil. There may be relevant differences also in the degree to which the beneficiaries will use their gains in ways that enhance general development.

### Back-up Programs for Export Taxes

While in principle the developing countries that export primary products could apply market management through export taxes without any cooperation from industrial countries, the system will work enormously better if they enjoy such cooperation. Thus, in a tax-focused commodity agreement the uniform export taxes of the exporting countries should be backed up by import taxes of the same amount per pound, with an arrangement under which previously paid export taxes could be credited against import taxes otherwise due. (It should be observed that there are already substantial import taxes in industrial countries on some of the commodities in question-- notably the "breakfast-table taxes" on tropical beverage products that are common in Europe, the incidence of which is presumably largely on overseas producers. The proposal being made here is that such taxes should be absorbed into the proposed uniform import taxes and that the import taxes should be designed so as not to be collected unless the corresponding export tax has been avoided.)

The advantages of such a back-up system would be substantial. In the first place, the administrative efficiency of import tax collection in industrial countries is high; and being assured that if they evaded the export tax at home they would subject their products to import tax on arrival in Europe, the United States, or Japan, the producing enterprises could readily be persuaded to pay export tax. In the second place, the back-up arrangement would do away with the temptation to smuggle out export goods from one developing country to a neighboring country where export taxes are less onerous or easier to evade. In the third place, the uniform back-up system would reduce incentives for governments of exporting countries to refuse to enter the agreement, since by doing so they would hand over revenues to the governments of importing countries. In the fourth place, the uniform back-up system would eliminate incentives to seek competitive advantage for a country's producing enterprises by undercutting a competing country's export tax rate.

Another respect in which a back-up by industrial importing countries could improve the system is by setting up standards for the handling of export tax proceeds. A multilateral body may be envisaged with representation of exporting and importing countries, with responsibility to certify export tax arrangements as warranting the credit against import taxes. It is plain that certain uses of tax proceeds should be taboo--particularly nullification of export taxes by payments to producing enterprises that are

proportioned either to their output or to their capacity.[*]  It
might be useful to stipulate that export tax proceeds should go
into development funds of some kind, in which case the
certifying body would have to scrutinize the expenditures
charged to such funds.  To ban all redistributive uses of such
funds (except as they were incidental to development programs)
would not be acceptable, but neither would such uses as
subsidies to the housing or education of elite groups that are
abundantly able to take care of their own.

Supervision of development programs by "donors" from the
industrial countries has such a bad record that it would be hard
to justify trying to graft it onto commodity agreements.  On
the other hand, a degree of supervision under multilateral
arrangements such as the U.N. Development Program does seem
to be acceptable and to some degree useful.  As compared to the
alternative of asking the industrial countries simply to
collaborate in price-boosting arrangements and ask no questions
about disposal of the proceeds, the use-certification aspect of
a back-up tax system would seem an enormous improvement.

## Make-up of Working Parties to Frame Agreements

One reason for the bad record of commodity agreements down
to the present time is that it has been customary to entrust
their design to "working parties" made up of people close to
the trade.  It is quite obvious that to go to the other extreme
and bar people close to the trade from membership in working
parties could be disastrous.  It is essential to take account
of the technicalities of the trade and of the way in which
producing and merchandising enterprises are likely to react to
changes in their incentive structure.  But to include few or
no participants from other backgrounds is to introduce a very
unfortunate bias.  The people now regarded as eligible have a

---

[*]Difficult problems are sure to arise in relation to state
trading.  It is clear that state trading operations such as
those of the cocoa boards in West Africa are in fact setting a
gap between their export prices and a lower price that they pay
to producing enterprises, and that such a trading gap (insofar
as it exceeds the operating costs of the cocoa board's transport
and shipping operations) has all the essential characteristics
of an export tax.  It would not make sense in terms of world
public policy to try to ban state trading of this type or to
set up obstacles to operation of mines and the like as state
enterprises.  On the other hand, criteria to determine
whether a state enterprise is being conducted in a way that is
strictly equivalent to the application of an export tax to a
privately owned industry will not be easy to agree upon.

natural tendency to identify with the profit takers in
producing enterprises and have little awareness of other viewpoints.  To a minor degree, this bias is mitigated by adding
commodity experts from importing countries.  But we should
not exaggerate the gains from this kind of "consumer
representation":  These people have a natural affinity for the
point of view of traders in primary commodities, and there are
so many ties of common interest between traders and "producers"
that it is altogether too easy for their representatives to
agree on programs that impose serious handicaps on people of
different sorts.

     One of the advantages of making taxation a central feature
of commodity agreements, and of a back-up tax scheme that
requires "certification" of the patterns for using tax proceeds,
is that to do so requires broadening the working parties to
include experts in taxation and in development finance.  The
presence of negotiators of these fresh types can go a long
way to ensure that this branch of economic planning will
genuinely consider how to serve real public interests, rather
than degenerate into a conspiracy to forward the interests of
small and unrepresentative elite groups.  The willingness of
governments in industrial countries to involve themselves in
the negotiation and operation of commodity agreements should
be very much affected by the willingness of governments in
developing countries to broaden the working parties in this way.

## Limiting the Domain of Commodity Agreements

     With minor exceptions, as indicated at the outset, this
chapter has been framed on the assumption that the primary
commodities for which commodity agreements will be considered
are of such a character that demand for exports from developing
countries will be inelastic with respect to price--not only
in the short run but also in the long run.  But this assumption
can be a trap if in fact demand is considerably more elastic
than supposed.  Allowance must be made also for the fact that
commodities can become obsolete.  Few people carry the fact
in mind, but a few generations ago dye stuffs such as indigo
and cochineal were major primary commodities.  Where are they
today?  What has become of the market for natural nitrates?
Where are the traditional markets for the original Brazilian
wild rubber, and for the original Asian varieties of coffee?
Such obsolescence is partly the unavoidable consequence of
the basic evolution of technology and tastes, but it reflects
also the "induced" changes in technique that result from
overaggressive price policies.  Would natural rubber from
Southeast Asia still be widely used had the governments and
business interests involved not seen the necessity of price
moderation ever since World War II?

An element of natural monopoly can be attributed to commodities based in tropical agriculture. Coffee, tea, cacao, bananas, pineapples, and the like have relatively secure positions (though even for coffee, substitution of the freeze-dried product may impair the position of the better grades). But all the major grains (including rice), the major natural fibers (except jute and sisal, for which synthetics offer direct competition), sugar, the major metals (except perhaps for tin), wood and paper pulp, the basic chemical raw materials--almost all primary products are produced on a large scale within the advanced industrial countries, which in many primary products are export competitive. Depletion of reserves tends to raise production costs, especially of minerals, in the advanced industrial countries compared with the developing countries, and makes it seem rather likely that apart from market management the overseas countries dependent on primary product exports will find their terms of trade improving over the next few decades. But this is not the same thing as having markets where demand is price-inelastic. Even though the demand for use of a given product may be inelastic, the demand for import can be elastic. If for example two-thirds of the supply of a mineral for use in industrial countries comes from within the industrial countries themselves, while the price elasticity of industrial-country demand for use is (minus) 0.5, the elasticity of demand for import will be three times as great-- (minus) 1.5-- if the elasticity of supply within the industrial countries is negligible, higher if the elasticity of supply is substantial.

In such a situation, it may be very risky for the governments of developing countries to engage in price-boosting commodity agreements. Insofar as these agreements stay within the bounds of the "natural" shift of terms of trade in favor of primary commodities, they may be in a position to claim credit for changes that would have happened without them. But to venture outside these bounds (even if an agreement's price policy is backed by tax instruments) may be to build up a position that will lead to a collapse within a few years. As a gauge of orders of magnitude, it is likely that market management may well be able to consolidate price boosts for many primary products of the order of, say, a fifth or a third as against the price ratios to industrial products we have experienced in the last few years--but that attempts to double the relative prices of primary products will backfire well before the end of the 1970s.

The risk of attempts at price raising through commodity agreements can be reduced if the agreements are tax-focused. If the producing enterprises in the developing countries are not misled by passing through to them a large share of the contemplated price increases, they will not develop cost

structures that make them extremely vulnerable.  If the price
increases prove unsustainable, it is feasible to absorb
unavoidable cuts by abating the tax rates rather than by
pulling the prices realized by producing enterprises down into
a range their cost structures cannot stand.  This type of
price/tax strategy would transform the risk of commodity
markets into a risk of finding the bulge in export-tax revenue
unsustainable.  This risk could be serious enough in itself.
But the risk can be abated further if overseas countries that
are heavily in debt to the industrial countries use part of
their perhaps unsustainable export-tax revenue to store up a
reserve of borrowing power by reducing these debts.  On the
other hand, this might be a poor use of funds in a world where
inflation tends in any case to erode the real value of
outstanding debts.

The possibility that it may be good policy to score major
short-term gains at the cost of permanent impairment of markets
cannot be disregarded.  If the overseas producers of copper
(for example) are in a position where with ample funds they
could diversify their economies and reach 1980 with a wide
range of industries in which their costs are competitive with,
say, the Japanese, it may be sound policy (if feasible) to
run a high-priced copper market for the rest of the 1970s even
at the risk that copper may have a weak market for the 1980s.
On the other hand, this kind of policy can pay off only if
the management of the copper market focuses on export taxes (or
equivalent management of state enterprises) that will enable
the governments involved to draw off a large fraction of the
copper proceeds for investment in other industries.  A high-
price policy that passes through the great bulk of the
additional export proceeds to the producing enterprises is all
too likely to fritter away the opportunity for industrial
diversification, without realizing the potential long-term
gains of a bold price policy.


THE POSSIBILITY OF MONETIZATION

In the present state of the world, those who hope to help
the developing countries by restructuring the markets for
primary commodities would do well to think of putting their
main efforts into a program radically different from the
cultivation of commodity agreements--namely, into tying stocks
of primary commodities into the world monetary system, as a
key feature of the much needed general monetary reform that
seems to be in the making.  In view of the character of this
volume, this is not the place to go into these monetary

possibilities at length.  But a sketch should be offered.[*]

    Part of the basic difficulties of the last few years in
international monetary policy has been the disappearance of
the landmarks that have traditionally been the guides to
"discipline" in the management of national monetary systems
and the adjustment of the national balance of payments.
Through most of the postwar period, the world has been
effectively on a dollar standard, and the United States has
displayed enough internal "monetary discipline" so that keeping
in line with the U.S. dollar has been a not too disreputable
"second choice" standard for other countries.  But the U.S.
inflation that grew out of the war in Vietnam, combined with
failure to taper off the process by which the U.S. balance-of-
payments deficit was the great generator of monetary reserves
for almost all other countries, made the dollar standard
untenable, and the events of the early 1970s brought it to an
end.  Experience since the Smithsonian agreements which made
it official that the U.S. dollar was only another of the world's
numerous "floating currencies" has been discouraging.  Even
apart from the extra fillip given to the process by the
financial disturbances surrounding OPEC management of the
market for petroleum, it is plain that the interplay of
different countries in the new process for generating
additional monetary reserves results in highly excessive
growth of aggregate reserves, giving a marked inflationary
bias to the whole international monetary system.  The hopes of
many monetary economists, including the present author, that
the internalized financial "discipline" of the directors of
national monetary systems would give stability to an international monetary system that lack any "standard" have been
dashed.  At the same time, experience has made it seem less
and less likely that there is any hope of reestablishing
monetary discipline by a "return to gold."  Gold itself has
moved further and further away from its one-time status as
the queen of commodities; it would not be unfair to say that
in the process of making money more and more abstract and
remote from the world of commodities, gold itself has become
an abstraction, moved more by flights of fancy than by
economic realities.

---

[*] A considerably more detailed account of the commodity
reserve possibility for monetary reform is presented in
A. G. Hart, "The Case as of 1976 for International Commodity
Reserve Currency," Weltwirtliches Archiv, March 1976.
Another quite distinct view of the commodity reserve
possibility (stressing management of commodities one at a
time, in a way with which this writer would disagree) is
being presented in a series of papers by Nicholas Kaldor.

The key idea of the commodity reserve proposal is to
reestablish an authentic monetary standard, tied into the real
economy by a "monetary commodity"--and to adopt as monetary
commodity a "basket" containing stated physical quanta of each
of a list of standardized commodities.  This standard would be
administered by an international organization, which would be
a branch of the International Monetary Fund (IMF), and the
value of the IMF's monetary unit would be tied to the value of
the composite commodity basket.  When the system was in full
operation, the IMF would be obligated (as national monetary
authorities used to be obligated in gold standard days) to
stand ready to buy or sell the monetary commodity at pre-
announced prices.  Since the commodity basket would have to be
a collection of wholesale lots, we may think of it as having
a large value--say a million special drawing rights (SDR) units
when at par.  Then the IMF's obligation might be stated in
terms of readiness to buy unlimited numbers of baskets if
offered at $950,000 and of readiness to sell unlimited
numbers of basket at $1,050,000.*  The effect would be to give

---

*Under a gold standard, it was left to private
initiative to determine when transactions in the monetary
commodity would take place.  Under a commodity reserve standard,
transactions would probably have to be initiated by the IMF's
commodity reserve agency.  Several dozen commodities would be
on the composite list, and the place of delivery for each
commodity (an essential part of the specifications of the
basket, along with tonnage and grade of commodity) would, for
reasons of cost, have to be located somewhere along its
ordinary channels of trade, so that there would be several
dozen locations in the world where part of the transactions
entailed by purchase or sale of a basket must take place.  It
would be too costly for each of a number of private
organizations to maintain a worldwide network for getting
price information, accumulating the ingredients of a basket
for sale to the IMF, or handling the sale of all the
ingredients in a basket bought by the IMF.  We must suppose
that the IMF itself would have such a network, with
responsible agents who know how to deal with rice in Rangoon,
wheat in Liverpool or Rotterdam, coffee in New York, and so
forth.  At times when market prices of commodities were
running so low that the composite value of the quanta making
up a basket was not far above 950,000 SDR units, agents would
be called upon for hourly reports as to the prices at which
their commodities could be bought (and the quantities
apparently available at the price offered to each agent).  Any
hour when the computer determined that the weighted sum of the
latest batch of price quotations added up to 950,000 SDR units
or less, instructions to buy would be flashed to all the agents

real content to the SDR unit and to stabilize a price index of
the commodities in the basket within a band of 5 percent on
either side of par value.  This index would be of such wide
interest to the business firms, banks, and governments of the
world that it would be widely publicized; at critical times,
frequent quotations would doubtless be flashed on the New York
Stock Exchange ticker and announced on news programs.  Hence
the linkage between the world's basic monetary unit and the
real world as represented by primary commodities would be
constantly in people's awareness.  Each national currency
would be seen against this background.  It would still be
open to a national monetary authority to devalue its currency
relative to SDRs, or to let its currency float.  But it would
be very plain that a devaluation or a "downward float" would
represent a diminution of the real content of the currency
unit, and general awareness of this fact would create the
public opinion context for a restoration of "monetary
discipline."

     What commodities would enter the basket would be a matter
of negotiation among governments and monetary authorities.
Plainly, it is not feasible to hold physical stocks of
cucumbers or oysters, and perishables would have to be
excluded from the basket on practical grounds, though such
items as frozen orange juice could be eligible.  Goods that
are physically durable in storage but are unstandardized or
subject to "fashion obsolescence" would be ineligible:  women's
handbags, for example.  There would be little or no scope for
including any items not quoted on organized markets, with a
grade-standardizing system such that an experienced dealer can

---

simultaneously, and each would buy the designated number of
wholesale lots.  Thus, the IMF would have bought whatever
number of baskets the computer determined the market could
yield according to the price quotations.  Since buy orders
would have to be "at the market," which can always diverge a
little from the last quotation--particularly when the relevant
market is closed over night--the price actually paid would
approximate 950,000 units rather than hit it exactly.  A
symmetrical process would operate when prices of the
ingredients of the basket were so high that its market value
was in the neighborhood of 1,050,000 SDR units.
     Payments for purchases and receipts from sales would be
in the currencies customary in the trade for each commodity.
Agents would presumably have working balances of local funds.
Emission of new SDRs when commodity baskets were bought would
buy local currency to replenish the agents' working balances
when purchases were being made.  When commodity baskets were
being sold, the agents would use excess balances to buy SDRs
from local central banks, and the SDRs thus coming into IMF
ownership would be retired.

make a buying or selling commitment on the floor of an exchange
or over the telephone and know with precision what is meant by
a briefly stated price quotation on a specified grade.  The
list of eligible commodities clearly includes the major grains
and fibers, the major nonferrous metals, the major tropical
beverage items (coffee, tea, cocoa), and a few standardized
chemicals.  Extending the list by finding other commodities
with suitably organized markets (or perhaps by organizing
markets that have been uncoordinated and standardizing price
quotations that have been incoherent) would improve the
proposed system, insofar as it did not add too much to costs,
by putting more meaning into the price index.

(The special case of petroleum deserves mention.  On the
whole, petroleum presents a set of rather well-standardized
commodities, on which a refiner or the owner of a tanker load
can give well-understood specifications and price quotations
to a potential buyer.  But, for most petroleum products, there
would be doubt as to whether they offer a two-way market on
which an agent could either buy or sell according to
instructions from the IMF.  Furthermore, the market is subject
to manipulation by OPEC actions--and to some extent still,
perhaps, by giant private companies.  If petroleum entered the
commodity reserve basket with a weight corresponding to its
importance in trade, it is easy to imagine situations in
which, say, a manipulated 50 percent rise in petroleum prices
could call for a drop of 10 to 20 percent in the average of
all other reserve commodities.  Petroleum should thus either
be kept outside the basket or brought in with a much diminished
weight.)

Before a commodity reserve plan could go into full
operation, there would have to be an initial period (3 to 10
years, perhaps, according to how one views the impact of
reserve accumulation) during which reserve stocks were built
up.  For, obviously, the announcement of a standing offer to
sell baskets at (say) 1,050,000 SDR units could not be
meaningful unless the agency had enough baskets to sell to be
insured against a rapid sell-out.  During these early years,
the IMF's commodity reserve agency would be a buyer but not
a seller.  Presumably, the underlying international agreement
would have to include a target for the reserve and some
general directives as to the pace of accumulation.  For
example, it might be agreed to open full operations only when
the reserve represented 25 percent of the average tonnage of
recent years in international trade for each commodity, and
the agency might be directed to buy each year a quantity
representing 6 percent of the previous year's tonnage.  But
the pace of accumulation could not be precisely predetermined:
One can readily imagine contingencies such as major crop
failures that would lead the governments of the countries most

affected to request IMF to slow down accumulation or even to
release part of the stock of this commodity so far built up.
The rate which preexisting governmental or commercial stocks
should be absorbed into the commodity reserve would have to
be worked out, and the time of year at which purchases were
concentrated would be important for agricultural commodities.
To set a predetermined price for the basket as a whole during
the buildup period is risky:  Unless the price is set so high
that commercial use of high-priced commodities will fall short
of release for export over the whole period of accumulation,
the desired quantum may simply not be offered to the reserve
agency.  To set predetermined prices at the outset for each
specific commodity would be not merely risky but fatal:  The
information available is insufficient, and the upshot would
be massive accumulation of some commodities and a failure to
find others for sale at the predetermined prices.  Considerable
discretion for the reserve agency as buyer during the buildup
period would seem to be an unavoidable part of the plan;
though of course there is scope for oversight by responsible
bodies of policy makers, and for directives that bar merely
arbitrary purchase policies.

During the accumulation period, adding the reserve
agency's demand for accumulation to the normal demand for
current consumption would clearly tend to strengthen primary
commodity markets considerably and thus improve the terms of
trade of countries exporting these commodities.  As compared
with the price increases likely under commodity agreements,
it should be remembered that those resulting from accumulation
of an international commodity reserve would be available
without the systematic restriction of output that is inherent
in commodity agreement planning.  Hence, the favorable prices
offered by the formative stage of a commodity reserve would
be available on a larger physical quantum than those under a
scheme of generalized commodity agreements, and export
proceeds could be larger even though prices were not so high.

When a commodity reserve scheme was in full operation, its
effect would be to provide primary product exporters as a body
with a guaranteed market in the sense that they could sell all
they wanted without pulling the price of the commodity-reserve
basket below its buying-price minimum set in SDRs.

(The precise composition of the basket would have to be
determined only at the end of the buildup period--taking
account of the stocks then in hand and presumably with some
buying and selling of individual commodities so as to permit
baskets to be defined as collections of wholesale lots of
commodities.  The size and the exact price of the basket would
also have to be given precision at this stage and could not
be fully predetermined.)

Since the price effects of accumulating the reserve would not have worn off at the time when the plan went into full effect, the initial price would presumably involve a degree of "overvaluation" of the commodity basket, in the sense that it would probably be so high relative to industrial prices and wage rates as to be slanted toward some further accumulation. The result would be some inflationary pressure on industrial economies, which would tend to raise their prices and wage rates relative to primary commodities, at least to the point where reserve accumulation would no longer outpace the growth of trade.

Stabilization of a price index, of course, is not equivalent to the stabilization of each individual price that enters the index. Grain prices could fall relative to the rest of the index, for example, on condition that some other prices (perhaps those of metals) were rising. But the commodity standard would block the process by which industrial depressions have sometimes led to a simultaneous downswing of the whole array of primary product prices. Within the family of primary-commodity-exporting countries, it would be possible to set up a mutual insurance scheme against shortfalls in export proceeds, without having to face the hazard of having all the prices that determine export proceeds low at the same time. For the developing world as a whole, it would be prudent to set in motion plans for general expansion of primary product output--relying on the commodity-reserve system to ensure that unless some commodity's expansion got seriously out of line, the required expansion of primary product markets would take place.

In terms of general economic strategy, the commodity-reserve plan has notable advantages for primary product exporters over attempts to negotiate an improvement of primary product prices and backstop the results with commodity agreements. Even if the agreements are focused upon export taxes in order to cure their normal fragility, they entail policies that brake the expansion of lines of output for which developing countries have great opportunities.* The commodity

---

*The problem of expanding primary production and industrialization is often presented as if developing countries must do one or the other but not both. But most of the success stories of industrialization in the last generation are of countries that have simultaneously industrialized and expanded their exports of primary products. Among them are Canada, Finland, Denmark, and the Netherlands.

It will be noted that the argument in this chapter for focusing commodity agreements upon taxes hinges largely on the incompatibility of high-price policies for specific

reserve plan does risk a relative decline of primary product
prices compared with industrial product prices in a period
beginning, say, five years after the initiation of the scheme.
But attempts to restructure markets through much wider use of
commodity agreements are also likely to yield short-term gains
followed by long-term losses.  And incentives for the
industrial countries to collaborate are much stronger for a
plan that promises to combine a foundation for monetary
stability with a plentiful supply of raw materials than for a
plan that rests on raising prices by inducing a scarcity of
raw materials.  Since major changes in the world market
structure can scarcely be avoided, all parties involved should
seriously consider the feasibility of the policy alternative
of monetizing primary commodities under a commodity reserve
system.

---

commodities with encouragement of the expansion of capacity
in the industries producing those commodities.  If the market
permits expansion of primary production, gains for profit
takers in primary production (who are much more readily
induced to invest in their own industries than in other
activities) become much more harmonious with general
development policy.

# 4

## POLLUTION TAXES
Richard E. Slitor

This chapter examines pollution taxes, or more precisely, the potential for using national revenue structures to further the objectives of controlling pollution and improving the quality of the human environment. The discussion does not attempt to reach hard and fast conclusions or delineate specific recommended directions of policy. Rather, it is designed to block out major areas for consideration in a broad, probing assessment of the state of the fiscal art as it is developing in relation to the pollution and environmental problems of nations and the world community.

Specifically, it discusses first in general terms the objectives and techniques of taxation to combat pollution, such as positive incentives for investment or other outlays to prevent or control pollution; environmental regulatory excise taxes designed to internalize the social costs of pollution so that environmental damages will be reflected in the market pricing and costing mechanisms, and incentives thus developed to reduce or eliminate the deleterious impact on the environment; tax measures to induce or finance private or public research and development in the environmental field; identification and correction of biases in existing traditional tax provisions that contribute to pollution problems or are inimical to conservation objectives; and problems and approaches in the fiscal field relating to international aspects of the pollution problem, including the coordination of different national and regional tax policies to improve the environment.

On the basis of this general review of pollution tax objectives, techniques, and rationale, the analysis proceeds to outline specific areas of application of fiscal devices to cope with a broad range of environmental problems, including

reduction or elimination of pollution of the ambient air, the
global atmosphere; companion or related measures to deal with
pollution of the earth's water supplies, including streams,
rivers, lakes, estuaries, and the seas; encouragement of more
appropriate and economic methods of solid waste disposal, with
particular emphasis on recycling of waste materials through
reuse or conversion into fuel, energy, building materials, or
other economically valuable end-products; stimulation of efforts
by government and private enterprise to develop more adequate
sources of "clean" energy, or to ameliorate the antienvironmental
impact of the generation and use of increasingly massive
amounts of heat and energy in the process of economic growth;
control of thermal pollution; measures to counter the
increasingly recognized problem of noise pollution; improved
patterns of land utilization and population distribution;
preservation of the world's "wetlands" and estuarial resources,
so vital to ecological chains important to marine life and
world food supplies; preservation of the national and international heritage of historic and aesthetically valuable
structures; and identification and control of forces operating
to produce the so-called doomsday effects of environmental
deterioration of concern to the world community.

International aspects of environmental problems and
fiscal measures to deal with them will receive specific
attention.  Just as externalities--effects and costs that do
not play a role in the self-regulating mechanisms of the
private enterprise economy--figure largely in the analysis of
pollution problems of national economies, so comparable
"externalities" of concern to the community of nations may be
overlooked or treated as imponderables in the more parochial
aspects of national policy.  The chapter will explore this
area and the range of possibilities for cooperation,
coordination, and international effort in harnessing the
world's revenue structures to the tasks of achieving a
better global environment.

Specific matters calling for attention in examining the
international aspects are dangers of national tax or other
policies that tend merely to "export" pollution; problems of
the competitive balance among national producers subject to
varying environmental control standards and to different
degrees of pollution-control taxation designed to "internalize"
social costs and pay for "clean-up" operations; and fiscal
measures related to monitoring the world, achieving cooperation
in the preservation and enhancement of ocean resources,
protecting and developing national parks and the world
heritage of buildings and areas of unique cultural and
historic value, and preserving endangered forms of life and
genetic pools.

Apart from the forces of public opinion and the autonomous development by industry of methods of making profit from use or sale of byproducts recovered by pollution control, two major approaches of public policy, at the local, national, and international level, are available:  direct regulatory control of polluting activities or emissions; and government grants, subsidies, tax incentives, tax penalties, and tax-revenue supported research to deal with particular or general environmental hazards.

Direct regulation for environmental quality operates in a new, uncertain, and technologically dynamic area.  Regulatory problems are in part technical, and in part economic and informational since costs and benefits of pollution and pollution abatement must be measured and balanced against each other for varying levels of control and, if possible, incrementally.  They are also in part political, since the imposition of wrenching and costly readjustments is involved in dealing even in a preliminary way with long-neglected environmental requirements.

Regulation does not foreclose the need or opportunity for fiscal incentive measures.  Contrary to the opinion of many, regulation and fiscal incentives may coexist in complementary fashion:  the tax incentives (1) aiding in the creation of profit incentives for control and the development or perfection of control technology, particularly in the initial transitional phases of control efforts, (2) making provision for persistent monetary motivation for industry to improve beyond the minimum control standards, (3) buttressing the enforcement of pollution control standards, and (4) providing both explicit recognition of the social costs of pollution in the production cost function, and at least transitional revenues to pay for the costs of clean-up and government-sponsored research and development.

The chapter will examine these considerations more fully and in specific policy situations, with particular attention to the potential implications for international as well as national policies.

OBJECTIVES AND TYPES OF POLLUTION TAXES

The breadth, complexity, and changing perception of environmental problems and goals call for a mixed strategy of response.  A first objective is, of course, reliable identification of ultimate environmental problems and needs. Much of this has already been accomplished, and the work is proceeding, though not without controversy and error.  The next primary requirement is the best attainable knowledge of technological and economic alternatives in light of the short,

intermediate, and long-term goals of environmental policy
and ecological balance.  The basic objective then becomes one
of resolving the conflicts between demands for the production
of goods and services and the social costs of depletion,
pollution, and environmental strain or deterioration they
generate.

To accomplish the latter objective, which is the proximate
motivation of pollution taxation policy, policy makers operating
within the framework of an at least partially free enterprise
system will look to the employment of the market mechanism,
with whatever additions and modifications are appropriate and
workable to help make the market structure of costs, needs,
and profits take into account the "externalities" of
environmental costs and benefits.

Taxes, including environmental excises and charges as
well as various other positive and negative incentives relating
to investment, process modification, research, and other
environmentally oriented adaptations of the economic process,
are one set of measures.  Taxes, including effluent charges,
are perhaps the most precise and yet the most flexible means
of making businesses, municipalities, other nonbusiness
organizations, and consumers take environmental cost factors
into their calculations.

Direct regulation, cash subsidies, government-prescribed
standards, and the actual conduct of environmental research,
monitoring, industry surveillance, and preventive clean-up,
and other conservation activities may also serve to direct
the economy into patterns of behavior similar to those that
could be followed if environmental costs and benefits were
reflected in the conventional monetary costs of the market
mechanism.

As suggested in the introductory section of this chapter,
these methods generally should be viewed both as policy
alternatives and as potential complementary components of an
effective policy mix.

### Tax Incentives to Reduce Pollution:  Cost Internalization Approach

In his State of the Union Message in 1970, the president
of the United States urged that the price of goods "should be
made to include the cost of producing and disposing of them
without damage to the environment."  He urged that a charge
on sulfur emitted into the atmosphere would be a major step
in applying the principle that the cost of pollution should
be included in the price of the product.

The principle of applying excise taxes, effluent charges, and similar fees or levies to reflect the external or social costs of polluting activity was enunciated by the early welfare economists, beginning with the tradition of Alfred Marshall and A.C. Pigou.

In simplest lay terms, while man cannot survive with excessive pollution, it is also true that he cannot survive without some minimal amount of pollution.  Pollution--or a potential for pollution--is created virtually every time a good or service is produced.  To eliminate any possible source of pollution, it would be necessary to restrict production to the level of very primitive living standards, and even that effort would not be successful since primitive human societies suffered from their own particular forms of pollution, generally tolerable because of the pollution-absorbing capacity of a relatively vast environment in relation to a comparatively sparse, low-energy, low-technology, low-output population.

The fact is that the capacity of the environment to absorb pollution and regenerate itself is a factor utilized in the economic processes of production and consumption.  The problem modern economies confront today is that, since there is generally no proprietary right that could restrain the use of the pollution-absorbing factor, it is, in the absence of public intervention, a free good.  The usual cost-price mechanism that would balance the social costs of pollution against the costs of preventing it, or the costs of cleaning it up, fails.

Theorists point out several alternative techniques for controlling pollution.

1.    Control by regulation would determine the overall or aggregate limit on pollution and would assign permissible levels of pollutant contribution to different producing firms, as well as the time schedule on which prescribed overall standards and emission or performance standards of particular firms were to be achieved.

2.    Control by taxation, if executed in accordance with theoretical norms, would in effect compel firms to pay the correct price for the right to pollute.  A tax or charge on the discharge of polluting effluents would give firms a clear monetary incentive to reduce their level of discharges.  The resulting new equilibrium would display not only a lower overall level of pollution but also an equation on a marginal or incremental basis of the costs of control and the fixed unit tax or effluent charge.[1]

The resulting allocation of the costs of pollution control among different firms would presumably be more efficient than under a broad regulatory requirement. It is possible to imagine situations in which it is not feasible to measure polluting effluents with sufficient precision to use them as a penalty tax base. In these circumstances, it would be possible to levy a pollution-type tax on the production process or on the consumption of the pollution-intensive goods. Such a tax would unfortunately not provide a sharply focused incentive to curb pollution or develop pollution-control technology, but it would cause the costs of pollution to be reflected in the marketplace. It would at least reduce consumption of pollution-causing items, shift productive factors away from the pollution-intensive activity, and thus assist in achieving an optimal allocation of resources. It is arguable whether the pollution tax under these conditions should reflect estimated pollution damage or the social costs of repair. This is probably a subordinate issue. The major objective is to internalize an approximately realistic cost measure in the economic decisions of the marketplace. If the government receives tax payment for these costs, it can then appraise the comparative benefits of pollution repair expenditures, possible subsidies to nonpolluters, or other uses of the money.

If market elasticities are such that even a heavy tax is not deemed sufficiently effective in shifting resources, the presumption is that the externalities are too great and too grave to be expressed in terms of production and market considerations. In practical terms this situation implies that no politically or administratively feasible tax could adequately measure pollution damage or make it register in the market process of factor allocation. Direct intervention and nonfiscal controls might then be called upon.

3.    Control by property right is analogous to the tax approach; it involves the sale of rights to pollute. More theoretical than practical, except in special environmental situations, this approach would involve sale by the government (or by a government concessionaire) of rights to pollute. Thus, if it is decided that the maximum amount of pollution of a given type is X million units per year, licenses for the X million unit permissible level could then be "auctioned off" to the highest bidders or marketed at a price that just "clears the market." Subsequently, rights to pollute might be allowed to be bought and sold, with the result that firms that discovered ways to reduce their pollution at a cheaper cost would dispose of some or all of their "rights" to firms that found it less expensive to buy rights than to control their pollution.

The limitation of pollution to the licensed total would
itself be a progressive step, lessening pollution and producing
revenue to the government.  The subsequent adjustments and
reallocation of licenses among firms would, as indicated,
tend to achieve an overall minimum cost solution from the
social standpoint.

The environmental excise and the license sale approaches
are similar in producing revenue, in creating incentives to
reduce pollution, and in assuring a balancing of marginal
cost and marginal benefits, since firms would control
pollution up to the point where the purchase of pollution
rights became less expensive.

## Some Basic Principles

An economic approach to pollution problems recognizes
that (1) the existence of pollution-causing activity imposes
costs on society, and (2) the reduction or elimination of
pollution also imposes costs on the various economic
activities that generate pollution and therefore on the
industries involved, their consumers, or both.

One obvious principle that may be derived from this
observation is that pollution should be eliminated when the
cost of eliminating it is lower than the social benefits or
reduction of social costs.  The universal optimizing
principle of economic analysis suggests that pollution should
be controlled only up to the point where marginal benefits
equal marginal costs.  Unless marginal costs of control are
virtually zero it follows that from the economic standpoint
not all pollution should be eliminated.  Pressing pollution
control beyond the marginal equation of costs and benefits
would involve net diseconomies and could be justified only
on the basis of values or value judgments that cannot be
translated into the monetary terms that permit the
calculation of the marginal optimizing point.

Another principle of efficient social decision making
in the environmental area is that pollution that is to be
eliminated should be eliminated in the most economical way
feasible.  Here, the choice is among the several alternatives
previously listed:  (1) regulation, (2) taxation, and (3) pro-
prietarization of the environmental factor, with sale of
"rights" to pollute.  The latter, despite the invidiousness
of selling rights to pollute, is very similar to the
environmental excise approach, one advantage being the
subsequent creation of a market for pollution rights, with
greater flexibility and economy in the resulting redistribution
of the rights among firms with varying pollution control
costs.

## Practical and Administrative Aspects

Tax incentive devices, including the regulatory excises
or charges designed to incorporate "externalities" in the cost
structure of the firm, work best when they can be reduced to
semiautomatic, self-executing standards and definitions, with
clear-cut lines of application that keep compliance and
administration within manageable limits.  This is not readily
feasible in some phases of pollution control, particularly
where there are numerous potential polluters who must be
monitored and their performance standards or emissions checked
and quantified as the base of a tax.

It is true that regulation and tax penalties on pollution
may coexist and complement each other.  But if the effective
operation of the tax depends on more continuous monitoring
and exact emission measurement than is required under
reasonably alert and effective regulation, the tax introduces
a new, extra burden that may or may not be acceptable,
depending upon the numbers of taxpayer-polluters involved and
the available technology for continuous automatic monitoring
and measurement of the emission or effluent.  In brief,
regulation may meet acceptable administrative standards with
less cost than the satisfactory and uniform application of a
tax or effluent charge.

## The Art of the Feasible Antipollution Excise Tax

At this stage of the fiscal effort against pollution, a
primary requirement for an antipollution excise tax or charge
is to avoid too cheap a "license to pollute," so that the cost
of continuing at least some part of preexisting pollution
levels would be higher than those of a reasonable effort at
control or substitution yet would fall short of an unreasonable
pressure that would involve excessive economic dislocation,
meet with difficulties of enforcement in communities dependent
upon the polluting industries, and involve de facto or de jure
exceptions that would seriously weaken the prestige and
public image of the regulatory process.

The capacity of the antipollution excise tax or charge
to operate more flexibly and economically than regulation
is an important consideration--that is, producers with high
costs of control may pay more tax than those in a position to
reduce pollution.  It would be difficult for regulation to
operate in this manner.

## Site and Seasonal Dimensions of Pollution and Pollution Control

A more difficult issue is raised by the fact that the
social costs of added pollution vary regionally (due to weather

conditions, differences of intensity of industrial development
or population distribution) or seasonally (for similar reasons).

Varying excise taxes (or charges) by region or season
involves practical and legal problems, since it introduces a
form of identification and discrimination not usually undertaken
in the tax laws.  Lowering charges in certain areas or at
certain times where or when damage inflicted by pollution
appeared low is one approach.

The "constitutionality," practicability, and acceptability
of varying cost-internalization taxes or charges by region and
season remains controversial.  To some, any encouragement to
additional pollution in relatively unspoiled or uncongested
areas is bad; also, the inherent nonuniformity of taxes or
charges based on the place or time of polluting activity is
too patently discriminatory and capricious by traditional tax
equity standards and would thus bring the whole environmental
tax mechanism, however well intentioned, into disrepute.

At least it may be said that sophisticated use of the tax
system in this guise partakes more of the nature of a user
charge system, which might need to be distinguished legally
and institutionally from the traditional tax collection agencies
or instruments of the government by transferring it to special
regional, water basin, or estuarial authorities.

## Transition Role of Antipollution Excises

One of the significant aspects of the antipollution excise
tax rationale is its promise of spurring new technology and the
production of antipollution control equipment.  In the absence
of economic motivation, there is little or no market for
antipollution technology and its reduction to practice in the
form of cleaner production processes and practicable control
equipment.

It is true that the scheduled introduction of regulatory
standards, particularly those that would call for emission or
effluent controls, would in themselves tend to stimulate
technology and a commercial control equipment industry.
However, the affected industry is frequently in the posture of
being able to say that it cannot meet standards because the
control technique or equipment does not exist.  This argument
in practice tends to postpone the effective data of the
standards--thus further reducing their credibility and
efficacy as stimulants to the supply of a practical working
technology for use on a commercial basis.

## Effluent Charges:   The Ultimate in External Cost Internalization

The most sophisticated and most difficult to implement tax device for pollution control via the internalization of costs is the effluent fee or charge.  Typically thought of as a means of water pollution control, it can be expanded conceptually to embrace virtually any form of pollution, including air emissions and solid waste.

In the field of water pollution control, the effluent charge is typically proposed as a fee geared to such major components as biological oxygen demand (BOD) due to organic wastes, acidity, thermal pollution, and specified other harmful effluents not completely prohibited.  Synergistic effects of combining harmful compounds (self-neutralizing and self-compounding) would be taken into account.

The effluent charge would then be based upon scales from sophisticated monitoring devices that would continuously measure the effluent in terms of the various tax components. The charge would be calculated and redetermined from time to time in relation to the environmental damage involved, the unit cost of control, and the overall goal of environmental protection.  The effluent charges would thus be set, as in the case of the simpler environmental excises, so that the marginal costs of control would equal the tax at a point at which the desired level of pollution reduction was achieved.

The effluent charge concept will be discussed in more specific terms in a later section.

## Environmental Control Tax Possibilities

The range of possible candidates for an environmental excise tax or tax incentive program is already quite wide. It includes--in  addition to sulfur in fuels, lead additives, phosphates in detergents, junk autos, and waste oil--such items as nonreturnable containers, discarded tires, and harmful fertilizers and pesticides.  As the previous listing suggests, several types of objectives may be identified: (1) discouraging the use of harmful products or processes, (2) encouraging use of better methods of disposal or recycling of materials, (3) providing revenue for government antipollution programs, and (4) forming a tax leverage to provide incentives for industrial research and development for better environmental technology.  Preliminary study has indicated that it would not be too difficult to develop programs that could yield substantial revenues during the transition phases. Yield would decline as antipollution incentives, plus related regulatory actions, became effective.  Taxation is to some degree an alternative to regulatory action, but it may support

it where regulation would be too crude and the criteria or time
schedules for control are uncertain.  In some cases, these
plans involve a rebate or incentive payment coupled with a tax.
However, unlike tax incentive plans, which cost money and are
a form of backdoor spending, the plans under study at least
produce transition revenues or break even over the long run.

## Some Basic Considerations in Antipollution Excise Policy

The pollution control objective calls for a basic
rethinking of tax policy.  Traditional goals of neutrality,
dubious at best in the excise field, are no longer appropriate.
Rather, the objective is to internalize and bring to bear on
both producer and consumer the external costs--the adverse
social externalities--involved in the inevitable pollution of
the environment by most forms of production and consumption.
This use of the tax system to recognize pollution almost as a
factor of production or operating cost serves to equate in
better fashion the marginal social costs and benefits.  This
use of taxes to recognize externalities and attain desirable
social benefits has long been an honored concept of tax design
in the tradition of public finance.  It has not played much
part historically in excise policies, despite the use of
regulatory and sumptuary excises.  The antipollution excise
field, and indeed the whole antipollution tax incentive area
generally, is made more complicated because of the highly
complex science and technology involved and the difficulties
of estimating social costs and evaluating adverse effects.

### Tax Incentives for Investment in Pollution
### Control Equipment

Tax incentives, in the sense of positive forms of
financial assistance for particular types of investment or for
investment generally, have a long and extensive background in
the fiscal systems of many countries.

In recent decades, there has been growing interest in,
use of, and critical analysis of the investment incentive
device as a tool for influencing the scale and direction of
investment.[2]  Along with a variety of other investment
incentive measures to help attain national economic and social
goals, incentives for investment in pollution control
facilities have received attention and have been adopted in
the United States.

Proposals in the United States have included various
forms of accelerated amortization as well as tax credits for
capital outlays on pollution control equipment.  The Tax
Reform Act of 1969 in the United States included specific

provisions for accelerated amortization over a five-year period
for approved pollution control facilities added to preexisting
industrial plants and installed prior to 1975. Various state
tax systems also have included property tax abatements as well
as fast income tax write-offs comparable to the federal
provisions for pollution abatement facilities.

Before undertaking a specific description and analysis
of the investment incentive device for pollution abatement
facilities, it will be helpful to review some of the general
principles and considerations relevant to the investment
incentive technique.

## Need for Automaticity in the Positive Tax Incentive Approach

Too often, tax incentives--particularly of the positive
kind which confer attractive tax benefits--are regarded as the
first and only approach to environmental problems. Basically,
a tax credit or accelerated depreciation for pollution
abatement plant or equipment is equivalent to a kind of
"backdoor expenditure"--differing from ordinary cash grants
or subsidies in that the tax route (1) evades ordinary budget
scrutiny and periodic review in the course of the public
decision-making process determining appropriations of public
monies, (2) relies on the virtually continuous "contact"
between the taxpaying business and the tax structure to assure
the automatic and general impact of the tax incentive, as
distinguished from the typically more complex process of
applying for cash grants and awaiting the receipt of a
government check, and (3) utilizes the administrative
machinery of the income tax to make appropriate factual checks
and determinations and to assure reasonable conformity with
the criteria for eligibility laid down in the statute.

This type of incentive works best when it can be reduced
to a semiautomatic, self-executing standard in the tax
statutes and regulations, prescribing clear-cut lines of
applicability, which keep problems of compliance and
administration within manageable limits. This may not always
be feasible in the more complex phases of pollution prevention
and control. Regulation and administration by highly technical,
changing, and sometimes judgmental standards, beyond the
capacity of the tax draftsman or tax administrator, seem to be
necessary in some environmental areas. For example, a five-year
write-off of tall smokestacks designed to dissipate smoke,
with particulates and other ordinary air pollutants, could be
readily administered by the tax authorities. This kind of
facility is easily identified, and its purpose and effectiveness
are readily checked. On the other hand, the application of tax
write-off privileges to a new, complex, untried water effluent
control system, rather closely integrated in some phases with

the production process and requiring specialized monitoring
and inspection, requires certification by pollution control
authorities.  The tax authorities can then accept and operate
on the basis of the certification.  But in these circumstances
the fiscal incentive device becomes barely distinguishable from
one involving payments or grants to firms that build certified
control equipment.  Actual writing of checks is avoided, and
the advantages are limited to taxpaying entities, but the tax
incentive is not self-operating; it requires the assistance or
intervention of a special skilled bureaucracy with environmental
expertise.

The latter situation may nevertheless be argued to be
favorable to the use of the tax incentive; though it may
involve a compromise of pure fiscal incentive principles, it
may be efficient if it can utilize more fully an already
existing environmental authority staff to carry out
certification procedures.  Its defects, if any, relate to the
distribution of benefits under the tax system as compared to
that under an explicit subsidiary payment system.

The present five-year amortization provisions under the
U.S. Internal Revenue Code rely on certification by both
federal and state pollution control authorities.

## Advantages and Weaknesses of the Tax Benefit Incentive Approach

Saving of Bureaucratic Overhead.  Tax incentives for investment
appear to have the advantage of avoiding another direct
expenditure, which calls for more tax money to take a "round
trip" to the national treasury and back to the taxpayer
undertaking the desired investment.  They also promise
freedom from an additional bureaucratic overhead associated
with the administration of an expenditure program.  There is
obvious appeal--not entirely superficial--in utilizing the
wide-ranging resources of the tax system and the taxpayers'
keen interest in saving taxes to harness business profit
motives and thus to form a "creative partnership" between
government and the private sector.

Inappropriate Allocation of Costs.  The investment incentive
approach--through tax credits or fast write-offs under the
income taxes--involves a reduction or postponement of
revenues.  Even if tax rates were raised adequately to offset
this drain and make the plan self-financing, the net effect
would be to charge a corresponding part of the costs of
protecting the environment to taxpayers generally.  It is
contended by some, however, that the tax burden should rest
more squarely on the producers and consumers of the polluting
industry, thus assessing the costs on the economic process
that causes the environmental problem.

Some critics of the investment incentive technique insist
that it is wrong in principle in that it renders financial
assistance to polluters and thus encourages them, even though
the tax benefit appears to be directed to the clean-up process.
If the pollution excise tax intended to internalize costs is
subject to derogatory characterization as a "license to
pollute," it is even more suitable to call the positive
incentive to control or prevent pollution a "pollution
subsidy."

Ambiguity of the Tax Incentive Concept as applied to
Unprofitable Pollution Control Equipment.  Tax credit and
accelerated amortization incentives, singly or combined, have
been proposed or adopted for a variety of social and economic
objectives, such as investment in housing, transportation, or
depressed areas, as well as pollution control.  A common
charge leveled against all these specific plans is that they
provide financial assistance not only to encourage investment
that would not otherwise have occurred but also for investment
that would have occurred anyway.  An incremental approach--
extending the incentive only to investment above some base or
norm (presumptively representing what would take place anyway)
is difficult to implement fairly and workably, whether on a
tax incentive or cash grant basis.

But pollution control investment presents special
problems for an effective tax incentive.  The pollution control
equipment is not ordinarily profitable, so the incentive does
not generally serve--as industrial investment incentives
typically do--to raise the rate of profitability on the
desired investment.  Moreover, if antipollution equipment is
required by regulation, the term incentive, it is argued, is
a misnomer.  The tax benefit is in effect only a financial aid
for what has to be done anyway.  It merely reduces the cost to
private industry of conforming to regulations, which to be
sure may be a particularly important aid during the initial
transition phases in securing acceptance of a new regulation.

Bias Toward Hardware.  A potential defect of the investment
incentive approach as applied to pollution control equipment
is that it extends its assistance only to the use of
pollution-controlling hardware, and even more narrowly, to
separately identifiable pollution control equipment.  It fails
to assist process or product changes, input modifications,
relocation, research, and other possible modifications for
reducing pollution that do not involve investment in
identifiable facilities for carrying out traditional pollution
control or prevention functions.  This bias may tend to
result in the misallocation of resources devoted to the
environmental effort and a related preoccupation of private
industry with the hardware approach to meeting environmental
standards.

The importance of this bias depends on the existence of options that involve less use of depreciable capital and more of other economic factors that would not qualify for the investment credit or fast tax write-off.  To those who see the correct ultimate technology of control as fairly well delineated and the worst hurdle for industry to surmount as being the capital outlay required, this objection may seem less real than to those who think of the adaptive process by which private industry may meet environmental standards as quite fluid, dynamic, and studded with options and "trade-offs." For the latter, tax assistance for control facilities encourages firms to overuse capital to the neglect of other forms of pollution control systems that would depend on the development and deployment of less capital-intensive methods.[3] The bias toward capital-using methods may be particularly harmful in the early phases of a pollution control system, since it may tend to freeze the shape of long-range efforts.

Lack of Incremental Incentive beyond Regulatory Standards. Another shortcoming of this type of incentive is that it does not provide a marginal incentive to undertake further pollution abatement, except in those cases where the pollution control installations are actually profitable or nearly profitable.  A loss investment generally remains a loss investment even with the tax credit or write-off.  The basic incentive remains the regulatory standard.  The tax assistance merely makes it less costly for the firm to achieve acceptable compliance.  It is not likely to induce improvement beyond that standard.

Lack of Incentive for Regional Cooperation.  The investment incentive approach fails also, at least in its conventional forms, to take advantage of potential economies in pollution control through collective action.  The investment incentive is a highly individualistic technique pitched to the tax outlook and control activities of the taxpaying firm.  It tends to encourage firms to build their own individual and possibly relatively inefficient abatement facilities.

Regional authorities, particularly in the field of water pollution control, have shown promise of greater efficiency in abatement through pooled efforts.  The complexity of such arrangements may defy provisions to include investment contributions to a collective effort.  Moreover, such regional authorities typically rely primarily on effluent charges to motivate participants.  The role of a positive investment incentive would accordingly tend to be limited. However, to the extent that there remains a role and that appropriate adjustments to the collective schemes are possible, the investment incentive plan could be used to cover capital investment shares in a regional authority or syndicate.

Limited Role in an Approach through a Combination of Solutions.
Methods of combating pollution vary with the nature of the
pollutant and the available technology. They include recovery
and reuse of materials and the pollutants themselves, generally
termed "recycling"; waste treatment, with possible modification
of the contaminants and their removal and disposition;
alteration of contaminant-using or producing processes to
elimination of the pollutants or reduction of their release;
use of alternative inputs with less polluting characteristics,
for example, sulfur fuels; development of alternative power
sources with lessened polluting characteristics; dispersion
of waste discharge over a larger area or as part of a larger
volume, reducing its concentration-related effects; transfer
of operations or discharge points to areas less sensitive to
pollution; holding of pollutants in detention for degradation,
loss of thermal pollution, and gradual release; and
environmental treatment to remove or neutralize the effect
of pollutants.[4]

The list could be expanded, but the important point is
that pollution control equipment used as an adjunct of a
private industrial plant is only part of a broader program of
interacting techniques, including public expenditure programs
and persistent, imaginative research. Tax incentives for
pollution abatement facilities may play a role, but they may
have no effect in assisting other important elements in the
effective policy mix, and even their role in encouraging
pollution control equipment tends to be subordinate to the
application of regulatory criteria and standards--a nontax
mechanism.

"Backdoor Spending". Tax incentives for pollution abatement
equipment are one of a large family of actual or proposed
tax concession provisions, aimed at encouraging desired
behavior, generally supported both by those concerned with
reaching certain economic goals and by those likely to benefit
in the first instance from the preferential tax treatment.

The most recent and sophisticated form of criticism of
the investment tax incentive route describes this kind of
incentive, and indeed any other special tax preference--
whether through additional deductions, speed-up of deductions,
credits, exclusions, exemptions, tax deferrals, preferential
rates, or other devices--as a form of "tax expenditure" or
"backdoor spending." This approach to the national budget is
condemned by critics in large part merely because of its
indirect and "backdoor" character--its evasion of normal
budgetary standards and periodic scrutiny by the legislative
committees with the best expertise and jurisdictional
authority in the area concerned.

On the other hand, it is argued that, in any specific functional area, the government may utilize direct expenditures, direct government loans, government loan insurance or guarantee, subsidized low-interest loans, and other financial assistance devices to attain the same objectives as these toward which the tax incentives are directed. In the circumstances, the tax expenditure and the direct expenditure are viewed as equally burdensome and are in effect alternative methods of utilizing the resources of the government.[5]

Impairment of the Equity of the Tax Structure. Any shortfall from a comprehensive base and from the unfaltering application of progressive rates bothers the purist, and this condemnation would apply to environmental tax incentives, credits, fast write-offs, and so on, or any other tax assistance or encouragement, no matter how high the social priority of the purpose. Cash grants would run through the progressive tax mill. By their nature, tax incentives constitute tax-free income. The distributional effects are different, and although the tax-exempt character of the tax incentives may in a rough way be taken into account in setting their level, the effect is inevitably uneven.

Efficiency Considerations. In addition to defending the conceptual purity of the tax base and the revenue structure, critics of the tax incentive method (1) deny that it is the better way to encourage the private sector to participate in social programs; (2) characterize the saving of government bureaucratic expenses and red tape under the tax device as illusory; (3) condemn the tax incentive as a loose, imprecise, sloppy, and wasteful way of administering government moneys; and (4) discount the idea that use of the tax system has special virtues in enlisting and promoting private decision-making or salutary "pluralism" in the campaign against pollution or for other purposes.

Eligibility by Certification. As far as efficient administration with a minimum of tax statutory language is concerned, the environmental investment is peculiarly well-situated. Provided that the investment is required or sought by environmental regulatory authorities, certification by them can become the standard and criterion of eligibility for the tax incentive. However, as previously indicated, the strictly incentive nature of the tax benefit would be limited to investments sought but not as yet actually required by the environmental authorities. Moreover, environmental authorities, not being directly responsible for revenue, will be tempted to certify outlays with only a minimal degree of effectiveness relative to the resulting loss of revenue.

Fiscal Incentives Pave the Way for Regulation. Here, it must be
conceded, as mentioned before, the role of the fiscal incentive
is ambiguous at best. It can hardly make an unprofitable
investment attractive by merely reducing losses. Its role in
some situations is perhaps one of making regulatory standards
more palatable and acceptable--the fiscal midwife, so to
speak, for the imminent regulation.

Short-Circuiting the Budgetary Process. The objections to tax
exemption, as foreshadowed earlier in this discussion, are
that it (1) approaches the budgetary decision by the back door;
(2) thus lowers standards provided by prescribed legislative
procedures for appropriations and expenditures; (3) puts the
decision within the jurisdiction of tax committees of the
national legislature whose knowledge and staff expertise is
presumably less adequate than those of the committees with
responsibility for appropriations in the environmental policy
area; (4) creates an illusion of costless social policy, which
in reality makes demands on the budget through reduction of
tax revenues as effectively as through an increase in public
expenditures; (5) baits the trap of overspending with the
nearly universal attraction of tax relief; and (6) tends to
facilitate and perpetuate (without as careful an annual
review as is typical of direct spending) so-called tax
expenditures that would not be acceptable politically or
technically if they were made directly.

### Pro- and Anti-Environmental Biases in the
### Revenue Structure

Another important phase of tax policy relative to
environmental objectives is the identification first of
existing provisions of the revenue structure that, possibly
quite unintentionally, affect the environment favorably or
unfavorably, and second of possible adjustments that would
remove or lessen undesired biases and create or enhance
favorable ones. Those charged with the fiscal policy
aspects of environmental programs need first to examine what
the present tax structure does in key environmental areas and
how the structure could be adjusted without undue violence to
general-revenue and tax-equity objectives in order to reduce
adverse environmental impact.

Some obvious examples of environmental bias provisions
appear below.

### Bias Against Recycling

Preferences in the natural resource provisions of
national revenue structures often favor new mineral and timber

production to the detriment of recovery and reuse of reclaimed materials, generally termed "recycling," a procedure that both alleviates the problems of litter and solid waste disposal and conserves primary resources.

## Land-Use Policy and Prevention of "Urban Sprawl"

A number of income tax features may unwittingly exacerbate tendencies to distort patterns of land use. Such distribution may involve growth "outward" rather than "upward"--extensive rather than more intensive use that would economize on scarce land resources.

"Disorderly" or "undesirable" development and utilization of metropolitan land areas may be due to the operation of the market system and monopolistic private property ownership in the context of the rather loose, sometimes sketchy, and often corrupt framework of zoning codes and governmental land-use planning. One aspect of disorderly use is so-called leap-frogging, which initiates development "further out" because of the difficulties of assembling closer-in parcels, thereby disrupting planned patterns of transportation, sewer, water and spatial development, and leaving closer-in and more "efficient" land areas unutilized. In addition, suburban growth is often criticized because of (1) its demands upon the commuter highway system, which involves heavy construction costs, lavish land use, and the imposition of a fixed and possibly ultimately uneconomical and obsolescent spatial pattern on the metropolis, (2) excessive costs of providing water, sewer, and other utility services, and the social costs of such environmental problems as traffic congestion and automotive commuter smog, and (3) its catering to middle- or upper-middle-class exclusiveness, land possessiveness, and general disengagement or flight from inner-city problems and dangers. Urban sprawl may involve lavish gobbling up of scarce land and irretrievable commitments of resources to an ultimately unsustainable spatial pattern. It has also been blamed for the precipitate decline in the vitality of many inner cities.

On the other hand, suburban and exurban developments can and sometimes do add green space, however private and exclusive it may be, as well as other esthetic values and satisfaction to the metropolitan environment. If the suburbanites themselves paid for the social costs they engender, it could be argued they had a right to the pattern of living they seem to prefer. Value judgments are ultimately involved in assessing whether the expansive pattern of development is worth its cost.

The following paragraphs summarize briefly, and possibly parochially, the principal ways in which a national tax system

may bear, favorably, unfavorably, or ambiguously, upon urban
sprawl problems.

Capital Gains and Depreciation.  Favorable capital gains and
real estate depreciation provisions in the United States
(accumulated over the years in response to complex economic
needs and urgent legislative pressures), tend to stimulate
tax-conscious investors to seek relatively quick returns in
real estate development and speculation with frequent turnover
rather than long-term holding.

Tax Preferences for Home Ownership.  The nonbusiness deduction
for home mortgage interest and property tax for individuals
has, generally as a matter of deliberate policy, encouraged
homeownership as against tenancy.  Corresponding deductions of
a portion of basic housing costs included in the rental are
not available to renters.  The basic feature of the tax law
that gives rise to this differential is the exclusion of
so-called imputed income from use and enjoyment of consumer
durables.  Inclusion of this income in the tax base would
justify the related interest and tax deductions.  While the
mortgage interest deduction merely equalizes the position of
homeowners with varying amounts of mortgage debt, and avoids
the creation of an incentive for borrowing on security other
than the home, the deduction for property taxes paid lacks
this justification.

     Technically, the tax law may be equally favorable to
owner-occupied detached single-family homes, duplex or row
houses, garden apartments, rural townhouse clusters, and high-
rise and other forms of owner-occupied construction.  In
practice, since condominium and cooperative apartments (and
indeed any form of homeownership) apparently do not appeal
strongly to inner-city dwellers in lower tax brackets, the
major force of the tax incentive to homeownership coincides
with the natural preference for the detached single-family
home "with a bit of land" on the part of those migrating
(from inner city or elsewhere) to the suburbs.

     Many consider that widespread homeownership is an
important and desirable objective--to give social stability,
a hedge against inflation, and on the whole more satisfying,
better maintained, and more economical housing, and that
these considerations outweigh whatever contribution this
feature of the tax law may make to suburban sprawl plus the
consequent impairment of the integrity and progressive
nature of the tax.

     The exclusion of imputed income derived from personal
assets is also a factor favoring automobile ownership, which
is required for living in low-density suburbs, as compared to
the use of mass transit.

In conclusion, the following observations should be made:

1.    To the extent that existing tax benefits for home-owners encourage "over-housing" (because it is a relatively tax-free use of income) or overextensive use of land (because some homeowners like to combine a little extra inflation hedge and land speculation with their basic housing requirements), consideration might be given to limiting the amount of housing and the mix of land and improvements that would qualify for the present favorable tax treatment.  However, this would be technically difficult and highly controversial.  Nontax approaches to sprawl would seem to be preferable.

2.    To the extent that further tax simplification is obtained by larger standard deductions or equivalent devices that obliterate the real significance of homeowner deductions, some muting of the tax bias toward sprawl could be secured with simpler tax reporting, avoiding the head-on conflict that would be involved in a direct denial or limitation of these tax benefits.

3.    Some concerted effort could be made to make cooperative or condominium ownership more attractive and appealing to persons who might well choose high-rise or cluster-type housing that economized on land and reversed tendencies toward sprawl.  One possibility would be particularly liberal rehabilitation amortization rules or credits for the restoration of multiple-unit housing for condominium or cooperative ownership.

4.    The quantification of the balance of tax advantages, including all government "levels" (national, state or provincial, and local), between owner-occupied and rental housing is not yet precise.  Neither is the burden of taxes on housing versus other cost-of-living items.  Because housing is so heavily financed by mortgage and direct owner equity, it generally is relatively free of corporate income taxes, which some experts regard as a distorting bias.  On the other hand, local property taxes, often at rates pushed close to the feasible limits by financially hard-pressed central-city governments, typically constitute an excise tax of 30 percent or more on basic housing costs in many of the larger central cities in the United States.  Rental housing on the other hand often enjoys the advantages of accelerated depreciation.[6]

5.    Various tax incentives or penalties could be applied to encourage economy in the use of land, specific types of location with reference to the metropolitan core, and better maintenance to combat deterioration and blight.  These could be built into the income tax or applied as exotic forms of excise tax, user charges, or even bounties (negative taxes).

6.   Localities could be encouraged to share their
property taxes in ways that would encourage land use and reward
improvements, which fit into local land planning.  Various
types of leverage might be used, depending on the prevailing
institutions.  In the United States, for example, compliance
with a program might be made a condition for allowing interest
on local borrowings to be exempt or for mortgage interest to
be deductible.

Real Estate Investment Trusts.  Real estate investment trust
provisions in the United States (extended "pass-through" tax
treatment without corporate tax), have encouraged investor
participation in real estate ventures, some apparently
speculative.

Unrealized Appreciation in Real Estate Values.  Capital gain
provisions, which ostensibly give preferential treatment, are
often criticized for lock-in effects, preventing the normal
investment turnover in both securities and real estate
markets.  Part of the problem is the deterrent effect of the
tax itself, which absorbs part of the realized gain, even
though it is differentially favorable as compared with full
ordinary tax rates.  Some observers consider the ultimate
exemption of unrealized capital gains at death under U.S. tax
law with tax-free step-up of basis in the hands of the heirs
as a major incentive for speculators or high-bracket investors
to seek capital appreciation, and a major deterrent to sale
during the lifetime of the owner of appreciated holdings,
especially of older persons.

Land Farmed as a Hobby and Agricultural Tax Benefits.  Various
agricultural tax deductions and benefits frequently help
gentleman farmers or those who farm as a hobby.  In the
United States, for example, these benefits consist of capital
gains on livestock, write-off of soil and water conservation
outlays, deducting expenses of development costs of orchards,
favorable depreciation, and so on.  Some believe the benefits
contribute to suburban sprawl.  On the other hand, they may
in effect slow the process of the subdivision and conversion
of farm land into suburban housing areas.  In some instances,
farm operations such as horse and cattle breeding, seem to be
not only a hobby but a way of covering carrying costs for
valuable land holdings.  Often they benefit not only from
income tax allowances but also from preferential local
property tax rates based on agricultural use.

These farm estates seem to have several effects--some
favorable, some unfavorable--on sprawl.

1.    They act as a kind of prestige magnet to exurban development.

2.    They form enclaves or barriers that divert or influence residential and other development, thus encouraging a kind of leapfrogging.

3.    Basically, they represent long-range land speculation, with whatever distortions and redispositions for type and timing of use this entails.

4.    They provide a kind of ornamental private greenbelt, but one that can readily deteriorate or undergo various undesirable changes unless subjected to effective land planning.

Tighter treatment might be applied, especially where the farm operation was evidently also a substantial speculative landholding venture, if it was desired to use direct tax devices to discourage land speculation.  On the other hand, favorable treatment might be allowed if the release of land to other areas followed or accorded with state or local planning requirements.

Scenic Easements.  The availability of a charitable deduction based on market value with respect to donation or sale below market value of scenic or similar conservation easements-- together with nonrecognition of the accrued capital gains-- may encourage reservation of undeveloped property.  On the other hand, uncertainty about dollar valuations in advance of the transaction, as well as the basic valuation approach, is said to hinder constructive policies for charitable transfers intended to preserve the environment against some of the onslaughts of urban sprawl.

Potential Leverage of Federal Income Tax on Local Property Tax Structure.  The deduction for local property taxes in the United States and other countries--available both on a nonbusiness basis to homeowners and to business taxpayers as business expenses--probably has some effect, as indeed it is intended to have, on the burden of the local property tax and on encouraging the financing of environmental improvement through increases in the general tax rate.  Particularly in the higher personal tax brackets, this, like other deductible state and local taxes, is absorbed to a substantial degree by the national treasury.  Some feel this gives the local governments too free a rein, especially in the smaller, wealthier suburbs.  On the other hand, deduction is denied for assessments specifically levied for local improvements primarily affecting selected parcels; the distinction is, however, often quite arbitrary and technical.

Deductibility of Carrying Charges on Unimproved Land. The
ability of land speculators to deduct charges for holding
unimproved land (interest on debt and local property taxes)
has been cited as a tax factor encouraging speculative land
ventures.  However, these deductions are generally available
to taxpayers under the U.S. and certain other national income
tax laws.  Denial of the existing treatment for owners of land
would be discriminatory, thus creating a clash between tax
equity and environmental objectives.

## Wetlands and Estuarine Areas

The coastal zones of the American and some other
continents are an important part of the world environment.
These ecologically vital coastal zones include beaches,
estuaries, tidal flats, bays, marshlands, lagoons, sounds, and
similar geographical areas.  The natural mixing of fresh and
salt waters makes the estuarine environment productive of a
variety of marine life, including microscopic species,
shellfish, birds, and mammals.  These areas aid the spawning
of some fish species and provide organic nutrients essential
to the ecological chain.  They provide nurseries for the young
and a needed habitat for migratory waterfowl, shore birds,
and other wildlife.  They are important esthetically and
recreationally.  On a more utilitarian basis, they absorb and
blunt onshore storm-driven winds and tides and provide
stability to the configuration of shore lands.  Pollution,
dredging, and filling for agricultural, commercial,
industrial, and residential use and for resort development
all threaten these so-called "wetlands."

Traditionally, development and conversion of swamplands
to "higher uses" have been regarded, in the light of the
limited knowledge and environmental insight, as a desirable
goal.  Thus, the tax laws inherited from an earlier era,
encourage this kind of development.  The tax bias typically
consists of favorable fast write-offs, or current expense
deductions, for expenses of ditching and draining (soil and
water conservation outlay) or clearing of land for
agricultural or possible other uses.  The generally available
tax allowances to assist construction and investment may, in
interplay with the special provisions relating to land
development or redevelopment, speed the exploitation and
depletion of the world's wetlands and estuarine resources.

Future tax policy should give increasing attention to
tax measures--possibly supporting more direct regulatory and
conservation action by governments--designed to remove tax
biases toward the conversion and effective destruction of
wetlands and possibly to develop tax incentives for their
preservation or for more conservation-oriented uses.

A great deal is at stake here.  Intelligent policies and
vigorous efforts are needed on all fronts--tax and nontax--
to preserve this element of the world's resources, until
recently so seriously underrated, against pollution and
harmful exploitation.  At stake are the following:  the supply
of edible fish and shellfish; sport and commercial fishing;
a healthy population of ducks and waterfowl; esthetic, scenic,
and recreational values almost beyond commercial "pricing";
and prevention of possible catastrophic effects of destruction
of the wetlands with unforeseeable impact on the ecological
balance of the oceans.

## Preservation of the World's Cultural Heritage

Tax laws also have an effect on the preservation of the
world's heritage of historic architectural treasures.  Despite
the work of national trusts and similar organizations, the
tempo of economic change and pressures for real estate
development have been leading to the demolition of many
architecturally and historically interesting structures.
Unfortunately, the marketplace does not effectively record the
values that may be lost as older buildings, which add so much
to our cultural enjoyment, are destroyed.  Tax measures to
compensate owners for loss of commercial value due to
preservation of their property as historic landmarks may help
stem this tide.

## Tax Incentives as Revenue Measures

As we have seen above, the regulatory excise tax
(possibly coupled with incentive rebates for recoveries of
pollutants) is a promising instrument in a number of ways.  It
registers the cost of pollution in the operations of the
producer and in the price to the consumer.  It thus
incorporates the pollution cost factor into the price and
market mechanism, curtailing consumption and motivating the
producer to use fewer taxable pollutant inputs and to reduce
taxable emissions.  It may hasten control or abatement
activities with or without accompanying regulatory action.
It may help the industries involved to achieve a better
position to comply with regulatory standards.  In the process,
it generates revenue either permanently on the part of the
pollution or pollutant-causing product that is not removed by
the tax or regulation; or temporarily in the transition phase
before industry and polluters have time to eliminate the
pollution-related base.

While the pollution excise tax or charge is perhaps the
most interesting from an economic and revenue standpoint,
there are other revenue aspects of the use of the tax system

for environmental purposes that call for attention in this
discussion.

## Revenue Gainers

Of the basic alternatives offered in the use of the tax
structure for pollution control, there are several with
positive revenue potential: (1) the regulatory environmental
excise tax just mentioned, imposed either on pollution itself,
measured in terms of effluents, emissions, or harmful
byproducts, or on the pollution-generating input, product, or
service; (2) user-charge-type excises, levied primarily on
consumers of an environmental resource, with the revenues
typically going to pay for the maintenance or improvement of
the resource (as in the case of a tax on fishing, hunting,
and camping equipment, with the proceeds devoted to park land,
recreational waters, and game supply programs); (3) a major
broad-based excise tax, such as an energy tax or a more
general value-added tax, used to finance environmental
research and clean-up or improvement programs; and (4) the
correction of tax biases, such as built-in tax preferences
for particular forms of economic activity that give rise to
special environmental problems, the removal of which would, in
the first instance at least, increase revenues.

## Revenue Losers

The use of positive tax incentives for investment in
pollution abatement facilities or plant adjustments involves
revenue losses or deferrals that decrease revenue within the
time frame in question. If tax rates were increased or the
general tax base expanded so as to compensate for revenue
concessions for pollution incentive purposes, the total
revenue would remain unchanged, but tax burdens generally
would be raised to finance the implicit subsidy or "tax
expenditure" to assist pollution control outlays.

## Transitional Revenue Effects

Where an environmental regulatory charge or excise tax
is imposed in a transitional phase of environmental policy,
the major revenue contribution is expected only for a
relatively short period. As the tax becomes effective in
carrying out the intended purpose of stimulating control
pressures, revenue gains will ebb and may even disappear
entirely.

There may, however, be a permanent revenue contribution
if the environmental excise (together with regulatory
requirements) leaves a taxable margin of uncorrected
pollution. The tax will continue to encourage a higher degree

of pollution control, provided the marginal costs of control
are less than the tax that the control measure would save.

## Contradictions between Revenue and Environmental Objectives

This underscores the basic contradiction in the
environmental and incidental revenue objectives of such a
tax program.  If the tax has the effect of totally eliminating
the pollution, there will be no revenue gain beyond the
transition.  However, in most cases, an optimal adjustment
will still allow some level of pollution the abatement of
which would cost more than the reduction in damage, and thus
some revenue would remain.  Even so, policy decisions on the
level of an antipollution excise tax need to consider the
trade-off between revenue, on the one hand, and the desired
level of constraint on pollution, on the other.

Fiscal charges, excise taxes, and effluent fees on
pollution may involve (1) a new tax on the output, on
polluting inputs, or on polluting emissions (possibly measured
directly or indirectly as polluting inputs minus recoveries);
or (2) a higher tax on a commodity or service already subject
to tax (the increase possibly proportioned to the pollutant
content of the particular product).

A new tax will always raise revenue, provided possible
negative effects on other revenues can be dealt with.  An
addition to an old tax may or may not increase revenues,
depending upon the elasticity of demand.  If demand for the
product is elastic, the amount demanded may fall off to such
an extent, as a result of the rise in price reflecting the
tax, that the overall revenues from the combined old tax and
the new addition thereto may be less than the revenue from
the old tax alone.  However, from the standpoint of
environmental control, the elastic demand that operates to
shrink revenues in the circumstances just assumed will have
the presumably desired effect of curtailing the production
and consumption of the pollution-causing item.

## Side Effects on Productivity

Pollution has adverse effects on productivity--shortening
the life of productive facilities, increasing morbidity and
mortality of workers, and probably reducing their efficiency.
To the extent that the tax incentive corrects these problems,
the economy will generate larger output and therefore a
broader revenue base.

The trade-off between ordinary goods and services and
the benefits of a cleaner, healthier environment will be
favorable, if the correct choices are made in balancing marginal

costs and benefits.  In the short run, it may be difficult to
translate some of the benefits into current fiscal revenues.
But, in the longer run, this difficulty should dissolve, and
a sounder economy and more productive revenue base may be
expected from a wisely conducted program.

## Acceptability of Pollution Excise Tax Burdens

The tremendous interest in and concern with environmental
matters has probably made citizens generally more willing to
accept taxes on consumer goods and industrial processes that
have recognized deleterious effects than other proposals for
new taxes.  However, the political resistance even to thoroughly
explored and justified measures should not be underestimated,
particularly where the tax approach is cast in an ambiguous role
along with regulatory authority that would seem to render
further tax burdens unnecessary.

## Substantive Revenue in an Antipollution Excise Package

Even a moderate package of excises directed at major
pollution problems of the air, water, solid waste disposal,
and other areas can produce substantial revenues relative to
the budget of most modern industrial economies.  Some of the
most promising candidates for such a package and their revenue
potential will be discussed in more detail below.

## Problems in the Pollution Tax Approach

The antipollution excise tax and similar devices
encounter a number of problems vis-a-vis revenue producers,
which are worth listing:

● Taxes that are especially good as revenue sources may
be the least effective in curtailing consumption or inducing
changes in industrial processes in order to reduce pollution;

● If public support of environmental excises is
subsequently confronted with evidence that the taxes, while
productive of revenue, are ineffective in curbing pollution,
the whole approach may be discredited (the "license-to-
pollute" criticism would in effect be substantiated);

● In conjunction with regulatory restriction or
prohibition of polluting activity, the excise tax may seem to
add little to the cutback of pollution actually achieved and
to add a tax burden to the substantial financial burdens of
compliance;

● The determination of the appropriate level and other specifications of the antipollution excise tax is a highly complex matter, involving as it does a relatively new and developing technological field and many imponderables; it follows that revenue estimates hinging upon the way marginal costs of pollution control interact with the tax to cause pollution reductions (removing part of the potential tax base) are especially uncertain;

● The transitory character of some substantial part of pollution tax revenues may complicate budgetary and fiscal planning;

● Conflicts of interregional interest within a country may plague the pollution excise: A tax, say, on nitrous oxide emissions designed to protect chiefly large metropolitan areas may be unpalatable to residents of thinly populated country areas; yet regional variation of the tax may also be difficult, legally and politically.

## Environmental Tax Earmarked for Research

The need for a more extensive and dynamic program of research and development in the environmental area, with particular emphasis on the energy field, has prompted various proposals for tax devices to stimulate research and development (R and D) under private auspices or to finance public programs of R and D.

## Use of Sulfur Emissions Tax Proceeds

An instance of this approach is the proposal by the president of the United States in his Environmental Message of 8 February 1971 to impose a "charge" on sulfur oxide emissions from smokestacks and use the money collected from this charge to finance environmental research. The tax would be paid primarily by the producers and users of coal and oil, the chief users being the electric utility companies. Other contributors to sulfur oxide emissions, such as copper and zinc smelters, might be included within the law's ambit. Technically, sulfur oxide emissions might be metered directly at the smokestack, although fully operational technology and equipment for this has not yet been developed for application on a commercial basis. The tax in general would therefore probably be based on the sulfur content of fuel, with a rebate for recoveries of sulfur from emissions, so that the tax would in effect rest on the emissions as measured by inputs less recoveries.

The research to be supported by the emissions tax might include intensification of government efforts to find an economic method of producing gas from coal (commonly called "gasification"), to develop a fast-breeder nuclear reactor, and to find other alternatives to conventional fuel use.  It has been estimated that such a tax, at a rate of one cent per pound of sulfur, could initially produce a revenue of $170 million a year in the United States.

## Use of an Energy-Related Pollution Tax

Another example of the R and D incentive approach, also oriented to the environmental aspects of energy generation, is one that would levy a special excise tax on some overall activity associated with pollution (such as electric power) and then allow against the tax liability a partial (but substantial) rebate for expenditures on research and development relating to the long-term "clean" energy supply and immediate energy-related pollution problems.  Net revenues from the plan after rebates or credits for eligible R and D expenditures could be earmarked or dedicated to various environmental purposes, particularly a government-sponsored energy research program.

The liberality of the rebate or credit for R and D outlays would determine the extent to which the plan involved either a combination private-incentive and public-funded R and D program or a virtually mandatory private R and D program spurred by credits that would give the private program a "free ride" on the special energy tax revenues.

A varient of this plan might provide that a portion of the net revenues from the tax (after rebate for private R and D) should be used to defray public costs directly connected with the fight against energy-related pollution--as distinguished from R and D in the strict sense.

## Rationale of Research Incentive

The basic rationale of incentives for environmental research and development is partly the same as that for any government incentive for R and D:  to supplement the market mechanism where the fruits of private R and D are not adequately "appropriable" by the research investor or where there are significant externalities (beneficial side effects from successful research efforts on the economy), which by their nature are not recapturable in monetary terms by the research spender, even if that spender is organized in the form of an industry-wide association or syndicate.

The problem of the inability to recapture the monetary
rewards of research is compounded in the case of environmental
research, since pollution control is not in itself generally
a profitable activity.  It is true that the existence of
environmental regulatory standards has helped to motivate
R and D effort on the part of the industries affected and
their suppliers of control technology and equipment.  A tax
stimulus would, however, supplement that incentive.

Since, next to the automobile, the energy-generating
industries are the largest single source of pollution, it is
appropriate that a substantial research stimulus should be
focused on them.  To ensure that the rationale of the plan is
effectively and efficiently carried out, the proposal should
include tax credits for joint or collective research efforts
by the energy industry as a whole or by groups of companies,
on an in-house basis or acting through nonprofit research
institutes or utilizing ordinary research contractors.

Since the electric utility industry is in general not a
research-active industry, the credit might not be effective
in some instances; namely, where companies preferred to pay
the full tax rather than mount and supervise research
programs at some additional cost to themselves, even though a
large part was borne by the public revenues.  The net revenue
resulting from this forfeit would permit the public funding
of government-directed activities.

Earmarking and Revenue Flow

The earmarking of pollution taxes for environmental
research impinges upon an important phase of fiscal and
budgetary policy.  Earmarking is here taken to connote the
provision for the automatic appropriation for specified
environmental uses of an amount equivalent to the tax revenues.
The use of special trust funds is a particular financial
procedure sometimes associated with but not necessary to
earmarking.

Earmarking, regarded as part of a method of assuring a
reasonably adequate and sustained flow of funds to an orderly,
planned research program, would have to operate with
reference to a reliable, predictable revenue inflow.  This
condition would not be forthcoming in the case of transitional
pollution control excise taxes or severely constraining
excise taxes, which had a strong effect in discouraging
pollution and therefore shrinking the particular revenue base.
This condition would be reasonably satisfied in the case of an
energy tax, as distinguished from a severe penalty charge on
emissions or effluents, which would be inconsistent with a
sustained revenue objective, as indicated above.

## Earmarking and Pollution Control

Earmarking is designed to provide an assurance that the pollution tax revenues will be used in the interest of a better, cleaner environment.  In dedicating these revenues to environmental research and development closely related to the problem area or areas created by, say, electric energy generation or the production of particular pollutants, the plan helps progress toward a solution that will reverse deterioration of the environment.  The tax is paid by the polluting industry and its customers, those responsible for the pollution.  In this whole process, the hidden environmental damage cost is added, as we have seen, to the actual monetary cost of production and sale of the polluting good or service.

If the tax is levied on a pollutant, the tax will encourage pollution control up to the point, in each particular firm's operations, where the marginal cost of control is equal to the tax.  Beyond this point, where marginal costs exceed the tax, the firm prefers to accept the tax liability.  In this situation, revenues represent the residual uncorrected damage to the environment for which control costs would be greater than the tax--and greater than the damage if the tax were set at a level that correctly re-flected damage.  Where controls are low, a successful program, presumably in combination with regulatory standards, will leave relatively little tax base and therefore little revenue.  The earmarked financial support for environmental research would at best be uncertain and attenuated, not necessarily adequate for the research tasks, though the more difficult the control under existing technology, the greater the revenues available to finance the research to lower these costs.  There is, in any case, no reason to suppose that the optimal level for R and D would correspond to the revenue from optimal pollution changes.

## Earmarking and Equity

Some regard an environmental control excise tax as a kind of user charge--a license fee to pollute, similar to a hunting fee.  Therefore, they consider it essential to the equity of the tax--otherwise possibly quite regressive by orthodox liberal standards--that it should be spent on behalf of those paying the tax.  They think of the ability of the atmosphere or bodies of water to absorb pollution as a costless natural resource to be used in particular by certain industries, such as the electric utilities.  Just as duck hunters may feel that the license fees they pay can quite properly be devoted in user-charge fashion to replenishing and nurturing the duck population, it is held that producers and users of electricity should be entitled to see their control excise money properly used to develop methods of preventing pollution, repairing damages, increasing the pollution-absorbing capacity of the environment, or finding alternative sources of energy that entail lighter pollution costs.

Others assert that the environmental control excise rates should be set in relation to damages (not merely control costs). In particular, they see pollution charges as compensation for injury and claim that any proceeds should be used on behalf of those injured by the pollution, insofar as they can be identified.

This difference between the "license" concept and the "damage" concept may be, for most purposes, academic,* though the level of excise indicated by the "damage" concept is more defined and is likely to be higher than the level that would be imposed under the "license" concept.

## Earmarking and Budgetary Policy

Earmarking--no matter how high the priority of the budgetary function involved--is subject to criticism from the standpoint of modern budgetary practice. The justification of earmarking is, of course, that it gives a basis of equity and political acceptability to the tax used to finance the program and an assurance that the moneys will be used as intended. Earmarking, so the criticism runs, tends to reduce budgetary flexibility, foreclose options that budget makers feel they should possess, freeze in programs at levels that may become inappropriate as time goes on, and create vested interests in the earmark-supported programs of expenditure.

These criticisms are not conclusive, however, and departures from the anti-earmarking rule may be warranted in order to win support and justification in the case of extraordinary programs such as those for the protection of the environment. If environmental programs are subject to continuing review and modification on both the revenue and expenditure sides, these objections to earmarking will be largely met. Such review and continuing adjustment may well be fumbling and uncertain, however, and earmarking pollution-based taxes for research in the face of varying requirements would lead to either inadequacy or waste or both.

---

*However, the question whether an environmental excise tax should reflect the one concept or the other may have practical policy implications in the area of international environmental policy, as will be pointed out below.

## AREAS FOR POLLUTION TAXES

This section examines specific types of pollution tax proposals in three major areas of the effort to improve the environment:  air, water, and land-use policy and human settlements.

In the field of air pollution, the immediate targets to be singled out for tax control measures appear to be the complex of smog-creating emissions from automobiles; sulfur oxide emissions, chiefly from the combustion of fossil fuels, in connection with electricity-generating plants, and also emissions from smelters; nitrogen oxide emissions from various combustion sources; and particulates.  These different immediate objectives are varyingly amenable to fiscal or tax incentive devices (for use in combination with regulatory standards).  A number of feasible environmental control taxes or tax incentives are available to deal with major sources of air pollution such as automotive emissions and sulfur oxides.

Water pollution problems can be expressed in terms of municipal waste treatment; industrial effluents, including toxic substances, organic wastes measured in terms of biological oxygen demand, excess acidity and alkalinity, dissolved solids, and thermal pollution; waste treatment on ships; oil and other polluting discharges and spillages from tankers and other vessels; oil leakage from offshore drilling accidents and natural earth faults; and ocean dumping.  Of these, the area with the greatest immediate promise for fiscal incentive devices is that of industrial (and municipal) effluents, including sewage.  The concept of effluent charges has received considerable attention, and there are inter-national precedents for the effluent charge approach on a regional basis.

The area of land use and human settlements embraces basically the problems of population distribution, including protection of the natural environment, urban congestion, suburban sprawl, and rural development.  A number of tax approaches have been advanced to further environmental objectives in this area.  These measures would include not only local property tax reform but also reform of the national income tax structure and other fiscal systems.

### Air Pollution

#### Sulfur Oxides

There is general recognition that sulfur oxides today are one of the most harmful air pollutants discharged into the

atmosphere of industrial nations.  U.S. estimates indicate that
they account for about half of the total damages from air
pollution.[7]

There is substantial documentation of their adverse effect
on human health (particularly, evidence of increased morbidity
rates for respiratory diseases, including permanent damage to
lung tissue leading to bronchitis and cancer), vegetation,
materials, and property.  Sulfur oxide emissions may have
international effects due to movements of the pollutant across
national boundaries and its precipitation in the form of "acid
rain," as has been experienced in Scandinavia.

U.S. studies put estimates of national health costs due
to sulfur oxide emissions at over $3.3 billion annually, and
damages to material, property, and vegetation at $5 billion
annually--making a total of $8.3 billion annually or about
$.20 for each pound of sulfur emitted into the atmosphere.

The estimated amounts and sources of sulfur emissions
in the United States at 1971 levels are shown below:

|                  | Million tons | Percent |
| ---------------- | ------------ | ------- |
| Power plants     | 20.0         | 55      |
| Other combustion | 8.2          | 22      |
| Smelters         | 4.0          | 11      |
| Refineries       | 2.4          | 7       |
| Miscellaneous    | 2.0          | 5       |
| Total            | 36.0         | 100     |

The severity of the environmental problem is underscored
by the fact that sulfur oxide emissions in the United States
are expected to quadruple, to an estimated 126 million tons,
by the year 2000.

With available technology poorly defined, genuinely
effective regulatory efforts will be hampered by arguments on
technical feasibility.  In this situation, an economic incentive
such as a sulfur emissions tax would put pressure on industry
to use technology as soon as possible, encourage industry to
achieve even higher levels of abatement than are required by
the standards, and create a market for technology, stimulating
commercial R and D for sulfur oxide control.

The incentive proposal recommended by the president of
the United States was to have been developed jointly by the
Council on Environmental Quality and the Department of the
Treasury.  The plan was for a charge on sulfur emitted into the

atmosphere from combustion or distillation of fossil fuels and
possibly from other sources, such as smelters.  The tax would
apply in the first instance to the input of fuels.  A rebate
would be granted for sulfur removals from the fuels or from
the smokestacks.  With 80 percent removal, for example, only
20 percent of the tentative charge would be required.

The tax rate might rise progressively over a transitional
period, starting at, say, one cent per pound of sulfur emissions
at the outset, and reaching 10 cents per pound by the end of
the period.  Revenues would then rise correspondingly from
about $400 million in the first year to $4 billion in the
final year, if emission levels remained the same.

Several strategies are available to industry to reduce
emissions and thus decrease or minimize the tax:  resorting to
lower-sulfur fuels such as natural gas or low-sulfur oil and
coal; desulfurization of fuels such as oil and coal; recovery
of sulfur in the combustion process by various means including
stack-gas cleaners; switching to nuclear energy and hydro-
electric methods for electricity generation; and relocation of
plants or purchase of power or services outside the country
(a possibility open to smelters and possibly to electric-
generating facilities).

It will be readily understood that higher prices of
electricity due to the tax and pollution control costs will
reduce demand for electricity, in accordance with price
elasticity of demand.  In the broad social sense, this
curtailment of output in response to a demand change is a
response strategy that eases environmental strain.

In general, these strategies represent adjustments that
contribute to an improvement in the environment.  However,
some may represent merely a shift from a taxed form of
pollution to as yet untaxed forms.  Others may involve
appreciable injury to the national economy.

One of the questions of policy in formulating this type
of emissions tax or charge is the matter of regional variation.
One somewhat cold-blooded view of rational environmental
policy is that it should utilize the spatial (and seasonal)
dimension of the environment to maximize its pollution-
absorbing capacity.  In this view, more favorable treatment
would be given to emissions in remote regions (or in seasons
with low total emissions or favorable prevailing winds for
dispersal).  The U.S. Clean Air Act, however, sets uniform
national standards that serve as minima for state regulation.
This approach means that air is nowhere permitted to be more
polluted than the national ambient standard, and that even in
sparsely populated areas emissions are to be limited.

Despite its laudable objectives, the sulfur emissions tax--like other more mundane revenue-raising measures--has met with vocal opposition. Some of the resistance comes from environmentalists who decry a tax or charge of this type as a "license to pollute." Much of it comes from the utility industry and other potential payers of the charge; their opposition is summarized here: the charge superimposed on already heavy capital outlays required to comply with air pollution standards means a double burden on the electric utility industry; no reliable tested technology is as yet available for sulfur emission control, so the tax is a penalty incentive with no practical escape; the coal (and other fuel) industries will suffer severe economic wrenches due to the premium placed on low-sulfur fuel with corresponding loss of income to high-sulfur coal and other fuel producers; damage data on sulfur emissions are dubious or exaggerated; it is inherently unfair and objectionable to impose a charge or tax on emissions of utilities in regions that are already meeting, possibly by a wide margin, ambient air standards--national and state; if there is a need to move to higher standards the regulations should reflect it.

## Automotive Emissions

From the standpoint of the commuter or resident of large metropolitan areas, particularly those cursed with geographical conformations and climatic conditions especially suited to the creation and entrapment of smog, air pollution from automobiles is the single greatest environmental problem.

Two facts make it difficult to approach the automotive emissions problem with a simple effluent-type tax: the complex interaction among ingredients of smog, the automobile emissions of carbon monoxide, hydrocarbons, and nitrogen oxides, plus particulates from various sources, and the damages caused are as yet imperfectly understood; the existence of the millions of potential taxpayers would make it administratively difficult to carry out the monitoring, measuring, and reporting required.

Conceivably, a special pollution tax could be imposed on motor fuels, with rebates depending upon the pollution rating of the motor, the efficacy of the control or abatement devices installed in the automobile, and the area in which the vehicle is operated. The fact that substantial taxes are already levied at national and state or provincial levels, the time schedule on which effective control devices are expected, their practical limitation to new cars used by the more affluent, as well as the compliance and administrative burden, all tend to cause this approach to be rejected.

In the United States, therefore, the primary reliance in
the automotive emission area has been on regulation such as
legislative provisions that require advanced pollution control
devices on all new automobiles.  It was not until the energy
crisis that fiscal measures that have significant environmental
implications have again been seriously considered.

One of the pioneering fiscal incentive plans, utilizing
the regulatory excise approach for environmental purposes, is
the tax on lead additives for motor fuel, initially proposed
by the president of the United States in May 1970.  So far, no
action at the national level has been taken, though some
cities (for example, New York) have placed restrictions on
the amount of lead permitted in gasoline.

The lead additives tax has a very special rationale.  Its
ultimate objective is cleaner air.  Its immediate (and in part
its long-term) goal is twofold:

1.    Encouragement of both demand and supply of low-lead
or no-lead gasoline.  Lead fouls the emission control systems
for automobiles using catalytic converters.  A supply of lead-
free gasoline in sufficient amount and quality for use with
these control devices was thus considered essential, though
doubts have since been expressed as to whether catalytic
control of carbon monoxide and nitrogen compounds would not
also entail oxidation of sulfur to more damaging sulfuric
forms, making the form of control unsuitable.

2.    Control of lead in the atmosphere.  Lead itself is
a pollutant; the contribution of lead from auto vehicle fumes
adds to the already rising background lead in the environment.
Some 95 percent of the total lead emitted into the ambient air
is derived from lead additives in gasoline.  Lead particles
can penetrate the lungs and be retained and absorbed in the
bloodstream.  Lead from the atmosphere can be precipitated
into water supplies, thus becoming diffused into the water
used for drinking purposes.  While this may be regarded by
some as a long-range problem, it cannot be ignored.  In urban
areas, the margin of safety between blood levels of lead in
humans and the levels at which lead poisoning symptoms
manifest themselves is narrowing.

But the main motivation for the lead additives tax plan
is the strategy for control of automotive emissions.  As
official discussions have pointed out, the U.S. Clean Air
Amendments of 1970 authorize control of lead levels in
gasoline.  Total prohibition is impracticable since over
one-half the vehicles now on the road require high-octane
gasoline, which, in general, can most cheaply be made using

lead additives. While the government can require unleaded gasoline to be available, it cannot require motorists to buy it--and substantial purchase is necessary to support an expanded capacity. The cost of low-lead or nonleaded gasoline is higher for an equivalent octane, so there is no clear microeconomic incentive, so to speak, to buy it and, unfortunately, the altruistic objective of helping to reach a cleaner environment is likely to be overwhelmed by everyday concerns, which lead to the purchase of the cheapest fuel of the required octane rating.

One problem with a lead tax is that smaller refiners would find it more difficult to adapt their production plant to the production of nonleaded fuel. One way around this would be to provide a specific exemption for each company of a given amount of lead incorporated in their product for a transition period.

Because even small amounts of lead could permanently foul a catalytic converter, a prohibition against the use of leaded gas in converter-equipped vehicles was to have been enforced by having special filling attachments on such cars into which only special pump-hose nozzles used for lead-free gas could be inserted.

In conclusion, the lead additives tax plan represents an ingenious and pioneering use of the environmental excise tax device to complement and assist regulation. Its acceptance has been made difficult by the already high tax on gasoline, by motorists' resistance to further fuel price increases, by the sharp collision with a cohesive industry that would suffer special hardship (the manufacture of lead additives), and by the prospect of its somewhat ambiguous coexistence with regulatory provisions that would accomplish the same thing. The detailed formulation of such a plan, involving estimates of cost and price differentials in the light of a changing technological scene, presents formidable problems.

## Nitrogen Oxides

The oxides of nitrogen present significant though somewhat less understood and recognized problems of pollution of the atmosphere. The most important of this family of pollutants from the atmospheric standpoint are nitric oxide (NO) and nitrogen dioxide ($NO_2$). There are other known oxides of nitrogen, sometimes of transitory existence and apparently not of great importance for the ambient air.[*] The term $NO_x$ is

---

[*]For example, nitrous oxide ($N_2O$) ("laughing gas"), nitrogen sequioxide ($N_2O_3$), nitrogen pentoxide ($N_2O_5$), nitrogen tetroxide ($N_2O_4$), and nitrogen trioxide ($NO_3$).

generally used to denote the atmospheric total of nitric oxide and nitrogen dioxide.

Nitrogen dioxide ($NO_2$) is apparently the most harmful to human health, exerting its primary toxic effects on the lungs-- causing lesions, emphysematous conditions, and other pathologic developments. Nitrogen dioxide ($NO_2$) also causes noticeable necrotic leaf injury and other injurious effects on vegetation including a slowing of plant growth. Both oxides ($NO_x$) affect materials adversely, including fading of textile dyes and the deterioration or corrosion of certain metals. While larger quantities of $NO_x$ are generated by natural than by human sources, the contribution to the atmosphere originating in human activities is concentrated in urban areas. In these concentrations it creates problems of air pollution in itself and also in its synergistic reactions with automotive emissions (themselves including $NO_x$) to help create smog.

Control of nitrogen oxide emissions is generally directed at combustion sources and chemical processes. In stationary combustion sources, the control techniques involve reducing the flame temperature and the availability of oxygen. These control principles are also applicable to automobiles. Catalytic techniques have been used to reduce $NO_x$ from chemical processes and are also usable in controlling the $NO_x$ in automotive exhaust gases.

With the deleterious effects of concentrations of $NO_x$ reasonably well established, the sources identified, and the control techniques available, it would appear that the nitrogen oxides are a potential candidate for an environmental regulatory excise tax.

One practical problem is that of systematic and accurate metering of $NO_x$ emissions. Unlike sulfur oxide emissions, the nitrogen oxides are derived not so much from inputs of nitrogen materials as from the "fixation" or absorption of nitrogen from the atmosphere itself under certain conditions of combustion. Consequently, the procedure used in the sulfur oxides tax plan of measuring the sulfur content of fuel inputs and subtracting out the recoveries from abatement procedures to arrive at a semipresumptive emissions base is not available in the case of the nitrogen oxides.

Direct measurement of a more or less continuous type, using metering devices for stack gases, would be required. While the technology for monitoring and sample checking of nitrogen oxide emissions seems to be available, it is not clear how available and practicable it is for continuous use or whether the cost of operating such measurement devices would prohibit their use for small and medium-size plants.

In formulating a pollution tax aimed at nitrogen oxide emissions, these matters would call for careful exploration, including study of the implications of a possible exemption for numerous smaller stationary combustion sources. The automobile contribution to the $NO_x$ problem, it can be assumed, would be handled as part of the regulatory approach to automobile emission control.

Significant considerations relevant to the merits and demerits of a pollution tax on nitrogen oxides would be the questions: whether regulation can handle the problem; whether tax penalties or incentives can adequately or significantly stimulate the development of commercially available control methods and equipment; whether the cost-internalization effects of a pollution tax could effectively supplement regulatory standards to bring nitrogen oxide control to a more effective general level, with greater efficiency and flexibility than by tightening general regulatory standards another notch or two; and whether control methods are feasible on a commercial basis for both oil or gas and coal-fired boilers and for chemical process industries.[*]

"Residence" time in the atmosphere for $NO_x$ and the capability of movement of $NO_x$ concentrations across national boundaries are matters for concern in approaching this source of air pollution from an international standpoint. The record does not show the equivalent for nitrogen oxides of the "acid rains" in Scandinavia caused by the international drifting of sulfur oxides. However, where urban concentrations occur near national boundaries, the problem of $NO_x$ is clearly interregional and international.

---

[*]Research and development seem to be going on actively in this field. Techniques for controlling $NO_x$ in oil and gas-fired boilers apparently involve two-stage combustion, low-excess-air firing, and furnace modifications. In general, the approach here is through reduction of peak gas temperatures, trends away from oxidizing and toward reducing atmospheres, and changes in the time history of the combustion gases. Feasibility is apparently demonstrable for oil and gas, but the extension of these methods to coal-fired boilers remains to be demonstrated. Various catalytic methods, stack cleaning, and other procedures seem to be usable in the chemical industries.

## Particulates

No discussion of air pollution problems from the standpoint
of possible tax incentive approaches would be complete without
some attention to particulates.  Welfare economics, which
contemplates the use of tax penalties and subsidies, has long
used soot and smoke as a typical instance in which the price
and market mechanism breaks down because of the failure to
recognize in the internal cost calculations of business the
external damages caused by their emissions.

Solid and liquid particles suspended in the air constitute
a major fraction of the pollutants found in urban atmospheres.
Air pollution control policy has to take into account various
descriptive criteria of particulate pollution relating to the
size distribution, concentration, and chemical composition of
the particles.  Various techniques are available for determining
the atmospheric concentration of particles of various sizes,
using optical measurement devices and volume samplers.  More
elaborate and expensive methods are used for analysis of
particulate pollution by chemical composition and particle
size.

Particulate air pollution affects the weather locally near
the pollution sources and both seasonal and weekly variations
are observed.  Pollution of this type may be causing the
gradual decrease in the average worldwide temperature that
started in the 1940s.

The effects of particulate pollution are matters of common
observation and relate not merely to plumes from smokestacks
but also to well-dispersed and well-aged stable atmospheric
aerosols.  Among the sources of those aerosols that cause
greatest concern are nominally nonparticulate emitters such
as automobiles, because the emissions may eventually become
particulates after photochemical reaction in the atmosphere.
The burning of fossil fuels is an especially important
source of particulate pollutants, and several of the most
serious air pollution episodes have been accompanied by high
concentrations of soot together with sulfur dioxide resulting
from the burning of bituminous coal.

Air-borne particles can, depending on their chemical
composition and physical state, cause a wide range of damage.
They may cause deterioration by settling on surfaces and
soiling them, thus creating a need for more frequent cleaning,
which in itself weakens materials.  Particles may also cause
direct chemical damage to nonresistant materials in two ways:
through their own intrinsic corrosiveness and through the
action of corrosive chemicals absorbed on their surface.
There seems to be little doubt that a number of dusts,

particularly certain fractions of cement kiln dusts, adversely
affect plants when naturally deposited on wet-leafed surfaces.
The injuries are due to direct chemical actions, which are not
clearly understood.

The health effects of particulate pollution are dependent
on the processes involved in the inhalation, retention, and
clearance of the particles from the lungs.  The inhalation of
certain particulates may be followed by their subsequent
clearance from the respiratory system and their entry into the
gastrointestinal system, so that organs remote from the
deposition site may be affected.

Particulate matter may exert a toxic effect in one or more
of three ways:  the particle may be intrinsically toxic; it
may interfere with clearance mechanisms in the respiratory
tract; it may act as a carrier of absorbed toxic substances.

Epidemiological studies lead to the conclusion that the
presence in community air of high levels of particulate matter
accompanied by other pollutant substances, notably sulfur
dioxide, is associated with several types of health effects.
Brief episodes of acute elevation of particulate and other
pollutant concentrations can lead to excess deaths detectable
in large population groupings.  These deaths are often
distributed among susceptible individuals having chronic
pulmonary disease or cardiac disorders.  However, the general
population is also involved.  Long-term residence of individuals
in areas of high pollution is associated with a greater risk
of mortality from respiratory diseases and, for certain
population segments, from cancer and "deaths from all causes."
There is apparently an association between the prevalence of
chronic obstructive pulmonary disease in a population and the
particulate pollution level.

It is important to emphasize the synergistic role of
particulates with sulfur and possibly with other automotive
emissions such as carbon monoxide, hydrocarbons, and related
photochemicals, which contribute to the smog phenomenon.

Particulate polluting materials found in the ambient air
originate from many sources.  In general, these are usually
grouped into mobile and stationary source classifications.
Internal combustion, industrial processes, construction and
demolition, and solid waste disposal are the major stationary
sources.  An estimate of particulate pollution made as of 1966
in the United States showed that of 11.5 million tons of
annual particulate pollution, the contributions to the total
were as follows:  6 million tons from industrial processes,
including industrial fuel burning; 5 million tons from power
generation, incineration, and space heating; and 0.5 million
tons from mobile sources.

A wide variety of techniques are available for controlling
the source or reducing the effects of particulate pollution.
They are gas cleaning, source relocation, fuel substitution,
process changes, good operating practice, source shutdown, and
dispersion.

The sheer complexity of the particulate pollution problem,
the variety of sources, the variety of forms of particulates
involved, and the difficulties of measurement and metering on
an economical basis that would be accurate and comprehensive
enough for the construction of a tax base, all point in the
direction of reliance on regulatory methods. The exclusive
or primary use of a tax on particulate emissions would seem
to be too difficult for serious consideration at this stage.
However, positive tax incentive approaches that would encourage
or assist industry to construct particulate pollution abatement
devices or redesign their processes so that the particulate
pollution problem was reduced or eliminated merit consideration.

Particulate pollution is of concern to the international
community because of the considerable residence time and
mobility in the atmosphere of many harmful particulates, the
impact on urban communities near national borders, and the
implications for the world climate of the pumping of millions
of tons of particles into the ambient atmosphere.


## Water and Marine Pollution

The problems of water pollution are not generally local
in character. Water supplies at any point are part of an
ecological chain or system that ultimately affects the seas,
the life systems, and the world's food supplies from oceanic
sources.

For the most part, the task of keeping these effects
within manageable limits is one requiring (1) large public
expenditures and financial aid--as in the case of municipal
sewage construction to keep up with expanding urban populations
and the more sophisticated processing treatment required to
cope with industrial wastes dumped into municipal systems--
and (2) alert, aggressive, well-informed regulation.

There are, however, several avenues of approach to water
and marine pollution via the tax structure. Among the most
relevant to the present situation are taxes applying the
principle of internalization of social costs: an excise tax
on the phosphate content of detergents; a general effluent
charge system on municipal and industrial discharges of wastes
into the water system; substantial taxes on harmful inorganic
fertilizers, pesticides, and herbicides; and taxes on waste oil
and spilled oil.

Each of these proposals has obvious difficulties.  But they
illustrate the potential contribution of specific pollution tax
devices to the reduction of multiple-source pollution, with
some economies in administrative costs and bureaucratic burdens.

Phosphates in Detergents

Excessive nutrient enrichment, algae growth, and eutrophication make up a syndrome constituting one of the most
difficult water pollution problems.  Apparently, removal of
gross organic waste loads by means of expensive treatment
plants will not necessarily stop eutrophication.  Other factors
continue to fuel it.  There has been disagreement among
scientists and technical experts as to the basic causes of
eutrophication.  Some have claimed that carbon is the chief
cause rather than phosphates, which were long suspected as the
controlling factor, but recent official studies in the United
States have concluded that phosphates are still the most
important nutrient to control if eutrophication is to be
successfully halted.[8]

Most phosphates reach water, in the United States at least,
from municipal effluent sources.  Phosphates in detergents are
said to account for approximately 50 percent of the total.
The runoff of phosphate fertilizers from the land is another
source, one difficult to control.  Nitrogen compounds, also
implicated in the eutrophication process, originate from both
municipal effluents and land runoff.

In view of the key role of phosphates in detergents as a
nutrient interfering with clean water programs, both regulatory
and tax approaches have been studied.  An incentive tax of the
excise type for reducing the phosphate content of detergents
would accelerate industry research toward a low- or no-
phosphate washing material; induce immediate economies in
phosphate use; avoid putting the government in the difficult
position of prescribing phosphate levels without full knowledge
of the problems of reduction; and allow the consumer to express
preferences but with a higher cost for higher phosphate content.

The tax could be phased in with gradually increasing rates
to carry out a transition to a goal of very low phosphate
content of detergents over, say, a five-year period.  The tax
could be developed either as a graduated tax on detergents
depending on their phosphate content or, more logically, as a
flat tax per pound of phosphates going into detergents, broadly
modeled on the proposed tax on lead additives for motor fuels
and phased in at increasingly restrictive rates.

## Effluent Charge or Tax System

On a grander scale than the specific type of environmental
cost excise tax, such as the plan for phosphates in detergents,
is the effluent charge system previously mentioned.

As stated repeatedly earlier in this chapter, from the
economist's point of view the control of water (or air)
pollution is facilitated in an optimum manner if a price is
charged for polluting the environment.  The advantage of this
solution is that in this way individuals and society explicitly
place a value on pollution abatement.  The internalization of
pollution cost by such tax pricing motivates movement in the
direction of a socially optional adjustment.

Full implementation of the pollution-charge approach
involves quantification and evaluation of the damages done by
polluting effluents.  Some data on abatement costs also
furnish helpful guidance in predicting industry (or municipal)
response to setting the effluent fee or charge at any
particular level.  Too low a charge will not provide sufficient
incentive to reduce the wastes disposed; too high will induce
uneconomic overcontrol.

The effluent-charge and user-charge approaches have been
particularly applicable to water or water basin pollution
control operations.  The term "effluent charge" or "emission
charge" generally refers to a price charged for direct
disposal to the environment--in short, pollution.  The term
"user charge" is reserved for the price charged for waste
treatment service provided by a treatment facility--in short,
organized pollution abatement.

There is considerable experience in different countries
(in some cases, associations handling international watersheds)
with user charges for industrial waste treatment by
collective or public facilities.  The collective approach may
obtain greater economies than individual plant waste discharge
treatment.  Regional facilities and procedures--operated in
accordance with the particular hydrological situation and
environmental standards--offer great advantages in water
pollution control.  Use of such facilities may be made
mandatory or may conceivably be induced by an effluent charge
system.

The system of effluent charges could be applied to any
polluter--private industry, municipalities, and tax-exempt
organizations alike--on the basis of their discharge of
specified polluting effluents into public water bodies.
Effluents would be measured on the basis of three
characteristics:  biochemical oxygen demand, total suspended

solids, and acidity.  Coverage of these pollutants would include the major wastes and would establish a satisfactory initial effluent charge system that could be elaborated to cover other pollutants or effluent characteristics as desired.

The plan would require that effluents be measured in an acceptable manner and that reports be submitted to the national treasury or effluent charge authority detailing the types and amounts of pollutants and submitting payments with the corresponding charges to be remitted to the treasury. Monitoring and surveillance would be required on the part of the national effluent charge authority, so that procedures and reports of waste charges by polluters would be subjected to periodic audit and checked, with penalties imposed for evasion similar to those under any other form of taxation.

Since the objective of the proposed effluent charge system is to build environmental costs into the cost schedule of business firms, these costs would be deductible as expenses for income tax purposes just as any other cost of production.

The operation of the plan would involve little or no specification as to how or to what extent firms or organizations are to cleanup their discharges so as to avoid the effluent charge.  Presumably, each plant or organization would use the available appropriate combination of its own treatment facilities, internal process change, recovery and recycling of materials, or delivery of effluents in the first instance to collective treatment facilities or to municipal plants that would have their own user charges.

The structure of effluent charges would alter production costs for different firms and industries depending upon the nature and amounts of their polluting effluents.  The impact would also vary depending upon the treatment facilities already in operation, which reduced or even eliminated taxable effluents entering the public water system.

By the same token, the prices of products, which would presumably incorporate the effluent charge expense, would be increased more for firms and industries that were heavy polluters and less for those that were light polluters or had already been controlling their pollution to a substantial degree.

An analysis in the United States of the comparative costs of the effluent charge method and alternative formulas for achieving a given target for water quality improvement using the "Delaware Estuary Model" produced interesting results. The following alternative methods or management procedures were compared, using a computerized model:  actual cost

minimization for the whole estuary; cost minimization by zones
in the estuary; uniform cutback in discharge at all "outfalls"
(a typical regulatory approach); and effluent charges.

The findings were that the uniform cutback cost about twice
as much as cost minimization.  However, a single effluent
charge based on BOD was found to achieve the target level of
water quality improvement at a cost in terms of real resources
only slightly higher than the programed cost-minimization
procedure.[9]

The formulation of appropriate damage and treatment-cost-
oriented charges is more difficult than would appear in the
enthusiastic presentations of proponents of the effluent
charge system.  A national effluent charge level might have
quite different effects in different locations, leading to
either under- or overcontrol by optimal standards.

Disposition of the receipts from the effluent charge--
presumably, though not necessarily, for environmental purposes--
would help to justify the tax as something different from an
ordinary government expense burden but would still present
problems of equity in regard to the alignment of burdens and
benefits.  Whether or not these equity problems were valid in
the context of academic theory, there would still be
conflicting group and regional interests.

Effluent charges have not only the theoretical merit of
being the means of an optimal, self-operating corrective, but
also the practical appeal of providing a clear-cut operating
mechanism to supplement or even replace a lumbering regulatory
process.

## Waste Oil and Oil Spills

The economics of waste oil collection and reprocessing are
now unfavorable to the salvage and re-refining of crankcase
oil, chiefly owing to the high labor costs of collection.  As
a result, a large volume of crankcase oil is dumped on vacant
lots or poured into municipal sewer systems, polluting the
underground water supplies and the streams or rivers into
which treated municipal effluents are discharged.  Waste oil
pollution of basic water supplies and streams can also affect
estuaries and ocean waters.

A simple excise tax or excise tax-subsidy plan could make
the recovery and reuse of waste oil profitable.  The purpose
of such a plan, which might tax new oil to finance a subsidy
for recycled oil, would be to reflect the "external" costs of
unrecycled oil and the "external" benefits of disposing of the
oil through reuse in a way that reduces water pollution.

International programs are already recommended or under way to control and clean up oil spills in navigable waterways.

Over and above existing conventions for compensation for damages caused by oil spills, a tax might be imposed on all international transportation of oil, the proceeds to be used for relevant research, for prevention, or to underwrite the cost of cleanup and repair of oil-spill damages. The plan might provide a rating system based on past experience of the particular transport firm, reducing the tax of those with good experience and raising it for those with unfavorable experience ratings. This would not only provide funds for combating marine oil pollution but also create a significant incentive for oil transporters to avoid accidents or spillage incidents.

## Harmful Inorganic Fertilizers, Pesticides, and Herbicides

While phosphates in detergents are an important source of water pollution, other sources include certain inorganic fertilizers with high nitrogen content. Various pesticides and insecticides also give rise to grave problems of pollution affecting birds, fish, and other wildlife, and directly or indirectly the human population. The pervasiveness with which some of these modern materials invade the water and marine environment and the related "ecosystems" of the world and the resistance to degradation and the tendency for many of them to be reconcentrated through biological food chains makes them matters of international concern.

While direct regulation is appropriate and necessary, an incentive tax to minimize the use of harmful materials in this general category would be helpful in initiating a transition to more salutary methods of fertilizing crops and combating insects, weeds, and so on. A statutory definition of items initially subject to the tax could be provided, subject to expansion from time to time on the determination of the appropriate government departments or agencies with expertise in the area in question. A special antipollution tax on the sales of such products would yield considerable revenue, depending on the exact definition of the regulatory excise tax base, which could be used for research on better and "cleaner" methods of achieving protection against insects and pests, for the repair of damages being done by these harmful materials, and for possible alleviation of hardship situations where agriculturists need transitional aid in adjusting to the reduction in their accustomed use of harmful compounds.

### Land Use and Human Settlements

The objectives of national land-use policy and population distribution are numerous and sometimes conflicting. They will vary between countries, but the international community as well as the individual nation has a stake in the wisdom of national decisions affecting optimal patterns of land use and the preservation of cultural heritage, wilderness, green space, and environmentally critical areas. Excessive concentrations of population, congestion, urban sprawl, and disorderly and wasteful patterns of land development are the enemies of healthy national societies and, within the limitations applicable to international intervention or assistance, are matters of concern to the world community.

What role can tax policy play in a comprehensive range of national programs--planning, implementation of plans, and creative use of regulatory powers at all levels of government-- to effect wise use of land and space?

Some observers argue that the sole legitimate aim of tax policy is to collect the revenue necessary to meet the government's bills--or, in more modern fashion, to maintain an aggregate withdrawal of funds from the national spending stream to avoid an inflationary or deflationary imbalance in the macroeconomy. In their view, tax policies distorting or modifying the allocation of resources, inadvertently or intentionally, are detrimental from the total welfare standpoint. This purist view tends to overlook the numerous defects in the market mechanism and the impact for good or bad that the far-from-neutral tax structure now extant has in most national economies. There is a soundly based contrary viewpoint that recognizes the possibilities of correcting biases in the present tax structure and introducing new tax incentives to achieve better land use.

### Relative Burden on Land and Improvements under Local Property Taxes

A major potential for control through the fiscal mechanism centers in the property tax. Here a central issue is the relative burden on land as opposed to improvements. Among economists, there is a strong body of opinion to the effect that the present local property tax systems rather systematically undertax land and overtax improvements. In part, the national income tax system may contribute to a valuation differential because of the preference of taxpayers to have value allocated to depreciable improvements that generate depreciation deductions rather than to land that is not depreciable for income tax purposes. Even in the absence of such discrimination, it is argued that tax rates on improvements should be lower or even zero, and rates on land increased.

## Effects of Taxes on Improvements

In general, it is contended, overtaxation of improvements and undertaxation of site value encourages low-density uses such as parking lots, benefits owners of run-down tenements and discourages both rehabilitation and replacement of dilapidated structures, and causes disorderly development because it encourages speculative holding of developable land.

## Proposals for Shifting Tax Burden from Improvements to Land

Proposals are frequently made to reverse or correct these undesirable tax effects by shifting a greater part of the property tax burden from improvements to land, with the hoped-for results of more orderly development on the whole continuum from core city to exurbia; savings to suburban communities because of the slowing down of hectic, disorderly expansion and the lessening of sprawl pressure on rural fringe areas; more economical use of urban land and increased supply of living and working space; reduction of transportation needs and costs; stimulus to investment in real estate improvements as against bidding up of prices of underutilized land; and incentives to the repair, rehabilitation, and replacement of deteriorated property.

All these claims on behalf of restructuring the property tax are subject to controversy, criticism, and counterclaim. Some expert critics allege that a lower tax on improvements as against land will have results that may not be entirely salutary, including the following: mushroom growth of high-rise structures in the inner city, squeezing out low-income housing and adversely affecting suburban growth; a shift of the tax burden to land-intensive uses such as low-income housing; higher land values in the inner cities balanced by lower land values on the fringe, resulting in development on the fringes with cheaper land (the capitalized value of the higher tax merely being thrust back upon the previous owners of fringe spaces); and possible overall rise in land value since land becomes a complement to more intensive (because lower-taxed) capital development.

Although an evaluation of the complex impacts of possible property tax changes cannot be made here, there is a presumption that capital development will be aided by a lower improvement tax, while the overall supply of land will not, by its nature, be altered by a higher tax burden.

## Other Proposals for Use of the Tax Structure to Aid Land Policy

Unduly favorable depreciation has been blamed both for overly hectic speculative building and for the perpetuation of

rundown slum-type properties.  Numerous proposals have been made
from time to time to adjust depreciation in various ways to
eliminate existing perverse incentives or create desired ones.
The speed of write-off determines the present discounted value
of the capital-recovery allowances for tax purposes, sometimes
termed the depreciation tax annuity.  This in turn affects the
profitability of the investment, the cash flow or liquidity
characteristics of the investment, and the time period within
which risk can be substantially reduced through return of
capital.

Some of these proposals take on quite unconventional forms,
as, for example, the following:

1.   To limit depreciation on any building to "one round,"
based on the original cost plus improvements in order to prevent
repeated resales and advantageous depreciation of slum
properties, which prolong their existence.  This would seem to
result in inequity on subsequent purchasers, but the reality may
be a loss to initial holders in terms of the resale value of
their property.  The "second-round" owners may, through the
working of the market, avoid any real penalty on their
operations by acquiring the property at a lower price in
recognition of the depreciation limitation.

2.   To cover taxes on excess depreciation through fuller
taxation of capital gains.

3.   To provide differentially favorable depreciation for
desired forms of construction and investment location.  This
approach involves a change of timing in allowances, which
defers revenue (permanently in an ongoing system) in a manner
equivalent to an interest-free loan.  In general, economists
occupying the left wing of the political spectrum disapprove
of capital investment stimuli through the tax system; those of
more conservative hue are inclined to find this a reasonable,
efficient use of the tax structure to accomplish society's
objectives as regards construction and land development.

Another proposal is fast write-off of housing
rehabilitation outlays to combat urban decay, increase the
effective supply of acceptable housing, equalize the
attractiveness to investors of rehabilitation and more
favorably financed new housing, and register some of the
externalities of better housing (social benefits not
appropriable by the individual housing investor).  This
approach does not require elaborate definitions or certification.
However, certain specifications such as maximum and minimum
amounts per housing unit may be appropriate to delimit
application of the provision so as to exclude routine capital
replacement spending and luxury expenditures.

The effectiveness of fast write-offs is probably limited to situations in which rehabilitation is not rendered utterly uneconomic by excessive local property taxes, disorderly slum conditions that make it impossible to collect rents, very high maintenance costs for the rehabilitated property, and similar factors making the investment inherently unprofitable or unmanageable.

Where the rehabilitation is marginally feasible, the tax write-off may spell the difference between continued deterioration and a new lease on life for older housing units--with consequent benefits for the urban environment. Some critics object to the inconsistency between tax-equity objectives and this incentive use of the income tax structure; for example, the 1969 Tax Reform Act in the United States included the excess of accelerated amortization for housing rehabilitation over straight-line depreciation in the list of "tax preference items" to which a minimum tax applies.

Tax credits, potentially more powerful than the tax write-off device, could serve the same purpose, with greater effect where the economic handicaps of rehabilitation were especially severe.

More generally, ecologists and environmental policy makers have looked with some interest at the possibilities of enlisting the income tax structure to restrict or slow the processes of development that impinge upon or threaten ecologically sensitive areas--coastal wetlands, steep slopes, scenic views, wilderness areas, and other unique natural elements.

One obvious approach is to deny to investment or development activity that adversely affects the ecologically sensitive area the otherwise applicable tax concessions, such as accelerated depreciation, expensing of land development costs, and capital gains relief. Desirable as they may be for the economy generally, these tax concessions do not seem appropriate where they are so directly counterproductive to environmental aims. The creation of a differential in favor of development elsewhere, and against development detrimental to the ecologically sensitive area, may assist in diverting economic activity. However, one important objection to this approach is that the tax disadvantage intended to discourage exploitation of the "eco-land" may merely be capitalized in the form of a lower value for its owners. "Exploiters" can then sidestep the tax hurdle, so to speak, by shifting the burden of the tax disincentive back to the landowners. While this argument has considerable merit, it is also likely that the reservation price of landowners, the price at which they become willing to surrender their economic interests, possibly

after long waiting for capital appreciation--will not fully
absorb the tax increase, and thus they will continue to hold
out, at least until the new tax handicap is overcome by further
economic pressure and upward trends in land prices.  In any
case, this type of tax disincentive measure is obviously not
strong enough to provide full protection for ecologically
important resources.

More tangible and probably more effective than the removal
of unwanted tax stimuli would be a positive tax benefit to
existing owners of ecologically sensitive areas, encouraging
them to maintain, protect, and manage them in accordance with
environmental goals; or donate them to governments, trusts, or
other protective organizations.

Positive tax benefits might include:  exemption or
preferential treatment under the local property taxes; and
special tax credits or deductions for prescribed forms of use,
maintenance, and management of the resource.

This type of tax incentive is akin to a direct public
expenditure for the purpose of acquiring the property or
subsidizing its owner in continuing appropriate use of it.
Where elaborate identification and prescription of acceptable
use and maintenance of the resource are required, so that the
tax incentive is not largely self-operating within the framework
of the administration of the tax laws, the advantage of the
fiscal device is weakened.  Defining some ecologically sensitive
areas with sufficient precision for the application of the tax
laws may be difficult.

Tax incentives may also be especially designed for the
historic and cultural heritage.  Because of the uptrend in land
values and carrying costs in most advanced countries, it has
become increasingly difficult to preserve historically and
culturally significant structures and traditional land uses.
There appears to be a need for some kind of economical but
effective and well-directed financial assistance to prevent the
decay, destructive transformation, or demolition of these
cultural treasures.

The chief area for tax policy is in dealing with such
treasures that are in private hands, typically in use as a
residence or part of a private estate.  The expense connected
with the maintenance and preservation of these structures may
be not only high, but also (pertinent to the tax incentive
approach under consideration) differentially higher than for
a new structure of equivalent functional value--apart from
(if such separation is possible) esthetic and prestige
considerations.

The problem of logically correct and effective tax
incentives to protect cultural treasures (or an alternative
direct subsidy program for that matter) is therefore to
distinguish between high costs of maintenance or restoration
per se and that portion that is over and above ordinary
expenditures for providing "equivalent" esthetic and prestigious
living quarters or estate ornamentation.  This excess portion is
in a sense a donation on the part of the owner-custodian of the
property.  It is this excess that may require offsetting by some
form of incentive, since many owners may not be prepared to make
the financial sacrifice involved in the appropriate handling of
a cultural heritage property without compensation.

Granted that it is not easy to surmount the problem of
identifying and measuring the amount of tax or other subsidy
called for, various tax techniques are nevertheless available
to serve the basic purpose, including property tax exemption,
income tax deductions, tax credits, special write-offs for
restoration outlays, and preferential treatment or exemption
under the estate, gift, or inheritance taxes.

One motivation in tax incentive policy may be to keep the
property in such private use that will preserve and enhance the
environment without converting the property into a public
museum.  In historic areas, so many culturally valuable houses
or business establishments may be worthy of restoration and
preservation that the public museum approach (sometimes
objectionable in itself) is not feasible.  The tax incentive
instrument is one that involves a minimum of intervention in
the orderly continuity of use and upkeep or restoration of
traditional structures.

Where public or trust ownership of the property or an
easement on it is desirable, the favorable income tax treatment
of donations (and possibly favorable bequest treatment) is
indicated.  In the field of donations, the valuation of the
property or the easement on it for measuring the deduction
becomes crucial.  Uncertainties or illiberal rules about
valuation may be a serious barrier to desired donations.

The use of the tax instrument generally assumes the
operation of a "national trust" organization that identifies,
classifies, and records the various architectural and historic
treasures.  This facilitates the administration of tax laws
designed to carry out the public purposes, which are best
understood and defined by the national trust.

Tax credits or similar tax benefits for the restoration
or upkeep of a national treasure property should be made liens
on the property, which would be subject to collection for all
prior years in the event of demolition, misuse, or destructive
modification of the property.

A main aspect of tax strategy for preserving cultural heritage properties relates to the difficulty of winning public support for a grant program to assist typically affluent persons in expenditures that might be interpreted as feathering their own nests.  The problem exists even in justifying tax preferences for this purpose, but it is probably less than for outright grants--particularly if opportunities for semicorrupt and favoritist administration such as are inherent in a cash grant program are more limited or absent under a tax relief or incentive plan that follows prescribed statutory rules, and reasonably objective management by the national or regional cultural trust authorities.

Another proposal related to methods of dealing with incorrect use of resources is tax on traffic congestion and noise.  Congestion and noise derived from the use of auto-mobiles are very closely associated with air pollution, and essentially the same tax mechanisms may be applicable in such a way as to deal with all three more or less coincidentally. One approach is to levy a special charge on vehicles entering congested areas during peak hours, payment of the charge being evidenced by the display of a suitable license tag or sticker. Levy of such a charge has been seriously considered by Singapore and other places as well.  The license can be for a prestipulated period of a month, a day, or a week, or, more flexibly, for a particular use by the user tearing off tabs or impaling the license on a holder just prior to use, so as to indicate the specific use for which the license is to be valid.

A more sophisticated approach that has been discussed but is as yet far from the implementation stage is to require each vehicle operated in the controlled area to be equipped with a transponder unit, which will permit the identity of passing vehicles to be recorded by wayside equipment.  These records can then be processed by a computer and appropriate bills submitted to the registered owner of the vehicle corresponding to the amount of congestion, noise, and air pollution damage the use of the vehicle has been estimated to have inflicted on the environment.  The technology has been tested and the necessary equipment is available at reasonable cost:  The remaining problem is simply to gain public acceptance of the concept and to formulate appropriate charges.

Probably the largest component of any such externality charge for motor vehicles would in most cases be the congestion cost; indeed it is to be doubted whether the gains from controlling noise and air pollution would by themselves warrant the costs of installing and operating such a system. Given that the system is warranted for control of congestion, however, superimposing additional charges to allow for these

other elements would involve little additional cost and would be
well worth while.  As compared with overall controls implemented
by the manufacturer, moreover, such a charge would have
beneficial impacts not readily achievable in any other way, such
as providing incentives for owners of high-pollution or noisy
vehicles to trade them off to users in sparsely populated areas
where the adverse effects of their use would be less, or
providing specific incentives for limiting the use of pollution-
producing vehicles on occasions when adverse air-quality
conditions are expected.

     To be sure, the difficulties of estimating the air pollution
and noise-generating potentials of various vehicles are somewhat
greater than those relating to their congestion-generating
potential, which is a matter depending on such relatively
immutable parameters as size, power, and weight.  The pollution
and noise characteristics are much more a matter of the manner
in which a vehicle is maintained and even operated.  Nevertheless, results that are considerably better than no control at
all are obtainable even with very crude methods of rating.  At
the very least, pollution and noise ratings for each make,
model, and year could be established on the basis of appropriate
samplings.  Such ratings could be made subject to automatic
annual degradation, with the proviso that any individual could
have his rating upgraded on the basis of a suitable test, if
he used his car sufficiently intensively in congested areas to
make it profitable for him to bear the cost and inconvenience
of the testing procedure.

     There is, unfortunately, considerable dispute over the
effectiveness of low-cost test procedures.  It is asserted that
a major part of the pollution emission occurs during warm-up,
and that determining the level of this emission for a car
requires that it be left idle for a considerable period and
tested from a cold start.  Even so, a relatively cheap test
covering only warm-engine conditions might show a sufficiently
close correlation with overall emissions as to make reliance
on such tests worth while as compared to no testing at all,
even if cold-start testing should prove excessively costly.
And voluntary testing, limited to those vehicles for which it
would be important to secure a higher rating than that
presumed in the absence of testing, would be less costly than
universal testing.


                    INTERNATIONAL AND REGIONAL ASPECTS

     The most urgent environmental problems--those that relate
to intolerable and dangerous forms of pollution of the
atmosphere and water--are common to all nations.  Although
they appear at the moment to be primarily matters of concern to

national policy in the more advanced industrial economies, they
must be shared also to some degree by the developing nations.
These too are involved as potential passive victims (since the
world's atmosphere and water supply are one), as incipient
pollution-plagued communities, as learners of the political and
technological techniques of pollution control along with other
lore of industrial growth, and as part of the international
economy, which is increasingly affected by pollution control
costs and their impact on prices and trade.

International cooperation is a pressing need in dealing
with the major pollution problems, which impinge on both the
politics and economics of national existence.

## International Economic Repercussions

In the economic policy area, the repercussions of pollution
control policies are becoming all too familiar:  when the U.S.
Food and Drug Administration finds unacceptable levels of
mercury in tuna and swordfish, the fishing industry of Japan
is affected; with the introduction of strict emission standards
on automobiles, the sale of European cars in the U.S. market
is potentially affected and European producers become
apprehensive that pollution control requirements may resemble
nontariff trade barriers; rising costs of pollution abatement
to meet U.S. regulatory standards seem to U.S. producers to
constitute another handicap vis-a-vis their competitors abroad,
along with high wages and a heavy burden of direct taxes.

## Work of International Institutions

Recognition of the fact that environmental problems are
inherently international is, however, relatively recent.  The
Environment Committee of the OECD for harmonizing national
policies with respect to this issue was established in
December 1970.  The United Nations Conference on the Human
Environment was held in Stockholm in 1972.  Since then,
international machinery for dealing with the issue and for
cooperation have greatly expanded.  A series of proposals were
adopted by the OECD following the meet of the committee at the
ministerial level in 1974.  A United Nations Environmental
Programme, together with a secretariat, was set up after the
Stockholm conference.

Trade and Payments Implications of Pollution Control

A new international issue arising from pollution control, either by regulation or by penalty excise taxes, is the implication for trade and balance of payments. Where the additional costs of pollution control are substantial, the industry of the country pursuing an aggressive antipollution policy may be made noncompetitive--at least on a considerable "margin" of output--not only with respect to its exports into foreign markets but also with respect to the ability of its domestic production to resist imports. To many observers concerned with domestic unemployment and balance of payments problems, it seems neither fair nor good economics to let people lose jobs and the international payments balance suffer because the country in question is in the vanguard in raising environmental standards and penalizing pollution.[10] Even though, in principle, the cleaner environment might be held to justify lower wage rates, labor markets are usually too rigid to permit the adjustment to take place in this way.

There are, of course, some possible means of protecting the domestic markets of the pioneering antipollution country, for example, restricting pollution-causing imports on sanitary grounds. This is reasonable enough if the pollution derives from consumption of the item (for example, phosphates in detergents); if the case is one where the pollution affects the producing country, this would be pressing the doctrine of sanitary controls into novel territory. There is also the danger of initiating a whole sequence of nontariff barriers to international trade, with reverberating chains of retaliation and counterretaliation.

The concerned observer sees a serious dilemma in this whole situation, which is little alleviated by the reminder that pollution control is not unique in this respect; similar problems have been created from time to time by restrictions on the labor of women and children, by minimum wage standards, by factory and mine safety regulations, by advances in social security costs and benefits, and possibly by social expenditure programs of various sorts that involve higher direct taxes.

Solution to International Cost Differences Due to
Pollution Policies

The Laissez-Faire Approach

There are those who believe that no particular solution is required for international trade impacts and competitive realignments resulting from additional production costs in a particular country, reflecting either the internalization of

external costs of pollution via pollution taxes or the costs of
compliance with regulatory standards.

In their view, international differences in environmental
situations (due to varying compliance standards, varying penalty
taxes on pollution, or varying need for or cost of pollution
control in different countries) will, if substantial, inevitably
lead to readjustments in trade patterns. Moreover, to continue
the outline of this view, the world economy will not suffer
from these changes. A certain amount of near complacency would
seem to be justified, according to this uncompromising freedom-
of-trade approach. If any solution is called for, it would be
argued, it is to proceed to international agreements whose goal
would be to encourage whatever readjustments seem to be called
for by the various "environmental cost differences," whatever
their precise causes. Again, in this view, ability or willingness to absorb pollution in the national or local environment
is very much akin to any other comparative advantage in
international trade and should be allowed to work its will on
the world's trade flows--imbalances, dislocations, and shock
effects notwithstanding. National policies to combat these
readjustments would be regarded, in this purist view, as
distorting the efficient pattern of trade.

## International Acceptance of Pollution Control Standards

The solution advocated by most pragmatists is the development and acceptance, on an appropriate international basis, of
standards for the control of pollution. There are rational
possibilities for flexibility in international standards,
although there is a presumption in favor of uniformity where
concessions and variances tend to weaken overall environmental
results. Environmental standard techniques are of several
types:

1. Ambient standards. These usually refer to ambient
air quality (as opposed to the quality of air in closed spaces
or emissions) but are conceptually applicable to the general
water supply.

2. Emission standards. These are typically applicable
to the amount or characteristics of air or water effluents by
industry (or conceivably by residential structures).

3. Design or performance standards. These apply to the
design of products, such as automobiles, sold for consumer
use, or to the performance or performance capability of
pollution abatement facilities or production processes
installed or in use by industry.

All these standards may exist side by side, mutually complementing or reinforcing each other. Ambient standards for most pollutants would lend themselves to national and regional variation, above some basic minimum that a reliable group of scientific experts could agree represented a level of air (or water) quality below which there would be a definite and substantial hazard to human health, livestock, vegetation, or property. Above this minimum, different air (or water) qualities might be tolerated, or even accepted, provided there was no problem of international pollution in the true sense by a pervasive, mobile, persistent, or especially hazardous type of contaminant.

The degree of flexibility or national variance implied by the above brief comments needs careful qualification, since (1) the extent to which one country can stand more pollution of the general body of air or water than another is limited, (2) international pollution is likely to be real, particularly in closely populated areas with numerous adjacent small or moderate-sized national areas, and (3) the leeway to be left for pollution cost-cutting by particular countries should be small, if unfair and unsocial competition is to be avoided.

Local emission standards can be somewhat more flexible than ambient air (or water) standards, provided the minimum ambient standard to avoid substantial risk of damage is met. Indeed, some theorists, eager to make the point that the overall capacity of the environment to absorb pollution should be utilized in the most economic fashion, would argue that "rational" nonuniformity is desirable. They also point out that, from the international standpoint, uniform emission standards do not impose equal burdens, are difficult to enforce, and would be difficult to secure agreement upon.

Design standards for products used in international trade (automobiles are the prime example) present the greatest single problem for international trade and commercial comity among nations. International standards, if attainable, would remove the possibilities of use, or suspicion of use, of especially high standards as a nontariff barrier to imports.

The difficulty of reaching agreement on an international design standard would depend in part upon the width of the disparity between felt domestic environmental needs in the countries of automobile exporters as compared with the felt needs in the countries that constitute their export markets.

## Compensatory Taxation

A third solution is the compensatory border tax. Where an environmental excise-type tax is imposed on a pollution-

causing or pollution-related product, a comparable border tax
on imports may be levied in the same manner as other domestic
excises with tariff equivalents on imported items.  If this is
feasible, the competitive problem due to differential
recognition of external environmental costs in the cost
structures of different countries is automatically erased.  The
difficulty is that the relatively simple, straightforward set
of circumstances under which a border tax equivalent to the
domestic environmental tax may be imposed on a product may be
relatively rare in this complex policy area.

Taxes imposed on emissions or effluents, as distinguished
from products, are difficult to translate into product
equivalents, legally and economically.  Tariff adjustments
designed to impose burdens on imports equivalent to estimated
pollution taxes paid by domestic producers, or to estimated
pollution abatement costs incurred to avoid taxes or to comply
with regulatory standards, raise the whole problem of the comity
of nations under General Agreement on Trade and Tariffs (GATT)
rules or their equivalent.  They raise the specter of a round
of environmental tariff adjustments that would usher in an era
of disguised protectionism.

Apart from the question of international comity favoring
no compensatory border tax, it is sometimes contended that if
the domestic pollution tax (or regulatory requirement) shifts
the production in question abroad--"exporting pollution"--
the country that can achieve this result would be gaining,
on balance, rather than losing.  The difference between the
"let's export pollution" view and the laissez-faire philosophy
discussed under a previous heading is a tenuous one.  In
addition, such a view cannot be accepted in good conscience
from the international standpoint of maximum utilization of
world resources consistent with orderly control and ultimate
"resolution" of major pollution problems.

## "Pollution Havens"

As has been indicated throughout the previous discussion,
international trade can be substantially affected by changes
in cost structures and prices attributable to pollution taxes
or similar measures (tax penalties or regulation) which
internalize the social damage cost of pollution through
environmental taxes, or induce higher costs for pollution
control incurred in the process of avoiding pollution taxes.

One possible outcome is merely an impairment of the
trade position of the country with (1) greater pollution
problems, (2) stricter standards, (3) more effective control
policies through taxes or regulation, or (4) higher costs of
pollution control due to scarcity of the resources or expertise

needed for efficient pollution abatement.  By the same token,
there would be an improvement of the trade position of countries
in which producers had a "favorable" pollution posture due to an
opposite set of conditions from those listed above.

With changes in the trade position, there would be shifts
in the pattern of trade.  But there may also be changes in the
location of industry and in international investment patterns.
One would expect that those countries with relatively low
pollution-control standards, lax enforcement, low or non-
existent pollution taxes, penalties, or charges, or simple
physical or economic advantages in absorbing or controlling
pollution, would attract location of industry and investment
flows.  Where the "favorable" situation was due to low
environmental standards or laxity in their enforcement by tax
or other means, these countries or regions could become what
might be termed "pollution havens," enjoying unfair
advantages over other more progressive parts of the world and
possibly contributing to truly international pollution problems.

## "Trade-neutral" Pollution Taxes

As noted earlier, one theoretical, but sometimes
operational, approach to incorporating the costs of pollution
damage into industrial cost structures is the "trade-neutral"
excise or sales tax on pollutant products or their use.  Such
a tax would be applied to all products of specified type,
whether produced at home or abroad, and rebated, refunded, or
not applied with respect to such products if exported.  Such a
tax would tend to reduce the domestic consumption, and therefore
the production, of such products, depending upon the
elasticities involved.  If foreign markets received the product
at a price that netted out the rebated excise tax in the
originating country and did not operate subject to a similar
environmental excise tax, the consumption of the polluting
product would tend to continue in such markets.  If the tax
brought some easing of the supply conditions relative to
demand in the originating country, exports might increase.

In this situation, with pollution costs not reflected in
export prices, the purposes of the tax would not be served or
would be frustrated with respect to exports.  If the pollution
in question was connected with production of the product, the
originating and exporting country would in effect suspend its
fiscal sanctions on the pollutant on exports, for the sake of
exports.  If the pollution was related to the consumption of
the product, the trade-neutral excise structure would work
satisfactorily for the originating country, since export would
mean no domestic pollution.

The weakness of this kind of pollution tax is that it does not penalize pollution per se, only the consumption related to it.  Its only incentive effect is in discouraging the consumption, generally limited to modest price elasticity responses of demand, unless a very heavy, punitive tax were involved.

To focus on pollution per se, there would need to be a rebate or credit against the tax for recovery of the pollutant from emissions or effluents, for recycling or similar corrective action.  If a rebate or credit is allowed for pollutant recovery or corrective action, there would be no net tax on the "cleaned-up" production to recover at the border on exports.  However, the higher costs due to correcting or cleaning up pollution would still be incorporated in the price, just as the tax would be in the case of the producer who merely continues to pollute and pays the license fee to do so.

## Antipollution subsidies

From the standpoint of the international implications, the subsidy technique for pollution control, ostensibly designed to absorb pollution control costs, mitigate the burdens of environmental regulation, or stimulate technological innovation, may in the process encourage exports and modify the international competitive balance.

If one country uses the subsidy technique to get its steel industry, for example, to clean up its pollutants, while another uses severe regulation or environmental control excise taxes, which increase costs, there could be a double-barreled effect on the relative competitive position of the two nations' steel companies.  The differential advantage of the steel industry in the subsidizing country vis-a-vis that of the regulatory-penalty tax country would be similar (although not necessarily quantitatively identical) to that of an industry that enjoyed the right of free pollution as against one that had to pay the costs of prevention or clean-up.

It is understood that, under the present trading rules of the GATT, (1) explicit export subsidies (or import levies) could be used to offset the competitive disadvantage arising from domestic controls or heavy charges, only if the subsidy (or import levy) was directly related to a domestic indirect tax on the product (excise, sales, purchase, and so on); and (2) an export subsidy to offset charges which increase the overall costs of doing business (such as direct taxes on producers) would not be permissible.

## Financial Assistance for Adjustment to Pollution Control Requirements

Pollution taxes and other approaches to environmental improvement may have such a severe impact on trade and investment in particular industries, reflecting alterations in the international competitive balance as well as the sheer burden of compliance, that some form of financial assistance may need to be extended to assist in the adjustment. This kind of assistance is itself a form of subsidy, but if the adjustment costs are largely temporary, such as the transitional costs of adopting new types of equipment or production methods, the effect may be to overcome or prevent any long-term competitive advantage to the industry of the environmentally activist country. However, if significant long-term increases in production costs result from pollution control, the adjustment aid may prevent disastrous transitional impacts but will not alter the long-run competitive imbalance created in the absence of international agreements or compensation. In any event, the absorption of capital in various sectors of the economy--even through government assistance--to meet pollution-control standards will tend to slow capital investment to improve productivity and make technological advances, thus impairing to some degree the competitive position of an environmentally progressive economy, unless there is a tangible payoff in terms of benefits from the improvement in the environment.

### Pollution Control and the Developing Countries

The whole gamut of pollution problems--harmful emissions, effluents, thermal pollution, solid waste disposal, noise, congestion--tends to increase with the level of industrial production and general economic affluence. Primitive agricultural societies have their unpleasant environmental aspects and limited sanitation, but these do not make the demands on social organization characteristic of the air, water, thermal, and refuse pollution problems of the modern industrial economy.

As economies develop, they encounter environmental problems. They also tend to seek to concentrate their resources on growth and productivity. Their lack of affluence may moderate their environmental problems, but it also tightly limits their capacity and willingness to devote resources to adjusting to environmental needs. For example, some have found it difficult to eliminate the use of DDT in favor of safer but more expensive substitutes. The capital required for pollution control equipment is difficult to provide. The initiative to control pollution before it gets

out of hand and damages the world's ecology is not likely to
be strong.

In a world system in which the more prosperous industrial
systems take the lead in environmental regulation and in the
imposition of pollution taxes that are reflected in their
producers' costs, the developing countries may appear to have
an opportunity to enjoy at least a transitory competitive
advantage through lower pollution control costs.  This
advantage may take the form both of greater ability to export
and greater attractiveness to capital investment.  Such
potential conflict between world environmental goals and growth
objectives for developing countries poses questions of policy
for a prosperous, orderly world community.

It would be unfortunate if the drive for growth resulted
in establishing pollution havens; yet it would be difficult
and probably not economic to insist on uniformity in all parts
of the world, since pollution (except the true international
or transnational type) does not involve the same costs and
damages everywhere, and rigid leveling through international
agreements or pollution tax standardization would reduce below
optimum the utilization of the world resource--the aggregate
capacity to absorb pollution with relatively little harm to
the global environment.

The problems outlined with respect to universal standards
or even minimal standards with respect to the developing
countries are applicable to some degree to other countries
(not classified as "developing") with varying levels of wealth
and income and different domestic environmental policies and
standards.

Conflicts between growth and environmental quality are
evident in any economy.  Capital and other resources, including
research expertise, devoted to pollution control are denied
other uses.  Any country with long strides to take industrially
to match the wealthier nations may find a temporary advantage
in keeping its pollution standards lower.

NOTES

1.    See Report of the Tax Policy Advisory Committee to
the Council on Environmental Quality (Washington, D.C.:
Government Printing Office, February 1973), especially pp. 1
and 12; and Pollution Control:  Perspectives on the Government
Role (New York:  Tax Foundation, 1971), especially pp. 16, 21,
and 31.

2.    See Tax Incentives, Tax Institute of America Symposium, Studies in Social and Economic Process (Lexington, Massachusetts: D.C. Heath Company, 1971).

3.    See, for example, Douglas B. Wilson, "Tax Assistance and Environmental Pollution," in ibid., pp. 246-56, especially pp. 251-52.

4.    Compare ibid., p. 252.

5.    Stanley S. Surrey, "Tax Incentives: Conceptual Criteria for Identification and Comparison With Direct Government Expenditures," in Tax Incentives, op. cit., p. 3.

6.    See Emil Sunley, "Tax Advantages of Homeownership Versus Renting: A Cause of Suburban Migration?" National Tax Association, Sixty-Third Annual Conference on Taxation, September 1970.

7.    See, for example, The President's 1971 Environmental Program Controlling Pollution (Washington, D.C.: Government Printing Office, 1971), p. 1.

8.    See Environmental Quality, First Annual Report of the Council on Environmental Quality (Washington, D.C.: Government Printing Office, 1970), p. 52.

9.    See Allen V. Kneese, "Environmental Pollution: Economics and Policy," American Economic Review (May 1971): 153-77.

10.   See Dan Throop Smith, "Improvement in the Quality of the Environment: Costs and Benefits," Tax Policy (Tax Institute of America) 37, nos. 3-4 (March-April 1970): 8.

# ABOUT THE EDITOR AND CONTRIBUTORS

N. T. WANG is assistant director of the Centre for Development Planning, Projections and Policies of the United Nations Secretariat. He was formerly leader of the United Nations Mission to Eastern Africa (1968-69) and the United Nations Mission to Jamaica (1968). He has lectured in many universities and educational institutions and served as visiting professor at City University of New York (1968), Pittsburgh University (1962) and instructor at Columbia College (1949-51). He is the author of books and articles on international economics, including Cooperation for Economic Development of Eastern Africa (New York: United Nations, 1971); New Proposals for the International Finance of Development: Essays in International Finance (Princeton, N.J.: Princeton University Press, April 1967); "The Role of Public Investment in Employment Promotion," in Fiscal Measures for Employment Promotion in Developing Countries (Geneva: International Labour Organisation, 1972). He is also the principal author of numerous United Nations studies, including Multinational Corporations in World Development (New York: Praeger Publishers, 1974).

JOHN F. DUE is professor of economics, University of Illinois. He has served as a consultant to the United Nations Department of Economic and Social Affairs on tax matters and as technical assistance expert to various countries. He is the author of books and articles on public finance.

C. LOWELL HARRISS is professor of public finance, Columbia University. He was president of the National Tax Association and Tax Institute of America and vice-president of the International Institute of Public Finance. He has served as a consultant to many governments and as visiting professor to a number of universities in the United States and abroad. He is the author of a number of books on public finance.

ALBERT G. HART is currently professor of economics, Columbia University. He has served as vice-president of the American Economic Association, United Nations expert on compensatory financing, United Nations technical assistance expert in Chile, consultant to the attorney-general of New York, and consultant-expert, U.S. Department of the Treasury. He is the author of many books and articles.

RICHARD E. SLITOR is currently engaged in consulting and writing in the field of taxation. He was Assistant Director of the Office of Tax Analysis, U.S. Department of the Treasury. He served as a professor at Amherst College (1967-68) and is the author of numerous articles on taxation.

BRAZILIAN ECONOMIC POLICY: An Optimal Control
Theory Analysis
                    Gian Singh Sahota

DEVELOPMENT IN RICH AND POOR COUNTRIES: A
General Theory with Statistical Analyses
                    Thorkil Kristensen

DEVELOPMENT WITHOUT DEPENDENCE
                    Pierre Uri

INCOME DISTRIBUTION POLICIES AND ECONOMIC
GROWTH IN SEMIINDUSTRIALIZED COUNTRIES:
A Comparative Study of Iran, Mexico,
Brazil, and South Korea
                    Robert E. Looney

TAXES ON DIRECT INVESTMENT INCOME IN THE
EEC: A Legal and Economic Analysis
                    Bernard Snoy